Vintage Aircraft

OF THE WORLD

Vintage Aircraft

Aircraft

OF THE WORLD

Gordon Riley

LONDON

IAN ALLAN LTD

First published 1983

ISBN 0 7110 1111 7

Published by Ian Allan Ltd, Shepperton, Surrey;
and printed by Ian Allan Printing Ltd at their works
at Coombelands in Runnymede, England

Contents

Photo credits

Air Portraits: 21B, 37, 45B, 63, 67, 69T, 71T, 72,
108, 129T, 185

P. N. Anderson: 47T, 74T, 126

G. Apostolo: 136T, 181B

Aviation Photographs International: 51,133T

Jeff Ball: 129B

Dansk Veteranflysamlung: 81T

Dornier: 142, 143T

A. E. Flanders: 116T

Peter J. Flint: 43B

Frederick G. Freeman: 25T

R. W. Harrison: 8, 23B, 55, 82B, 84, 87, 88, 123,
125T, 127, 146, 156, 165T

Hawker Aircraft Ltd: 92

Stuart Howe: 7T, 9T, 9B, 13B, 14, 15B, 25B, 27, 28,
29T, 30, 31T, 32, 33T, 33B, 36B, 38B, 42, 49,
52, 53B, 65B, 66, 70, 73T, 86B, 90, 102T,
106B, 117, 121T, 130B, 131, 136B, 137, 138,
139T, 140T, 140B, 143B, 144T, 144B, 147B,
153B, 154, 155, 165B, 167, 168T, 178, 180,
184T, 188, 189T, 190T

Kozlekedesi Museum: 93B

Ian Lawson: 45T

Ed Maloney: 50T, 50B, 175T

A. R. C. Mathie: 104B

R. G. Moulton: 13T, 18B, 20, 41T, 61B, 96T, 99T,
106T, 128B, 163T, 175B

J. Moriceau: 54B, 73C

National Aviation Museum: 89T

*National Museum of Science & Technology
(Ontario):* 19, 24, 29B, 39 , 40, 80, 97 T ,176B

Clive Norman: 48B, 53T, 145, 177

Bob Ogden: 10B, 11, 12B, 17B, 22, 44, 54T, 77B,
78B, 81B, 91T, 111B, 119T, 134, 162, 166T,
181T, 183T, 187B

L. E. Opdyke: 35B

S. W. Pope: 18T

RAF St Athan: 160B, 163B,172 T, 176T

S. G. Richards: 10T, 82T, 120, 132, 133B, 135T,
149, 150, 159, 170, 171, 173, 189B

R. E. Richardson: 85B, 166B

Gordon Riley: 6, 7B, 12T, 16, 17T, 35T, 43T, 47B,
48T, 56B 57T, 57B, 58, 62T, 64, 68, 69B,
71B, 75B, 76, 77T, 78T, 94T, 94B, 97B, 101T,
102B, 103, 104T, 105, 107, 109T, 110, 112B,
113, 116B, 118, 119B, 122T, 124, 130T, 135B,
139B, 148B, 151T, 153T, 158, 160T, 176T,
179B, 183B, 184B, 186, 187T

Rick Rokicki: 61, 93T, 111T, 121B, 168B

Science Museum: 74B

C. F. E. Smedley: 100

John Stride: 79, 83, 125B, 161

P. A. Tomlin: 95

USAF Museum: 41B, 59T, 62B, 75T, 99B, 115,
151B, 164, 169

USMC: 190B

C. S. Vangen: 174

Verkehrshous der Schweiz: 96B, 147T

Bo Widfeldt: 15T

Wiltshire Newspapers: 89 B

Introduction

The aim of this book is to review and illustrate the majority of the surviving aircraft types which were in production between 1903 and 1945. As there is no definition of what constitutes a 'vintage' aircraft these dates are, of necessity, arbitrary but they have enabled me to include a great number of types which range from the Wright Flyer I to the Grumman F8F Bearcat. Comments from readers on whether they would prefer to see later types included would be particularly welcome and will be borne in mind should a second edition be prepared.

The layout of the book is that it is divided into four parts which put types into broad eras: Part 1 covers 1903-1913, Part 2 covers 1914-1918, Part 3 covers 1919-1938 and Part 4 covers 1939-1945. Aircraft have been selected that are representative of each section and even though many of the more obscure types have been omitted those that are featured include virtually every significant type still surviving on a World-wide basis. If a type exists in store or is otherwise not available for viewing it has been omitted in favour of types which are on public exhibition. Types have been put into sections depending on the date of their first flight except in a minority of cases where the type may have flown during one era but made its name in another — this is particularly true of World War 2 types. In these cases the type is listed in the later section. Within sections the types are listed in alphabetical order of manufacturer and then in chronological order of development, thus the Hurricane is followed by the Typhoon and then the Tempest.

In any book of this sort the help given by many organisations and individuals is invaluable and the following are particularly worthy of mention: Col T. M. D'Andrea, US Marine Corps Museum; Paul Armstrong; R. W. Bradford, Canadian National Museum of Science & Technology; David Davies, Air Portraits; Stuart Howe; Philip Jarrett; R. W. Harrison; Ed Maloney, Planes of Fame Museum; R. G. Moulton; Bob Ogden; Leo Opdycke; Phil O'Keefe, Bradley Air Museum; Cole Palen; Robert G. Rawe, US Air Force Museum; E. A. Rokicki; Jerry Scutts; and Grover Walker, US Naval Aviation Museum. Considerable thanks must also be extended to my wife Jacqueline, without whose continual support and encouragement this book would not have seen the light of day.

Gordon Riley

Part One: 1903–1913

Blackburn 1912 Monoplane   UK

Photo: The 1912 Blackburn Monoplane taxying at Old Warden.

Powerplant: One 50hp Gnome rotary
Span: 35ft 8in
Length: 26ft 3in
Height: 8ft 9in
Wing area: 236sq ft

Robert Blackburn was a civil engineer who happened to be working in Rouen at the time of Wilbur Wright's demonstration flights of 1908. He immediately came home and constructed the 'Heavy monoplane' which was completed in the spring of 1909 but which crashed on its maiden flight. His next aeroplane was an elegant tractor monoplane which was developed into the 'Mercury' monoplane, several variants of which were built and sold between 1910 and 1911. One single-seater based on the 'Mercury' design was built in 1912 for Mr Cyril Foggin. It was sold the following year to Mr Francis Glew who put it in store at Wittering on the outbreak of war in 1914. Here it remained until discovered by Richard Shuttleworth in 1938. It was restored to flying condition just prior to the outbreak of World War 2 but not flown, this event taking place in 1947. It has remained airworthy ever since as the oldest airworthy British aeroplane and is based with the Shuttleworth Collection at Old Warden.

Bleriot XI   France

Photo: This Type XI was built from new parts and spare components and is now exhibited at the Imperial War Museum's Duxford Airfield.

Powerplant: Various including the 25hp 'Fan' Anzani
Span: 25ft 7.125in
Length: 26ft 3in
Height: 8ft 6.75in
Wing area: 150.7sq ft

Louis Bleriot was one of the greatest figures in the European aviation scene in the years before World War 1. He had a successful motor car accessory business at the turn of the century and built his first experimental model ornithopter (Bleriot I) in 1901–1902. During the next few years he experimented with differing degrees of success before producing the Bleriot XI which was shown at the Paris Salon of December 1908. It was flown for the first time at Issy on 23 January 1909 and was subjected to a programme of continuous development until by July it had made one flight lasting over 50min.

Bleriot's name was, however, catapulted into the headlines when he took-off from Les Baraques on the morning of 25 July 1909 and landed at Dover just over half an hour later, winning the *Daily Mail* prize of £1,000 offered for the first flight across the English Channel. From then on Bleriot did not look back and the Type XI went into immediate production for both private and military use, developed versions still being in widespread use both in England and France during the early part of World War 1.

The Type XI was copied widely and examples of both the genuine article and copies are exhibited, and occasionally flown, world-wide. Two other Bleriot types have also survived: the fuselage of the large 100hp Type X is preserved in the Musee de l'Air at Chalais Meudon, Paris and the Type XXVII, originally produced for the 1911 Gordon Bennett Cup, is with the Royal Air Force Museum, Hendon.

The actual cross-Channel machine is exhibited at the Conservatoire National des Arts et Metiers in Rue St Martin, Paris.

Cody Military Biplane UK

Photo: The 1912 Cody Military Biplane, No 304, in the Science Museum.

Powerplant: One 120hp Austro-Daimler
Span: 52ft
Length: 44ft

Samuel Franklin Cody started his career in aviation as a kiting instructor to the Royal Engineers at the Balloon Factory, Farnborough, at the very end of the last century. From his work on man-carrying kites he progressed to his first powered aeroplane which is known to have flown in September 1908. On 16 October that year it covered a distance of 1,390ft before crashing and this is recognised as the first *sustained* powered flight in the UK.

Cody severed his connections with the Army but continued his experiments at Farnborough from 1909 and in 1910 qualified for his aviator's certificate on a biplane of his own design. He won the 1911 Michelin and *Daily Mail* prizes and then built a new machine for the 1912 Military Trials. This was wrecked a month before the trials and he hastily constructed a further biplane based on his successful 1911 machine. This won the trials and £5,000 and two production machines were ordered with serials 301 and 304. Aircraft 304 was flown for a very short time and was presented to the Science Museum in 1913 where it remains on display as the only surviving Cody aircraft.

Curtiss Pusher   USA

Photo: Curtiss Pusher flying at Old Rhinebeck, New York.
Data: Model D

Span: 33ft 4in
Length: 25ft 9in
Height: 7ft 5.5in

Following the cessation of activities by the Aerial Experiment Association Curtiss spent the years 1909-1912 evolving the type which has become universally known as the 'Curtiss Pusher'. The final production versions were the Models D and E and Curtiss himself sold well over 100 of these popular little biplanes. The aileron and tricycle undercarriage were innovative and helped to swell its popularity. A Model E mounted on floats became the first successful seaplane and, designated the A-1, became the US Navy's first aeroplane. Several examples of the Curtiss Pusher, both land and seaplane variants, exist in the USA together with several replicas, one of which has recently been constructed in Germany by Arthur Williams; whilst another is under construction by Mike Beach at Twickenham, Middx.

Deperdussin   France

Photo: The 1913 Gordon Bennett racer, Musee de l'Air, Chalais Meudon.
Data: Monocoque 1913 racer

Powerplant: One 160hp Gnome
Span: 21ft 9.75in
Length: 20ft 0.125in
Height: 7ft 6.5in
Wing area: 104sq ft

The Societe Pour les Appareils Deperdussin first came into the limelight with the Type B single-seater of 1911. It was powered by a 50hp Gnome and was an elegant monoplane which was capable of some 56mph. The early Deperdussins were very successful and no less than seven were entered in the Circuit of Europe race of June 1911. The type was also developed for military use, four being ordered by the French government and nine being in service with the Royal Flying Corps at the outbreak of World War 1.

Two original 'Deps' are known to survive: the Shuttleworth Collection has aircraft No 43 which was built in 1910 and powered by a 35hp Anzani. Sold to the Naval Wing of the Royal Navy it was disposed of in 1914 to Mr Grimmer of Ampthill, Beds. He stored it for many years and it was rediscovered and bought by Richard Shuttleworth in 1935, restored to fly in 1937 it has been maintained in airworthy condition ever since. The other original aircraft is the winner of the 1913 Gordon Bennett Cup at Rheims, this superb example of the designer's art is preserved in the Musee de l'Air at Chalais Meudon but flying replicas of it are based at La Ferte-Alais with Jean Salis and at Old Rhinebeck, New York, with Cole Palen.

Donnet-Leveque Type A   France

Photo: Type A in the Musee d l'Air, Chalais Meudon

Powerplant: One 50hp Gnome
Span: 31ft 2in
Length: 27ft 10.625in
Height: 11ft 2in
Wing area: 183sq ft

The Type A was designed by F. Denhaut and first flew from the Seine at Juvisy on 15 March 1912. It was the first really practical European flying-boat and was soon put into production at Argenteuil. By the Paris Salon of October 1912 the Type A had become amphibious, a wheeled undercarriage which was capable of being wound up above water level being fitted. The Type A was looked on with considerable interest by many foreign governments, one was acquired by the Royal Navy and during 1912-1913 the type was delivered to Austro-Hungary, Denmark and Sweden. A development of the design, the FBA Type H was one of the most widely-used flying boats of World War 1.

Three examples of the Type A have survived at Chalais Meudon, Stockholm and Helsingor whilst three FBAs have survived at Chalais Meudon, Brussels and Lisbon.

Dufaux IV
Switzerland

Photo: The Dufaux IV at Lucerne

Powerplant: One 60hp Antoinette
Span: 8.5m
Length: 9.5m
Height: 2.7m
Wing area: 25sq m

The Dufaux IV biplane was designed and built by A. & H. Dufaux at Geneva in 1909. It was a conventional tractor biplane, powered by a 60hp Antoinette V-8 water cooled engine and was intended for pilot training. The Type IV was demonstrated to the Swiss Military authorities in May 1910 but was deemed to be unsuitable for military purposes and a new aircraft, the Dufaux V, was developed to take its place. The Type IV has been preserved and is exhibited in the Museum of Transport and Communications at Lucerne.

Ellehammer
Denmark

Photo: The Ellehammer VI 'Standard' at Hensingor.
Data: Ellehammer II semi-biplane

Powerplant: One 20hp Ellehammer 3-cylinder radial
Span: 30ft 11.75in
Length: 20ft 4.25in
Height: 19ft 8.375in
Wing area: 398.26sq ft

Jacob Ellehammer was Denmark's pioneer aviator, having built several models, his first full-scale aircraft, the Ellehammer I monoplane, was completed in 1905 and tested the following year on the tiny island of Lindholm. Because of the restrictions on size the monoplane was tested on a circular track and was tethered to a pole with rope! The Ellehammer I was then modified, becoming a 'semi-biplane' which was again tested around the circular track from August-September 1906. This historic aeroplane is now preserved in the Danish Technical Museum at Helsingor.

The Museum also houses two more Ellehammer designs, the Ellehammer helicopter and the last Ellehammer product, the Mk VI 'Standard' monoplane of 1909. This was to have been the first aircraft to attempt the flight across Copenhagen Sound but Count Moltke was beaten by another machine and the Standard was never flown.

Etrich Taube   Austria

Photo: Rumpler-built Taube in the Deutches Museum.

Powerplant: 120hp Austro-Daimler or 100 or 120hp Mercedes
Span: 46ft
Length: 27ft 3in
Height: 9ft 9in
Wing area: 301sq ft

The prototype Taube (Dove) appeared in 1910 and was the design of the Austrian engineer Doktor Igo Etrich. After considerable success the design rights were sold to Rumpler Flugzeugwerke of Johannisthal, Germany. Although the original was fitted with the 120hp Austro-Daimler most of the early Rumpler machines were powered by the 100 or 120hp Mercedes. Following a dispute with Rumpler, Etrich gave up his copyright in the design with the result that at least nine other German companies built Tauben of various types and the probable total output was in the order of 500 machines for both civil and military customers. At the outbreak of World War 1 more than half of the aircraft serving with the German army were Tauben of various sorts and at least two remain on display in museums; one with the Deutches Museum and another in the Vienna Technical Museum.

Farman MF7 Longhorn and MF11 Shorthorn   France

Photo: MF7 Longhorn in the Musee de l'Air, Chalais Meudon.
Data: MF7

Powerplant: One 70hp Renault or 100hp Sunbeam
Span: 58ft 8in
Length: 32ft
Height: 11ft 4in
Wing Area: 646sq ft

The brothers Henri and Maurice Farman were two of the greatest exponents of the aeroplane in France before World War 1 and Maurice's MF7 was one of the earliest and more successful aircraft to be adopted for military purposes in both France and England. The first Longhorn — so-called because of the long extensions which acted both as skids and to support the front elevator — appeared at the Military Review on Laffans Plain in 1911. By the outbreak of

war in 1914 most Longhorns had been relegated to to the training role as they were eminently unsuited to any warlike purpose; despite this they were used for observation during the early part of the war.

The MF11 Shorthorn was a development of the earlier type which dispensed with the front elevator and associated skid/supports. It formed part of the fighting equipment with which the RFC was equipped but was largely ineffective and by 1915 had been retired to the training role although the French continued to use them operationally on the Western Front as late as 1917.

Grade Monoplane   Germany

Photo: The 1909 Grade Monoplane on show in the Verkehrsmuseum, Dresden.
Data: 1911 racer

Span: 39ft 3in
Length: 33ft
Wing area: 480sq ft

Hans Grade is significant as the first German to fly in a German aeroplane, this he achieved at Magdeburg in a triplane of his own design which was built in 1908. He later founded his own company at Bork where he concentrated on producing monoplanes which bore a general similarity to the Santos Dumont Demoiselle (qv) with the engine mounted on the leading edge of the wing and the pilot sitting beneath it.

Two Grade monoplanes have survived, one is exhibited in the Verkehasmuseum in Dresden and the other is with the Deutches Museum in Munich.

Langley Aerodrome   USA

Photo: The Langley Type A Aerodrome after restoration.
Data: Not available

The Langley Type A Aerodrome was built by Charles Langley, one of America's pioneer aviators, and was a large tandem monoplane. The original flight trials

were made from the roof of a houseboat moored on the Potomac river, the aircraft being catapulted off, but the engine did not develop sufficient power and the Aerodrome crashed into the water.

Some years later, during a legal dispute between Langley and Glenn Curtiss, the Aerodrome was obtained by Curtiss and rebuilt in a new configuration in an attempt to both make it fly and to prove Langley wrong. The rebuilt aircraft differed in a number of respects from the original and was mounted on floats. It is believed that the Aerodrome made some short hops in this configuration.

The Aerodrome has recently been totally restored to its original form by staff of the National Air & Space Museum, Washington, DC, and is currently displayed at Silver Hill, Maryland.

Levavasseur Antoinette   France

Photo: The Type VII in the Musee de l'Air, Paris.
Data: Type VII

Powerplant: One 50hp Antoinette
Span: 42ft
Length: 37ft 8.75in
Height: 9ft 10in
Wing area: 538.2sq ft

The Antoinette monoplanes were some of the most elegant aeroplanes to be built in the years before World War 1 and the Antoinette aero-engines powered a great variety of European aeroplanes. The first of the classic Antoinette monoplanes was the Type IV which was tested at Issy on 9 October 1908 and which managed a flight of 2,953ft on 18 November that year. It was modified during that

13

winter and after the wings were enlarged it recorded a flight of three miles at Mourmelon on 19 February 1909. From then on the monoplane was flown by Hubert Latham and on 19 July 1909 he attempted a crossing of the English Channel but engine failure caused him to ditch some seven and a half miles from the English coast. The Type IV was salvaged and figured prominently at the Rheims meeting later in the year. The Type VII was the most successful of the various Antoinettes and went into production both in France and at the Albatross factory in Germany. Three genuine Antoinettes have survived, one is on show at the Musee de l'Air, Chalais Meudon, another is stored at Krakov, Poland and a Modified Type VII which was built for Robert Blackburn is exhibited in the Science Museum, London.

Morane-Saulnier Types G and H France

Photo: The M-S Type G at the Musee de l'Air was originally owned by Robert Morane.
Data: Type G

Powerplant: One 80hp Gnome
Span: 30ft 6.125in
Length: 21ft 5.875in
Height: 9ft
Wing area: 160sq ft

The definitive pre-World War 1 Morane-Saulnier monoplanes were the Types G and H which appeared in 1912 and which differed because the G was a two-seater and the H a single seater. Both were produced extensively and 94 Type Gs were delivered to the French Aviation Militaire together with 26 Type Hs. The monoplanes were widely recognised as amongst the most advanced of their day taking the World Altitude Record (18,405ft) in 1912, winning the UK Aerial Derby in 1913 and becoming the first aircraft to cross the Mediterranean (460 miles) on 23 September 1913. The first official French air mail was carried in a Morane on 16 October 1913 and in early 1914 a remarkable flight was made from Cairo to Khartoum and back between 4 January and 3 February. A Type G is exhibited in the Musee de l'Air, Paris, and a Type H is on show in the Chicago Museum of Science & Industry.

Nieuport IVG France

Photo: The sole surviving Nieuport IVG at Linkoping.

Powerplant: One 50hp Gnome
Span: 38ft 0.875in
Length: 25ft 7.125in
Height: 8ft 2.375in
Wing area: 188.37sq ft

The two-seat IVG monoplane appeared in 1911 and was powered by a 50hp Gnome rotary. The type was put into quantity production for both civil and military purchasers and was operated by the Italian Army Air Corps — in one of whose Nieuports the second-ever military reconnaissance was flown on 24 October 1911 — and by the air arms of France, Great Britain and Russia. A developed version for military purposes was known as the VIG and it was in one of these that Lt Nesterov of the Imperial Russian Air Service performed the very first loop on 20 August 1913.

One Nieuport IVG was presented to the Swedish armed forces in 1912 and formed the first equipment of the Swedish Army Air Force. It was still maintained in flying condition as late as the mid-1960s but is now retired to the Swedish Air Force Museum at Linkoping.

REP Types D and K   France

Photo: The Gnome-powered Type K at Chalais Meudon.

Powerplant: One 60hp REP
Span: 47ft 6in
Length: 36ft 5in
Height: 9ft 7in
Wing area: 290sq ft

The REP machines were built by Robert Esnault-Pelterie during the years leading up to the outbreak of World War 1. Technically they were uninspiring and sold in fairly small numbers although Esnault-Pelterie is credited with first installation of ailerons on a full-scale aircraft (on his second glider) and the first use of a seat belt (1911). The two aircraft types which were built in the greatest numbers were the Types D and K which were fairly conventional two-seat monoplanes powered by the 60hp REP (D) or the 80hp Gnome (K). One example of each is preserved in the Musee de l'Air at Chalais Meudon and another REP monoplane is with the Conservatoire National des Arts ets Metiers, Paris.

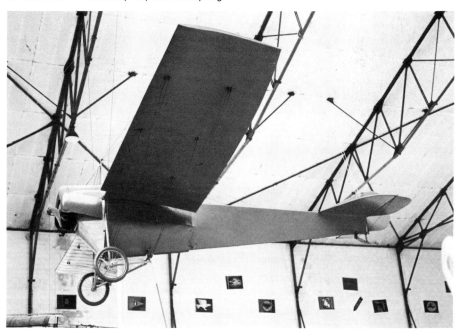

Roe I Triplane   UK

Photo: The Roe I Triplane in the Science Museum, London.

Powerplant: One 9hp JAP
Span: 20ft
Length: 23ft
Height: 11ft
Wing area: 217.5sq ft

The Roe I Triplane was Alliott Verdon-Roe's second full-sized aeroplane and it was built in a workshop beneath a railway arch on the Lea Marshes in East London during 1909. It was a fairly conventional machine with both wing and tail surfaces of the triplane layout and both acting as lifting surfaces. Powered by a two-cylinder 6hp JAP engine and covered with varnished brown paper it was successfully 'hopped' in May and June 1909 and on 23 July it managed a flight of about 900ft. The 'Bull's eye' — as it was later named — was then rebuilt with a 9hp engine and managed a flight of about half a mile at Wembley Park the following December. Retired from flying, the 'Bull's eye' was stored at the Avro works in Manchester until restored and presented to the Science Museum, London, in 1925 where it has been an exhibit ever since. It is historically important as the first totally British aircraft to fly successfully.

Santos-Dumont Demoiselle   France

Photo: The Demoiselle at Chalais Meudon.
Data: No 20

Powerplant: One 35hp Darracq-built Dutheil-Chalmers
Span: 16ft 8.75in
Length: 26ft 3in
Height: 7ft 10.5in
Wing area: 110sq ft

Alberto Santos-Dumont was an ex-patriate Brazilian who settled in Paris in 1898 and became another of the leading figures in the European aviation world in the years leading up to 1914. His first experiments were with airships and it was not until 1906 that his first powered aircraft, the 14bis, appeared. Santos-Dumont continued development work and eventually produced his delightful little No 19 Demoiselle (Dragonfly) in 1907 which was the first successful light aeroplane in the world. The fuselage frame was of bamboo, as were the wheels, and the engine was mounted on the centre-section with the pilot crouched underneath it. A number of Demoiselle developments appeared during 1909 and 1910 and several were built for pioneer sporting pilots, Santos-Dumont having relinquished any rights to the design and throwing it open for anyone to build. The original 1908 Demoiselle is preserved in the Musee de l'Air at Chalais Meudon and several replicas have been built and flown world-wide.

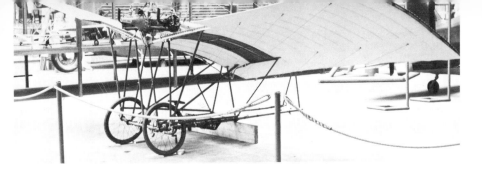

Voisin-Henry Farman Ibis

France

Photo: Voisin-Henry Farman Ibis at Chalais Meudon, Paris
Data: Standard Model

Powerplant: One 60hp ENV
Span: 32ft 9.75in
Length: 34ft 5.375in
Height' 11ft
Wing area: 445sq ft

The Voisin-Henry Farman No 1 was built by the Voisin brothers in 1907 to the order of Henry Farman and was used by him to make his first flight on 20 September that year. It was powered by a 50hp Antoinette and was the third powered Voisin that had been built. Various modifications were carried out to the machine and on 9 November 1907

Farman won the Ernest Archdeacon prize by covering 3,380ft, well in excess of the stipulated distance of 150m! This flight lasted for 74sec and is significant as the first flight by a non-Wright machine to have lasted for longer than a minute, as well as being the first 1km closed circuit flight made in Europe. The aircraft was then used to win the Deutsch-Archdeacon prize on 13 January 1908 and rebuilt with a 50hp Renault engine as the Ibis, making its first flight as such on 14 March 1908. A programme of continuous improvement was carried out on the machine and it was eventually sold to an Austrian buyer in early 1909. This historical machine has survived and is preserved in the Musee de l'Air at Chalais Meudon. An American-built 1908 model has been rebuilt to fly and is based at Old Rhinebeck, New York, with Cole Palen.

Watkins Monoplane

UK

Photo: The Watkins Monoplane 'Robin Goch' at RAF St Athan.

Powerplant: One 40hp Watkins-built Anzani
Span: 32ft

Length: 21ft 6in
All up weight: 600lb

There is a certain amount of confusion over the Watkins Monoplane which is said to have been built

by C. H. Watkins at Mynachdy Farm, Maendy, Cardiff between 1907 and 1909. It was probably 'hopped' in 1909 but its first real flights were not made until a new rigid wing was fitted sometime between 1911 and 1913. There are reports that it was seen flying over Whitchurch. Glamorgan, in 1910 but these are not substantiated. Other cross-country flights are said to have taken place to Caerphilly Mountain. It was progressively modified and is believed to have been flying as late at 1918 when a cracked cylinder head caused its grounding. Stored by the builder until 1959 it was removed and taken to RAF St Athan where it was restored to static display condition where it remains to this day.

Wright Brothers aeroplanes   USA

Photo: The Flyer I in the National Air & Space Museum, Washington, DC.
Data: Flyer I

Powerplant: One 12hp Wright
Span: 40ft 4in
Length: 21ft 1in
Height: 8ft
Wing area: 510sq ft

The Wright brothers, Wilbur and Orville, are recognised world-wide as the true pioneers of powered flight, their 1903 biplane having made the first powered and sustained flight on 14 December 1903 at Kill Devil Hills, North Carolina. Their first aeroplane, the Flyer I, was exhibited at the London Science Museum for many years but was eventually dispatched to the National Air & Space Museum, Washington, DC, in 1948 where it now hangs alongside Lindbergh's *Spirit of St Louis* and the Apollo 11 command module in the 'Milestones of Flight' exhibition.

The Wrights continued their experiments until late 1905, producing the Flyers II and III, the major components of the Flyer III were unearthed in 1948 by Orville Wright and were rebuilt for exhibition at Carillon Park, Dayton, where it was unveiled in June 1950.

Although several replicas of various Wright aeroplanes have been built and occasionally flown the only other surviving Wrights are a 1910 Military Flyer and the 'Vin Fiz' trans-America Flyer, both with the National Air & Space Museum, Washington, DC; a modified Wright B in the USAF Museum, Wright-Patterson AFB; and 1910 Baby in the Musee de l'Air, Chalais Meudon which is the only genuine Wright in Europe.

Part Two: 1914-1918

AEG GIV

Germany

Photo: Sole surviving GIV at Rockcliffe, Ontario.
Data: AEG GIV

Powerplant: Two 260hp Mercedes DIVa
Span: 60ft 4.5in
Length: 31ft 10in
Height: 12ft 9.5in
Wing area: 675.36sq ft

The GIV bomber followed the precedent set by earlier products of the Allgemeine Elektrizitas Gesellschaft in that the majority of the load-bearing structure was formed of steel tube. This meant that the relatively small GIV was overweight when compared with the contemporary Gotha and Friedrichshafen products. Although accommodation for a crew of four was provided it was normally operated with three men on board, the front cockpit being left empty on account of the type's excessive longitudinal sensitivity.

The type was used for both daylight and night short-range tactical bombing of Allied targets as well as for long-range reconnaissance and photography work.

The surviving GIV is unique in that it is the only surviving twin-engined German bomber of World War 1. It was shipped to Canada in May 1919 as war reparations and it was restored to static display condition at CFB Trenton during 1968-69. A total refabric was necessary and much of the fuselage ply was replaced, the engines were found to be the wrong type of Mercedes, 180hp units instead of 260hp and these have been installed as temporary fittings only. The main wheels had deteriorated so much that units from a CF-100 have been fitted to enable it to be displayed at the Canadian National Museum for Science & Technology's outstation at Rockcliffe, Ontario.

Albatross DVa
Germany

Photo: DVa at the NASM Washington, DC.
Data: Albatross DVa

Powerplant: One 180 or 200hp Mercedes DIIIa
Span: 29ft 8.25in
Length: 24ft 0.5in
Height: 8ft 10.25in
Wing area: 229sq ft

Introduced in the summer of 1917, the DV was the German answer to the Allied SE5 and Spads, however it was not sufficient to restore the balance of power in Germany's favour. The DV was developed from the earlier DIII and was characterised by its predecessor's tendency to shed its wings in a prolonged dive and even after modifications were incorporated its pilots were instructed not to over-dive the type! The DVa was a modification of the basic type which had aileron controls running through the bottom wings rather than the top ones, they were thus interchangeable with those of the DIII and the only certain way of distinguishing a DV from a DVa was by looking for the aileron control runs.

Despite its shortcomings the type was in large-scale production up until 1918 when it was discontinued in favour of the Fokker DVII, over 1,000 of them being in service in May 1918. Today two are known to survive, D5390/17 which is on show at the Australian War Memorial at Canberra, and D7161/17 which is preserved at the Smithsonian Institution's National Air & Space Museum, Washington, DC, USA. Several replicas of the type have been built in recent years and one of these, G-BFXL, flies from Thorpe Water Park, near Chertsey, Surrey.

Avro 504K
UK

Photo: Avro 504K at the Shuttleworth Collection.
Data: Avro 504K

Powerplant: One 110hp Le Rhone or alternative
Span: 36ft
Length: 29ft 5in
Height: 10ft 5in
Wing area: 330sq ft

Possibly the greatest training aeroplane of all time, the immortal Avro 504 traces its origins to the Avro 500 racing biplane of 1913. In the opening phases of World War 1 it was used in an offensive role by both the RFC and the RNAS but from 1915 onwards it was used in the training role. Both the Avro 504J and K carried on after the war, the J until 1921 and the K until the late 1920s and many hundreds served as the equipment of joyriding companies all over the British Isles throughout the inter-war period.

It was the 504, in its Monosoupape-powered J version, which formed the equipment of the school of Special Flying which was formed at Gosport under the command of Maj R. R. Smith-Barry and where the basics of the system of flying training still in use today were worked out.

The 504K appeared in 1918 and if differed from the earlier version in having an open-fronted cowling and engine-bearers which were suited to take a variety of rotary engines including the 110hp Le Rhône, 130hp Clerget and 100hp Monosoupape.

Over 8,000 504s of various types were built during the period 1914-1918 and at the Armistice the Royal Air Force had some 3,000 on strength, 2,267 with Flying Schools and over 200 on Home

Defence duties, those in the flying training role being eventually superseded by the postwar Lynx-powered 504N.

At least nine original 504Ks are in existence today, several of which are preserved in the UK with one at the Science Museum, two with the Royal Air Force Museum and one with the Shuttleworth Collection, of these only the Shuttleworth machine is maintained in an airworthy condition.

Bristol F2B Fighter   UK

Photo: Bristol Fighter at the Shuttleworth Collection

Powerplant: One 275hp Rolls-Royce Falcon III
Span: 39ft 4in
Length: 25ft 10in
Height: 9ft 9in
Wing area: 406sq ft

The Bristol Fighter was one of the classic aircraft of World War 1 and one which managed to soldier on with the peace-time Royal Air Force into the 1930s. For such a successful machine its early operations were a complete disaster as a result of its being flown as a traditional two-seater, ie as a platform for the observer's gun. When, after some pilots started to fly it in the manner of a single-seater, its true capabilities became known the Bristol rapidly established a name for itself in a great variety of roles, which included offensive patrols, photographic sorties, escort patrols, reconnaissance, ground attack and contact patrols. The leading exponent of the type was Lt A. E. McKeever of No 11 Sqn who scored a total of 30 enemy aircraft between 29 June 1917 and the end of the war, most of them won on the Bristol.

At the Armistice some 3,100 had been delivered and a further 1,369 had been built when production came to an end in December 1926. The peacetime RAF used the type mainly on Army Co-operation duties, the first postwar variant being the Mk II which featured tropical gear for overseas use, this was followed by the Mks III and IV which were progressive refinements of the basic airframe. The last operational Bristols were those of No 6 Sqn which had given many years' valuable service in Iraq and india and which were replaced by Fairey Gordons in 1932.

Two aircraft survive today D8096, which still flies regularly with the Shuttleworth Collection at Old Warden, Bedfordshire, and E2581 which is preserved by the Imperial War Museum, South Lambeth. In addition to these two machines a third is being built up from spare parts by staff of the Royal Air Force Museum at Cardington and several replicas have been built for film use in the USA.

Bristol M1C

UK

Photo: Bristol M1C replica at Thorpe Park, Surrey.

Powerplant: 110hp Le Rhône
Span: 30ft 9in
Length: 20ft 4in
Height: 7ft 9.5in
Wing area: 145sq ft

The Bristol M1C was a victim of officialdom's distrust of monoplane fighters which could be traced back to the 'monoplane ban' of 1912. As a result of this prejudice, and despite its commendable performance, only 125 were ordered and none were delivered to the Western Front — the excuse being that the landing speed of 49mph was excessive.

Those which did see operational service were relegated to the Middle East, 35 aircraft being dispatched to that theatre, not enough for the type to form the sole equipment of a single squadron. The first aircraft to see action were in Palestine in 1917 with No 111 Sqn but even here their short endurance prevented their use on escort duties.

In 1917 six were sent to Chile in part-payment for two Chilean battleships which had been taken over by the Royal Navy and after the Armistice four M1Ds were bought back by the manufacturers for demonstration and racing purposes. Their lives were very short and today only one of these machines, which were exceptionally advanced for their day, survives. This machine is the civil registered VH-UQI which, as C5001, was bought in July 1919 by Capt Harry Butler and shipped to Australia. Following Butler's death in 1924 the aircraft was stored and then purchased by 'Horrie' Miller in 1930. He modified it considerably with a DH Gipsy II engine and a flat-sided fuselage, in which condition it won the 1931 and 1932 Adelaide Aerial Derbies.

After many years storage it was located in 1956 and presented to the town of Minlaton, South Australia, Harry Butler's home town, and it is now on permanent exhibition at the Captain Harry Butler Memorial, albeit in a rather confused state of construction which combines a Le Rhône rotary and RFC markings with the flat-sided fuselage and red colours of its days with Miller!

A static replica M1C with serial 'C4912' is displayed at Thorpe Park, Surrey.

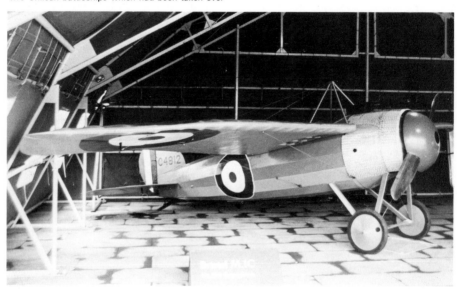

Caudron GIII and GIV

France

Photo: Caudron GIII in the RAF Museum, Hendon.
Data: GIII

Powerplant: 100hp Anzani
Span: 43ft 5in
Length: 22ft 6in
Max Speed: 71mph
Cruising Speed: 56mph

The Caudron GIII was a French two-seat training machine which was designed in 1912 and which was powered by a variety of engines. It was licence-built by the British Caudron Co Ltd at Cricklewood and the type was used fairly extensively by the Royal Naval Air Service which had 124, most of which were used as trainers at the school at Vendome, France, although a few also saw service as seaplanes

at coastal air stations before 1914. The prewar machines were fitted with either the 80hp or 100hp Gnome engine but the wartime aircraft had the 100hp Anzani.

Several examples exist today, at the Musee de l'Air, Chalais Meudon and the Salis Collection, La Ferte Alais, France and also in the Royal Air Force Museum at Hendon. The latter machine was imported from Belgium in 1936 by Ken Waller, Chief Flying Instructor of Brooklands Aviation Ltd. It never wore its civil registration G-AETA and passed from Waller to the Nash Collection, the Royal Aeronautical Society and finally the RAF Museum where it has been restored as aircraft '3066' of the RNAS Flying School, Vendome, 1917.

The GIV was a twin-engined derivative of the GIII, one example of which is exhibited at the Musee de l'Air, Chalais Meudon, France.

Curtiss Jenny   USA

Photo: Curtiss JN-4H at Old Rhinebeck, New York
Data: JN-4D

Span: 43ft 7.375in
Length: 27ft 4in
Height: 9ft 10.625in
Wing area: 352sq ft

The JN series began with the amalgamation of the best features of the Models J and N to create a new type which became universally known as the 'Jenny', North America's answer to the British Avro 504K. The first Jennies were ordered in 1914 by the US Army for observation work but the type achieved immortality as a trainer, becoming the principal US and Canadian trainer of World War 1. Its popularity increased during the 1920s when thousands of war surplus Jennies, and its Canadian equivalent the 'Canuck', were released on to the civilian market and were used by barnstorming pilots across North America. Many Jennies and Canucks survive in North America, some in airworthy condition, and one derelict example is held in store by the Royal Air Force Museum.

Although development of the Model J ceased in favour of the JN the Model N did continue its development and one example of the N-9H, basically a JN-4B fitted with a float undercarriage, enlarged windows and a 150hp Wright-Hispano engine, is preserved at the Naval Aviation Museum, Pensacola, Florida.

Curtiss Model MF

USA

Photo: Curtiss Seagull in the Canadian National Aeronautical Collection at Rockcliffe

Span: 49ft 9in
Length: 28ft 10in
Height: 11ft 7in
Wing area: 402sq ft

Standing for Modernised F the Model MF was a much improved, two-seat, training flying boat which was evolved from the Model F via the experimental BAT and BAF machines. Twenty two were built during 1918 at Garden City with a further 80 being built by the Naval Aircraft Factory. Limited production was undertaken after the Armistice for the civil market under the type name Seagull and several ex-US Navy machines were converted for civilian use by the Cox-Klemin Aircraft Co of College Point, Long Island. Of the three examples known to exist today USN No 5483 is preserved at the Naval Aviation Museum, Pensacola, Florida; a civil Seagull is on show at the Henry Ford Museum at Dearborn, Michigan; and a third is displayed by the Canadian National Aeronautical Collection, Rockcliffe, Ontario.

De Havilland DH4B

USA

Photo: Paul Mantz's DH4B

Powerplant: One 400hp Liberty 12
Span: 42ft 5.75in
Length: 30ft 6in
Height: 10ft 3.625in
Wing area: 440sq ft

The DH4B was an American-built version of the outstandingly successful Airco DH4, the prototype of which had flown at Hendon in August 1916. One of the complaints about the original DH4 was the separation of the pilot and gunner by the main fuel tank, a feature which earned it the name 'Flaming Coffin' in some quarters, this feature was alleviated in the Liberty-powered DH4B as the pilot's cockpit was moved back to be adjacent to that of the observer/gunner.

The aircraft is best remembered for its service with the US Postal Department on pioneer Air Mail contracts. The first machine entered service on 12 August 1918 and the mail pilots — one of whom was a young Charles Lindbergh — pioneered the routes in both day and night and all weathers between Washington, New York, Cleveland, Chicago and Omaha, the final coast-to-coast link to San Francisco being opened in August 1920.

Five of these important aircraft survive today in museums in the USA with N489 on display at the US Air Force Museum, Wright-Patterson AFB, Ohio.

De Havilland DH9

UK

Photo: De Havilland DH9 in the Musee de l'Air.

Powerplant: One 230hp Siddeley Puma
Span: 42ft 6in
Length: 30ft 6in
Height: 10ft
Wing area: 436sq ft

By the summer of 1917 there was an obvious need for a new aircraft which would be faster than the DH4 and which could carry a heavier bomb load over greater distances. At the same time it was reasoned that it would be a great advantage if the new type could be built using existing manufacturing facilities which had been developed for the earlier type. Thus was born the DH9 which used the same wings and tail surfaces as its predecessor but had a modified fuselage to bring the pilot and gunner into much closer communication and without the separation

caused by the 60gal fuel tank of the DH4.

The new type was powered by the Siddeley Puma engine, a lightweight version of the 230hp engine which should have produced 300hp. Teething troubles with the Puma resulted in its being de-rated to 230hp as a result of which the DH9 was seriously underpowered and consequently inferior to the aircraft which it was supposed to replace.

Over 2,000 were built and many were given a new lease of life at the end of hostilities when they were sold to many overseas air forces — their low initial cost being more important than their military potential!

Three DH9s survive today, F1258 in the Musee de l'Air, Chalais Meudon, Paris; IS-8 at the South African Museum of Military History, Saxonwold; and G-EAQM, ex-F1287, which is being restored with the Australian War Memorial at Canberra.

De Havilland DH9A

Powerplant: One 400hp Liberty 12
Span: 45ft 11.375in
Length: 30ft 3in
Height: 11ft 4in
Wing area: 486.75sq ft

The failure of the Puma-powered DH9 led to the construction of a new type, the DH9A, which combined the best features of the DH9 and DH4 with the extra power of the 400hp Liberty 12 which was imported from the USA. The re-design was in the hands of the Westland Aircraft Works at Yeovil and the Westland design team, aided by John Johnson of the Airco company, managed to produce the most outstanding strategic bomber of the Great War.

The first unit to receive the type was No 110 Sqn at Kenley, the cost of re-equipping being borne by His Serene Highness, The Nizam of Hyderabad, and an inscription to this effect was painted on each aircraft. On 31 August 1918 the unit left for France and, based at Bettencourt, began long-range day bombing of 14 September. On the sixth raid, on 5 October, the squadron went astray in cloud and haze and diverted its attention to Kaiserlautern where it ran into heavy flak and fighters. Bombs were dropped and four aircraft went missing. One of these was F1010 'Hyderabad No 12A' which was forced down intact and which was eventually put on show in the great Berlin Air Museum. Following the destruction of the Museum by Allied bombing the surviving exhibits were evacuated to Poland and the fuselage and tail of the DH9A eventually surfaced at Krakow as part of the Polish Museum of Aviation & Astronautics. Here it stayed until June 1977 when it was exchanged for a Spitfire XVI by the Royal Air Force Museum. Arriving at Cardington on 28 June 1977, the staff of the Museum are now well on the way to completing a restoration which has involved building all new flying surfaces and obtaining a new Liberty 12 from from the USA.

Fokker Eindekker

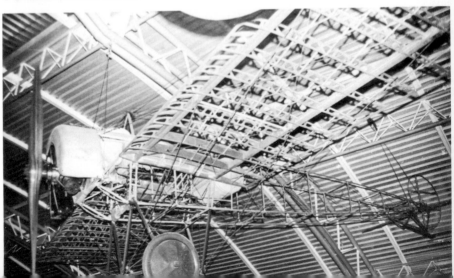

Data: EIII

Powerplant: One 100hp Oberursel UI
Span: 37ft 9in
Length: 24ft
Height: 7ft 6in
Wing area: 172.8sq ft

The success of the E series Fokker monoplanes was largely due to their being the first machines to be fitted with a reliable interrupter mechanism which allowed the machine gun to be fired through the propeller arc. The main production version was the

EIII, powered by the 100hp Oberursel UI, and of which some 120-150 were built.

The 'Fokker Scourge' reigned supreme over the Western Front from the autumn of 1915 until the spring of the following year when improved British types such as the DH2, FE2b, FE8 and Vickers FB9 — all of which were pusher types — came on the scene to give the Royal Flying Corps aerial superiority by the summer of 1916.

A number of famous German aces began their careers on the Eindekker including Boelcke and Immelmann but today only one original machine is known to exist, in the Science Museum, South Kensington, although several flying replicas have been built in Europe and the USA.

Fokker DVII   Germany

Photo: Fokker DVII in the RAF Museum, Hendon.

Powerplant: One 160hp Mercedes DIII or one 185hp BMW III.
Span: 29ft 3.5in
Length: 22ft 11.5in
Height: 9ft 2.25in
Wing area: 221.4sq ft

The most famous of all the German fighters of World War 1 was probably the Fokker DVII, winner of the competition held at Adlershof in January 1918 to find a new fighting scout to replace the Albatros DVa and Fokker DrI. Initially it was fitted with the 160hp Mercedes DIII powerplant and its car-type radiator was something of a departure from previous German practice. Later in 1918 the new 185hp BMW unit was fitted to enhance its already notable performance.

The success of the type can be attributed to the fact that it was fairly easy to fly yet very responsive — especially at its service ceiling of 22,900ft where its opponents were liable to be rather sluggish.

Throughout the summer of 1918 the DVII was met in increasing numbers and by November a total of 775 were in service. A pointer to the respect which was felt for the type can be found in the fact that it was the only aircraft to be mentioned by name in the Armistice agreement which designated which items were to be handed over to the Allied powers.

Today eight original examples are preserved world-wide including 2319/18, built by Albatross at its Schneidemuhl works, which is preserved in the Royal Air Force Museum, Hendon, and 6796/18 which is on show at the Musee de l'Air, Chalais Meudon, Paris.

Halberstadt CV

Photo: Halberstadt CV in the Musee Royal de l'Armee, Brussels.
Data: CV

Powerplant: One 220hp Benz BzIV high-compression
Span: 44ft 8.375in
Length: 22ft 8.5in
Height: 11ft 0.25in
Wing area: 464.6sq ft

The CV appeared during the first part of 1918 but did not become fully operational until mid-summer as a high-altitude, long distance reconnaissance machine.

Its high-altitude role is belied by the long span, high aspect-ratio wings and high-compression 220hp Benz Bz IV engine. Alongside the Rumpler CVII the Halberstadt CV gave sterling service in providing intelligence photographs during the closing months of the war, being faced with the awkward combination of frequently retreating positions and increasing Allied fighter opposition. One CV survives, 3471/18, in the Musee Royal de l'Armee, Brussels whilst the remains of a CLII is stored at Krakow, Poland and a CLIV is undergoing restoration with Doug Champlin's 'Falcon Field Fighter Air Museum', Mesa, Arizona, USA.

Hanriot HD-1

Photo: Hanriot HD-1 in the Royal Belgium Army Museum.

Powerplant: One 110hp Le Rhône
Span: 27ft 6in
Length: 19ft 8in
Loaded weight: 1,333lb
Maximum speed: 116mph

Although French in origin the attractive little HD-1 was almost totally ignored by the French forces during World War 1 and most of those built were delivered to either the Belgian or Italian Air Forces, in fact the type was so well thought of in Italy that it was licence-built there by the Macchi company.

Of the five known to survive one, No 75 of the Belgian Air Force, has recently been presented to the Royal Air Force Museum and was placed on display at Hendon in December 1979. This aircraft was built

in 1918 and served with No 1 Sqn, Belgian AF at Les Moors before being assigned to the 7eme Escadrille de Chasse after World War 1. In 1922 it actually won the World Aerobatic Contest at Nice and it was not retired from the Belgian Air Force until 1934 when it was bought by the three Drossaert brothers and registered OO-APJ. In October 1937 it was bought by Richard Shuttleworth and registered as G-AFDX, flying from Old Warden until badly damaged in an accident in 1939.

Stored until 1962 it was sold to Marvin Hand of California who rebuilt it to fly, this being achieved in 1968, and he eventually presented it to the RAF Museum in 1979. Other examples exist with the Italian Air Force Museum at Vigna di Valle, the Swiss Transport Museum at Lucerne, Planes of Fame Museum, Chino, California and the Royal Belgian Army Museum, Brussels.

Junkers J4 (JI)   Germany

Powerplant: One 200hp Benz BzIV with high
compression cylinders
Span: 52ft 6in
Length: 29ft 10.375in
Height: 11ft 1.5in
Wing area: 533.52sq ft

Bearing the manufacturer's designation J4 this
extremely large, all-metal, single-engined
sesquiplane was also known by its military
designation which was JI, this has led to some
confusion in the past with the earlier J1 of 1915
which was an all-metal cantilever monoplane.
The massive J4 appeared in 1917 and was

intended as a successor to the AEG and Albatross J
types which had always been intended as interim
models. It was a technical masterpiece and it was
the first aircraft to be covered with the revolutionary
corrugated metal skin which was to become a
hallmark of Junkers technique. It was intended for
contact-patrol duties, which necessitated plenty of
low flying over Front Line positions in order to report
back to HQ, and was therefore provided with an
armoured compartment to enclose the 200hp Benz
high-compression engine and two crew.

227 were built and, remarkably, one survives with
the Canadian National Aeronautical Collection where
it is on view at Rockcliffe Airport on the Northern
outskirts of Ottawa.

Junkers J9 (DI)

Germany

Powerplant: One 185hp BMW
Span: 29ft 6.375in
Length: 23ft 9.375in
Height: 7ft 4.5in
Wing area: 159sq ft

This all-metal, single-seat fighter was ordered into production in 1918 and was a development of the J7 prototypes of 1917, from which it differed mainly in its length and the installation of a BMW engine rather than the 160hp Mercedes. Only a few reached the front-line units before the Armistice and the type never got a chance to prove itself in combat. One of these interesting machines survives in the Musee de l'Air at Chalais Meudon, Paris.

LVG CVI

Germany

Photo: The Shuttleworth Collection's LVG CVI.

Powerplant: One 200hp Benz BzIV
Span: 42ft 7.75in
Length: 24ft 5.25in
Height: 9ft 2.25in
Wing area: 375.68sq ft

The CVI was a two-seat reconnaissance and artillery observation machine which appeared in 1918 and of which some 1,000 examples were built by Luft-Verkehrs Gesellschaft mbH at Johannisthal, Berlin. It was a successor to the earlier CV from which it differed very little, although it was lighter and more compact. Armament comprised a fixed, forward-firing Spandau and a Parabellum on a flexible mounting in the rear cockpit. Two examples are known to survive, one in flying condition with the Shuttleworth Collection at Old Warden, Bedfordshire, and the other with the Royal Belgian Army Museum, Brussels. In addition to the surviving CVIs the damaged remains of an earlier LVG BII are stored with the Polish Museum of Aeronautics & Astronautics at Krakow.

Martinsyde F4 Buzzard

UK

Powerplant: One 300hp Hispano-Suiza
Span: 32ft 9.375in
Length: 25ft 5.625in
Height: 10ft 4in
Wing area: 362sq ft

The F4 Buzzard was the production version of the F3, the first single-seat fighter in Martinsyde's F series, and from which it differed by the installation of the 300hp Hispano-Suiza and a cockpit which was slighly further aft. Tested in June 1918, large orders were placed for it but none had reached the

squadrons before the Armistice was signed. It was the fastest British aircraft in production at the time and would surely have had a tremendous influence had it been given the opportunity to prove itself in combat.

When the Martinsyde company ceased trading surplus F4s were offered for sale by the Aircraft Disposals Company, which later produced its own variant known as the Martinsyde ADCl and powered by the Armstrong Siddeley Jaguar radial. Finland operated the F4 as a single-seat fighter and one of these aircraft, MA-24 ex-D4326, is today preserved and on show at Jyvaskyla.

Nieuport Scout

France

Photo: The Nieuport 17 in the Royal Belgian Army Museum.

Data: Type 17

Powerplant: One 110hp Le Rhône rotary
Span: 26ft
Length: 19ft
Height: 7ft
Wing area: 158.8sq ft

Built in a wide variety of models the Nieuport Scout, with its characteristic 'V' interplane struts, was one of the most outstanding aircraft of World War 1 and will always be associated with such memorable aces as Ball, Bishop, Navarre and Nungesser. The prime variants were the Models 11, 17, 23, 24 and 28 which were progressively more powerful and refined, the last Type 28s remaining in service with the Swiss Air Force until the spring of 1930.

The Type 11 was in service in 1915 and this was superseded the following year by the Type 17 with the more powerful 110hp Le Rhône engine in place of the 80hp engines of the earlier model. The Type 23 was broadly similar to the Type 17 and powered by the same 110hp Le Rhône but the Type 24 introduced rounded instead of flat sides to the fuselage and the even more powerful 120hp Le Rhône engine. The final derivative was the elegant Type 28 which appeared in 1917 and of which 297 were delivered to the American squadrons fighting in France — virtually the entire factory output. This was the type flown by Eddie Rickenbacker to obtain his early victories and it was easily recognised by the slim, tapering fuselage, rounded wingtips and tailplane and its 160hp Gnôme-Rhône 9-N engine.

Several examples survive world-wide and a number of replicas have been built, particularly in the United States; a Type 11, N976, is exhibited at the Musee de L'Air, Chalais Meudon, a Type 17 at the Royal Belgian Army Museum, Brussels and two Type 28s in Switzerland — one at Lucerne and the other at Dubendorf.

A largely original Nieuport 28 which was once owned by MGM, and latterly by the Wings & Wheels museum in Orlando, Florida, was purchased by Guy Black in December 1981 and shipped to the UK in early 1982 for eventual restoration to flying condition by Skysport Aviation.

Pfalz DXII

Germany

Photo: The Pfalz DXII at Chalais Meudon.

Powerplant: One 160hp Mercedes DIIIa
Span: 29ft 6.375in
Length: 20ft 10in
Height: 8ft 10.25in
Wing area: 236.3sq ft

Appearing with front-line units during August 1918 the Pfalz DXII was a very definite late-comer on the combat scene and was almost totally overshadowed by the Fokker DVII. Although bearing a superficial resemblance to the Fokker product it differed appreciably in its mode of construction, the fuselage being a semi-monocoque as opposed to the welded

steel tube of the Fokker. Its double-bay wings made it unpopular with ground crews as, although it gave it added strength, it made the type more difficult to rig. Once the pilots had got to know the machine it gave a good account of itself in combat and, if the war had lasted longer, would have probably gained in popularity, by October 1918 there were some 180 Pfalz DXIIs in service on the Western Front.

Surprisingly, four of this little-known type survive today, one at the Australian War Memorial, Canberra, one with the Musee de L'Air, Chalais Meudon, one with the Champlin Fighter Museum in the USA and another loaned to the EAA Air Museum by its owners the National Air & Space Museum, Washington DC.

Royal Aircraft Factory BE2C   UK

Photo: BE2C in the Musee de l'Air.
Data: BE2C

Powerplant: Various engines were fitted including the 90hp RAF Ia
Span: 37ft
Length: 27ft 3in
Height: 11ft 1.5in
Wing area: 371sq ft

The BE2C was developed during 1914 from the earlier BE2 which had been designed by Capt

Geoffrey de Havilland of the Royal Aircraft Factory, Farnborough. The 2C differed from its predecessor in that wings of a new design were fitted which gave the type inherent stability — a factor considered of paramount importance at that time. With the outbreak of war looming on the horizon it was decided to order the 2C into mass-production, a decision which has often been criticised with the benefit of hindsight but which, at the time, was a decision of some courage and faith as the type had yet to complete its trials.

In the event the 2C proved an ideal

reconnaissance type and was even used for bombing missions but, with the advent of true aerial combat, it was soon outclassed as a fighting machine, its inherent stability making it extremely cumbersome in a dog-fight situation and it was withdrawn from Front-Line duties and relegated to training and Home Defence use.

In an attempt to improve the type the BE2E was introduced in the summer of 1916, joining the RFC during the Battle of the Somme. Although a better machine than the 2C in many ways it was still outclassed by the opposition and was eventually replaced by the RE8 and Armstrong Whitworth FK8 in the artillery observation role.

Three BE2Cs are preserved today, 2699 with the Imperial War Museum, Duxford, 4112 at the Canadian War Museum, Ottawa; and 9969 with the Musee de I'Air, Chalais Meudon, Paris. Two BE2Es survive in Norway; No 131 ex-AI380, is kept at Gardermoen AFB following its restoration at Kjevik in 1978-80 where the second, A1325, is currently undergoing a rebuild.

Royal Aircraft Factory RE8   UK

Powerplant: One 150hp RAF 4A
Span: 42ft 7in
Length: 27ft 10in
Height: 11ft 4in
Wing area: 377.5sq ft

Designed as a replacement for the cumbersome BE2 the RE8 was produced in considerable numbers from 1916 onwards, some 3,000 being built of which over 2,000 saw action on the Western Front. Despite the known shortcomings of the BE2 its successor managed to retain its inherent stability and was thus as unpopular in this respect as had been the earlier type. Despite this lack of popularity with both air and ground crews alike the type served in considerable numbers, it had an unpleasant tendency to spin if handled by inexperienced pilots and would readily burst into flames on impact — the engine being thrown into the fuel tanks by the force of impact. Various modifications were incorporated to make the machine more pleasant and it ended up comparatively viceless but the 'Harry Tate' was never loved and most crews would have given their right arms for the opportunity to re-equip with Bristol Fighters.

Two RE8s survive, F3556 is exhibited at the Imperial War Museum at Duxford, Cambridgeshire and another example, possibly ex-A4719, is with the Royal Belgian Army Museum in Brussels.

Royal Aircraft Factory SE5A   UK

Photo: Shuttleworth Collection's SE5A, G-EBIA/ F904.
Powerplant: One 200hp Wolseley Viper or one 200, 220 or 240hp Hispano-Suiza
Span: 26ft 8in
Length: 21ft
Height: 9ft 6in
Wing area: 247sq ft

Alongside the Sopwith Camel the SE5A, designed around the 150hp Hispano-Suiza, was one of the most well-known British aircraft of World War 1. The aircraft was designed to be flown by pilots with limited experience and incorporated the traditional inherent stability of previous RAF designs which meant that it was not as manoeuvrable as the Camel but provided a more stable gun platform in combat.

Early models had the standard Hispano-Suiza but later versions had the geared Hispano, when this engine proved troublesome it was replaced by the 200hp Wolseley Viper which was a British-built derivative. The 5A differed from the 5 in several other points including a long exhaust pipe, modified windscreen and wider track undercarriage.

Despite the Camel scoring the greater total of victories the SE5A was outstandingly successful and was the mount of some of the greatest British aces including Mannock (73 victories), Bishop (72) and McCudden (57), all of them were awarded the Victoria Cross for their exploits.

Five SE5As survive together with two American-built SE5Es, examples preserved within the UK are F904, jointly preserved by the Royal Aircraft Establishment and the Shuttleworth Collection in flying condition; F938 with the Royal Air Force Museum, Hendon; and F939 at the Science Museum, South Kensington.

In addition to the above the Hon Patrick Lindsay has obtained an SE5A AS 22-296, from the defunct Wings and Wheels Museum at Orlando, Florida and this is now under restoration at Booker, Bucks.

Rumpler CIV   Germany

Photo: Rumpler CIV in the Deutches Museum.

Powerplant: One 260hp Mercedes DIV
Span: 41ft 6.5in
Length: 27ft 7in
Height: 10ft 8in
Wing area: 361.8sq ft

The Rumpler CIV was mainly used in the strategic role for long-range reconnaissance and photographic duties, frequently flying well behind the Allied lines and using its excellent ceiling and duration (21,000ft and $3\frac{1}{2}$-4hr) to keep out of the way of attacking fighters, few Allied aircraft could catch it above 15,000ft.

Constructionally it was quite similar to the earlier CI and CIa but it certainly looked far more racy with its moderately swept-back wings and elegantly pointed engine cowlings which hid its 260hp Mercedes. It was popular with its crews and efficiently performed its vital, if unspectacular, tasks. Two CIVs survive, one is currently under restoration with the Royal Belgian Army Museum, Brussels while the other is with the Deutsches Museum, Munich.

Sopwith Baby

UK

Photo: Sopwith Baby 'N2078', FAA Museum, Yeovilton.

Powerplant: One 110hp Clerget
Span: 25ft 8in
Length: 23ft
Height: 10ft
Wing area: 240sq ft

The Baby was a more powerful development of the Sopwith Schneider, fitted with the 110hp Clerget in place of the 100hp Gnôme Monosoupape, the first batch of 100 Babies being built and delivered by Sopwith between September 1915 and July 1916. Production was transferred to the Blackburn company where 71 so-called 'Blackburn Babies' were constructed, most of which were fitted with the 130hp Clerget, and the Fairey company produced what amounted to an almost new design which was known as the Fairey Hamble Baby.

The Babies operated from seaplane carriers in the North Sea and Mediterranean on anti-Zeppelin and bombing missions and they also flew fighter patrols from Dunkirk until replaced by Sopwith Pups of the Royal Naval Air Service in July 1917. One Baby survives in the Fleet Air Arm Museum at Yeovilton, Somerset; serialed N2078 it is mainly a new aircraft although it does incorporate parts of two original Babies, Nos 8214 and 8215.

Sopwith 1½-Strutter

UK

Photo: The Sopwith 1½-Strutter at Chalais Meudon.

Powerplant: One 110hp or 130hp Clerget
Span: 33ft 6in
Length: 25ft 3in
Height: 10ft 3in
Wing area: 346sq ft

Bearing perhaps the oddest name of any British aeroplane the 1½-Strutter owes its name to the unusual arrangement of the inner-most wing struts which connect the upper wings to the top longerons rather than to the lower wings as would have been the case in a conventional two-bay biplane. It was a two-seater and with its fixed, forward-firing Vickers machine gun, which was the first to be standardised on a British type with interrupter gear, and a rear mounted Lewis on a flexible mounting, it set the style of the two-seat fighter which was to persist for the next 20 years.

The type was originally specified by the Admiralty, which knew it as the Sopwith Type 9700, but it was also delivered to the Royal Flying Corps and following the first deliveries in 1916 it gave sterling service well into 1917 and even at the Armistice nearly 170 were in service with the Royal Air Force, of which nearly 40 were embarked at sea with the Grand Fleet.

Two of these significant aircraft, the first Sopwith to become widely-known, survive today, S85 in the Royal Belgian Army Museum and 556 in the Musee de L'Air, Chalais Meudon. In addition a flying replica which was built by V. H. Bellamy at Land's End has been bought by the RAF Museum and is displayed at Hendon.

Sopwith Pup

UK

Photo: The Shuttleworth Collection's Sopwith Pup.

Powerplant: One 80hp Le Rhône
Span: 26ft 6in
Length: 19ft 3.75in
Height: 9ft 5in
Wing area: 245sq ft

Although officially known simply as the Sopwith Scout the little Pup was regarded with affection by all who flew it and it has been said that it was '...probably the most perfect flying machine ever made'. The name Pup was probably coined as its pilots thought of it as the offspring of the larger 1½-Strutter and like its bigger relative it too was used by both the RNAS and the RFC, being pioneered on the Western Front by squadrons of the RNAS a full three months before the RFC units went into action in December 1916.

Despite the low power of its 80hp Le Rhône it was markedly superior to the German Albatros because of its lower wing-loading, it could hold its height better than any other existing type on either side and was not surpassed as a fighting machine until mid-1917. Over 800 were on charge at the Armistice but it was declared obsolete in December 1918 and vanished from Service use with astonishing rapidity. A two-seat derivate, the Sopwith Dove, was built for civilian use and one of these, G-EBKY, was re-converted to Pup standards for the Shuttleworth Collection where it flies as N5180. Several replicas have been built world-wide but the last genuine Pup was probably C476 which survived in Australia as G-AUCK until dismantled on 21 September 1945.

Sopwith Triplane

UK

Photo: The RAF Museum's Sopwith Triplane.

Powerplant: One 110hp or 130hp Clerget
Span: 26ft 6in
Length: 18ft 10in
Height: 10ft 6in
Wing area: 231sq ft

The Sopwith Pup was followed by the Sopwith Triplane, one of the great aeroplanes of World War 1 which, owing to its triplane configuration, had a remarkable rate of roll and a very fast climb. Such was its impact with the RNAS squadrons, with which it entered service in February 1917, that it gained total supremacy over all enemy types in the heavy fighting of 1917. The Triplanes of 'B Flight', No 10 (Naval) Sqn — or 'Naval Ten' — were named *Black Death, Black Maria, Black Roger, Black Prince* and *Black Sheep*; commanded by F/Sub-Lt Raymond Collishaw they struck terror into the hearts of the enemy and in two short months brought down 87 German aircraft, Collishaw bringing down 16 in 27 days!

Their operational career was a brief but glorious seven months, being replaced by the Camel from November 1917, but one of these exclusively-Naval fighters survives, paradoxically in the Royal Air Force Museum, Hendon, and a second, possibly N5486, is

exhibited in the Soviet Air Force Museum at Monino, East of Moscow. Several replicas exist, including two flying versions one of which is airworthy with the Hon Patrick Lindsay at Booker and the other is under construction for the Shuttleworth Trust by the Northern Aeroplane Workshops at Harrogate.

Sopwith Camel UK

Powerplant: Several types were fitted but commonly the 130hp Clerget or 150hp Bentley BR1
Span: 28ft
Length: 18ft 9in
Height: 8ft 6in
Wing area: 231sq ft

Unquestionably the most famous British fighter of World War 1 the Camel was, in the right hands, the supreme fighting aeroplane and accounted for 1,294 enemy aircraft the greatest number to be brought down by a single type on either side during the four years of the war. It was a conventional biplane and a logical development of the smaller Pup but probably the main factor which brought about its extreme

manoeuvrability was the concentration of engine, guns, fuel, ammunition and pilot all within the first 7ft of fuselage.

Deliveries began in the early summer of 1917 and the first to see action were the RNAS machines from Dunkirk in July, later in the same month the type entered service on the Western Front in time for the Battle of Ypres. Although its use was extensive its disappearance from the Royal Air Force was sudden, the decision to re-equip with Snipes having been

taken before the Armistice, and the tenacious little fighter had virtually no peace-time use with the Royal Air Force.

Today two survive in the UK F6314 with the Royal Air Force Museum, Hendon and N6812, a Naval 2FI, which is preserved at the Imperial War Museum, South Lambeth. Several replicas have been built of which two are flyable at the Leisure Sport collection, Thorpe Park, Surrey, and a number of original and replica Camels are exhibited world-wide.

Sopwith 7FI Snipe   UK

Photo: The Canadian National Aeronautical Collection's Sopwith Snipe.

Powerplant: One 230hp Bentley BR2
Span: 31ft 1in
Length: 19ft 10in
Height: 9ft 6in
Wing area: 271sq ft

With the entry into production of the 230hp Bentley BR2 rotary engine it was natural for the Air Board to specify a new fighter to replace the Camel and equally natural for the Sopwith company to tender a new design. The first prototype Snipe looked very much like a more bulbous Camel but the eventual production version differed considerably, especially with its horn-balanced ailerons, two-bay wings and enlarged fin and rudder. The Snipe proved to be no faster than the Camel and slower than the Dolphin, when tested in February 1918 but it outclimbed both of them by a considerable margin and was selected

for quantity-production.

Comparatively few Snipes reached the Western Front before the Armistice and it saw very little operational flying but one action deserves mention, that being the remarkable battle of Maj W. G. Barker, fought in Snipe E8102 on 27 October 1918, who managed to dispatch four enemy aircraft singlehanded despite wounds in both legs and one arm. He was awarded the Victoria Cross for this action and his Snipe's fuselage is preserved in the Canadian War Museum, Ottawa.

The Snipe soldiered on for nine years after the Armistice, being used as the RAF's standard fighter for some years. Several survive today although none are extant in the UK, E6938 is maintained in airworthy condition by the Canadian National Aeronautical Collection at Rockcliffe, E8105 flies with Cole Palen's collection at Old Rhinebeck, New York state, and the fuselage of Barker's aircraft is preserved in Ottawa as mentioned above.

SPAD S7 and derivatives

France

Photo: The SPAD in the Canadian National Aeronautical Collection.
Data: S7

Powerplant: One 150hp Hispano-Suiza
Span: 25ft 6in
Length: 20ft 3in
Height: 7ft
Wing area: 200sq ft

Built by the Societé pour Aviation et ses Derives the S7 Scout and its later derivatives shared the honours with the Nieuport series as France's most famous fighter of World War 1. Its use was not restricted to the French forces however and 120 aircraft built under licence by Mann, Egerton Ltd of Norwich were diverted from the RNAS to equip RFC units on the Western Front during early 1917. Many American units were also equipped with the type and its greater structural strength compared with the Nieuport made it particularly popular with these pilots.

It was a difficult machine to master with a very steep glide angle which necessitated its being flown on to the ground with considerable power compared to the flatter glide-approaches adopted for its contemporaries, but its ability to stay together when pulling out of a dive made up for its lack of manoeuvrability. Over 5,000 were built in various models ranging from the S7 through the SXII and SXIII to the SXVI.

At least 13 original aircraft of various types are known to exist with examples of both an S7 and SXIII being preserved at the Musee de l'Air, Paris, whilst a flying replica SXIII, G-BFYO, is owned by Leisure Sport Ltd and based at Thorpe Park, Surrey.

A genuine SPAD XIII which had been displayed in the Wings and Wheels Museum at Orlando, Florida, was sold to a European buyer in December 1981 and is now statically displayed at the Imperial War Musuem, Duxford, Cambs, although it will eventually be rebuilt to flying condition.

Standard J-1

USA

Photo: Standard J-1 in the NASM Washington.

Powerplant: One 90hp Curtiss OX-5 or suitable alternative
Span: 44ft
Length: 26ft 6in
Gross weight: 2,206lb
Wing area: 433sq ft

The J-1 was a primary trainer, designed by Charles H. Day, and which was put into production for the US Army flying schools during 1916, a total of 1,601 being built eventually by a number of companies. Powerplants were varied, ranging from the 90hp Curtiss OX-5 up to the 150hp Hispano-Suiza, the 125hp Hall-Scott powered version gaining notoriety as a fire-trap! After the Armistice surplus J-1s were

converted into three-seaters for barnstorming and joy-riding, Lincoln Aircraft being active in this field, the aircraft being known as the Lincoln-Standard. At least 10 survive in North America, a Lincoln-Standard (N1375) being exhibited by the National Air & Space Museum, Washington DC, and at least two, N2825D and N2826D, being maintained in airworthy condition.

Thomas-Morse S4C Scout

USA

Photo: S4C Scout in the USAF Museum.

Powerplant: 80hp Le Rhône
Span: 26ft 5in

Length: 19ft 8in
Gross weight: 1,330lb
Wing area: 145sq ft

Following its rejection as a fighter late in 1916 the Thomas Morse Aircraft Corporation put the S4 into production early in 1917 as an unarmed, single-seat advanced trainer for the US Army. 597 Tommies were delivered to the Army and six float-equipped seaplanes were delivered to the US Navy. Eight examples of this attractive little aeroplane exist in the United States of which one, N74W an S4B model, remains airworthy with Cole Palen's collection at Old Rhinebeck, New York state.

Vickers FB27A Vimy   UK

Photo: Alcock and Brown's Vimy in the Science Museum.
Data: Vimy IV

Powerplants: Two 360hp Rolls-Royce Eagle VIII
Span: 67ft 2in
Length: 43ft 6.5in
Height: 15ft 3in
Wing area: 1,330sq ft

The prototype Vimy made its maiden flight on 30 November 1917 but the definitive production version, the Rolls-Royce Eagle VIII-powered Vimy Mk IV, did not fly until mid-1918 and only one of these superb machines managed to reach France before the Armistice was signed in November 1918. After the cessation of hostilities the Vimy was adopted for Service use with the peace-time Royal Air Force and gave many years of faithful service but its greatest achievements were in the sphere of long-range flights. Of these pioneering flights the one which is best remembered is that of Alcock and Brown who crossed the North Atlantic from Newfoundland to Ireland in June 1919, their modified Vimy is today given pride of place in the Science Museum, South Kensington. Another long-range Vimy, Ross and Keith Smith's G-EAOU is preserved at Adelaide, South Australia, and a full-scale flying replica is preserved at the Royal Air Force Museum, Hendon.

Part Three: 1919-1938

Aeronca C3 and 100   USA & UK

Photo: Aeronca 100 G-AEXD which is stored by Roy Mills in Hanworth.
Data: Aeronca 100

Powerplant: One 40hp Aeronca JAP J-99
Span: 36ft
Length: 20ft
Height: 7ft 10in
Wing area: 142.2sq ft

The C3 two seater made its debut in the USA in the early 1930s and 205 C3 'Collegians' were built

during 1932-33. A successor, the enclosed-cockpit C3 Master, was introduced in 1934 and 290 were built in the US with a further 21 built at Peterborough, England, as the Aeronca 100. With its diminutive proportions and comic looks the Aeroncas never really caught on in the UK but their undoubted popularity in the US is reflected by the numbers built and the fact that the Master held more records than any other type in its class. Several C3s survive in flying condition in the USA and five aircraft remain in the UK, two C3s and three 100s, of which only G-AEFT is currently airworthy.

Arrow Active II   UK

Photo: The solitary Arrow Active II, G-ABVE.

Powerplant: One 145hp DH Gipsy Major 1C
Span: 24ft
Length: 18ft 10in
All up weight: 1,325lb
Max speed; 144mph

Two Active single-seat sporting biplanes were built in 1931 and 1932 by Arrow Aircraft Ltd of Leeds. The Active I, G-ABIX, was powered by the 115hp Cirrus Hermes IIB and was written off in December

1935 when it caught fire in mid-air. The Active II, G-ABVE, was powered by the 120hp DH Gipsy III and was flown in the 1932 and 1933 King's Cup Air Races by Flt Lt H. H. Leech. It then seems to have been put into store and was rediscovered in 1957. Bought by Norman Jones it was rebuilt at Croydon for the Tiger Club and flew again on the power of a 145hp Gipsy Major 1C the following year.

The Active was a star performer at Tiger Club displays for more than 20 years and is now enthusiastically flown by new owner Desmond Penrose.

Avia B534

Czechoslovakia

Photo: H-6 preserved at Kbely, Czechoslovakia.

Powerplant: One 850hp Avia-built Hispano-Suiza 12 Ydrs
Span: 30ft 10in
Length: 26ft 7in
Height: 10ft 2in
Max speed: 226mph

The prototype of the elegant Avia B534 made its first flight in August 1933 and following trials an initial batch of 100 was ordered, to be powered by the Hispano-Suiza HS 12 Ydrs of 850hp. Early models had open cockpits but sliding hoods soon became standard. The armament was also revised in that two of the four guns were relocated from the wings to the sides of the forward fuselage. Various other refinements included the addition of wheel spats and the Bk534 mounted an additional 7.7mm machine gun between the cylinder banks.

A total of 445 B534s was eventually built, the first Czechoslovak squadrons becoming operational on the type in the summer of 1935. Following the German invasion four years later large numbers were transferred to the Slovak Air Force and were used against the Soviet forces whilst others were used for second-line duties by the Luftwaffe. The B534 was also exported in small numbers, 14 going to Yugoslavia in 1937 and a small number to Greece.

One B534 has survived and has been restored to display condition at the aviation museum at Kbely where it is marked as H-6.

Avro Avian

UK

Photo: VH-UQE is owned and flown by Albert Murrell of Penola, South Australia, and is the sole Type 616 IVA with 30ft span wings and DH Gipsy II engine.
Data: Type 616 Avian IVM

Powerplant: One 105hp Cirrus Hermes I
Span: 28ft
Length: 24ft 3in
Height: 8ft 6in
Wing area: 245sq ft

The prototype Avro 581 Avian, G-EBOV, was built for the 1926 *Daily Mail* light aeroplane trials in which it was piloted by H. J. 'Bert' Hinkler who later bought the aircraft outright, modified it, and flew it solo from Croydon to Darwin, Australia in February 1928. This historic aeroplane is now preserved in the Queensland Museum at Brisbane alongside Hinkler's diminutive Avro Baby G-EACQ.

The prototype had been all-wood and a small batch of production aircraft was then laid down as the Type 594. Two Avian Is were built to be followed by several Avian IIs and IIIs, the major production variant being the IIIA of which 58 were constructed, before the final wooden version, the Mk IV appeared. 90 Mk IVs were built before production was switched to the Type 616 which featured a welded steel tube fuselage and other refinements.

At least nine Avians of various Marks are known to survive in the UK, Australia, New Zealand, Canada and Sweden. Of these VH-UQE is thought to be the sole survivor in airworthy condition but a Genet-powered IIIA, G-ACGT, is being rebuilt at Yeadon, Yorks by Mike Rockcliffe.

Avro Tutor, Cadet and Prefect
UK

Photo: Tutor K3215 (ex-G-AHSA) is operated by the Shuttleworth Collection at Old Warden, Bedfordshire.

Data: Tutor 1

Powerplant: One 215-240hp Armstrong Siddeley Lynx IVC
Span: 34ft
Length: 26ft 6in
Height: 9ft 7in
Wing area: 300sq ft

The Type 621 Tutor was produced in 1930 to replace the immortal 504 in RAF service. It was of fabric-covered metal construction and the prototype was powered by the 155hp Armstrong Siddeley Mongoose IIIA radial. The production aircraft was powered by the 240hp Lynx radial and 394 were built for the RAF, the last one leaving the line in May 1936.

A variation of the basic airframe was the unnamed Type 626, large numbers of which were sold to overseas air forces. When fitted with a Cheetah engine and other mods this became the Avro Prefect, seven of which were built for the RAF as navigation trainers in early 1935.

The Cadet was basically a scaled-down Tutor which first appeared in 1931 as the Type 631, although bearing an external similarity to its larger relation it could be identified internally by virtue of its wooden wing structure. The Cadet was basically a civil aircraft but some were delivered to the Portuguese Air Force as basic trainers. The improved Type 643 appeared in September 1934 to be followed by the final version, the Cadet II, several of which served with the Royal Australian Air Force.

One Tutor survives with the Shuttleworth Collection at Old Warden and several Cadets survive in Eire, Portugal and Australia while one Prefect, ZK-APC (ex-NZ203) has been acquired by the Royal New Zealand Air Force Museum and is under restoration following many years of storage at Havelock North, New Zealand.

BA Swallow II   UK

Photo: Swallow II, G-AFCL landing at Old Warden.

Powerplant: One 90hp Blackburn Cirrus Minor 1 or
Pobjoy Cataract III
Span: 42ft 8.5in
Length: 27ft
Height: 7ft
Wing area: 215sq ft

The Swallow II was an extensively redesigned
version of the German Klemm L25 which was built
at Hanworth, Middx, from 1935 to 1939, by the
British Aircraft Manufacturing Co Ltd. 105 were built,
initially powered by the 85hp Pobjoy Cataract radial

but later aircraft had the Cataract III, Niagara and
Cirrus Minor 1, the latter being an in-line engine
instead of a radial.

The Swallow II was renowned for its low speed
handling and was exceptionally docile, being virtually
stall and spin-proof so that even the most inept
student pilot should have been able to handle it. Nine
Swallow IIs are to be found in the UK and Eire with
other examples in Australia. Of the British aircraft
four are currently maintained in flying condition:
G-ADPS with the Strathallan Collection, G-AFCL
with A. M. Dowson at Old Warden, G-AFGE with Don
Ellis at Sandown, Isle of Wight, and G-AFGD at
Shobdon, Herefordshire.

BA Eagle   UK

Photo: VH-UTI was rebuilt to fly by the Challinor
brothers at Murwillumbah, Queensland.
Data: Eagle 2

Powerplant: One 130hp DH Gipsy Major
Span: 39ft 3in
Length: 26ft
Height: 6ft 9in
Wing area: 200sq ft

The Eagle was a low wing, cantilever monoplane
featuring a retractable undercarriage and which
carried a pilot and two passengers on the power of a
130hp DH Gipsy Major. The prototype was built at
Hanworth in 1934 and five more aircraft were built
before the manufacturers were reorganised to

become the British Aircraft Manufacturing Co Ltd.
The Eagle was then refined and the deluxe Eagle 2
appeared in 1935, 37 production examples being
built.

The Eagle had an outstanding performance on the
relatively low power of the Gipsy Major and it was a
popular mount of prewar sporting pilots. The
retractable undercarriage was the only weakness
and several were written-off following undercarriage
collapse, one fixed undercarriage variant, G-AFAX,
was built and this survives in flying condition with
Cliff Douglas at Chewing Gum Field, Queensland,
Australia, as VH-ACN. Two other Eagle 2s survive,
both in Australia, VH-UTI has been rebuilt by the
Challinor brothers at Murwillumbah and VH-UUY is
being rebuilt.

BAC Drone

UK

Photo: BAC Drone, G-AEDB, prior to its maiden flight with new owner Mike Russell.
Data: Drone de Luxe

Powerplant: One 30hp Carden Ford
Span: 39ft 8in
Length: 21ft 2in
Height: 7ft
Wing area: 172sq ft

The single-seat Drone was a powered derivative of the two-seat BAC VII glider designed by C. H. Lowe-Wylde and manufactured at Maidstone. With the death of Lowe-Wylde in May 1933 the company was taken over by the distinguished Austrian glider expert Robert Kronfeld and the Drone was put into production by Kronfeld Ltd at Hanworth. Powered by a variety of engines, including the Douglas Sprite and Carden Ford, the Drone was exceptionally cheap to operate and was quite popular with some of the ultra-light clubs which were formed in the mid-1930s. Development of this promising aeroplane stopped when Kronfeld Ltd was declared bankrupt and very few survived World War 2.

One Drone is maintained in flying condition today, Bristol Cherub-powered G-AEDB with Mike Russell at Duxford. A Carden-Ford example, G-AEKV, is undergoing restoration with John McDonald at Booker and parts of several Douglas Sprite-powered versions have recently been acquired by P. G. Dunnington following long term storage by G. Eastell at Thetford.

Blackburn B-2 UK

Photo: G-AEBJ is maintained in flying condition by British Aerospace.

Powerplant: One 130hp DH Gipsy Major
Span: 30ft 2in
Length: 24ft 3in
Height: 9ft
Wing area: 246sq ft

The final derivative of the Blackburn Bluebird sporting biplane was the B-2 trainer of 1932. Powered by a variety of engines of Gipsy and Cirrus parentage the B-2 was unusual in that the fuselage was covered in Alclad metal cladding which made the aircraft incredibly strong.

The main user of the B-2 was the Blackburn Company itself, through its two Reserve Schools at Brough and Hanworth. All of the 42 production aircraft were civil registered with the exception of the last three which were serialed L6891, '92 and '93 and with the outbreak of war they were all camouflaged and continued their normal duties until retired in 1942 and given to ATC squadrons as ground instructional airframes. Two survived the war to fly again but with the loss of G-ACLD in June 1951 the sole survivor is G-AEBJ which is maintained in immaculate flying condition by British Aerospace at Brough. The fuselage of G-ACBH is to be found in an Essex scrapyard, where it has lain for over 30 years, and the forward fuselage of G-ADFV is in the possession of The Aeroplane Collection Ltd, Stockport, Cheshire.

Beechcraft Model 17 Staggerwing USA

Photo: Duxford-based N18V is a prewar D17S owned by Robert Lamplough.
Data: D17S

Powerplant: One 450hp Pratt & Whitney R-985 Wasp Junior
Span: 32ft
Length: 25ft 9in
Height: 9ft
Wing area: 296sq ft

Designed by Ted Wells the magnificent Model 17 first flew in November 1932 and was immediately dubbed Staggerwing on account of the characteristic negative stagger of its wings. Based on a specification for the personal use of Walter Beech the first Staggerwings were the 17R (420hp Wright Whirlwind) and A17F (700hp Wright Cyclone), both of which featured fixed and spatted undercarriages. The first model to boast a retractable undercarriage was the B17L with the 225hp Jacobs.

The type was the ultimate in personal transport throughout the 1930s and successive models were the B17B, C17B, C17L, E17B and E17L with the 285hp Jacobs L-5; the F17D with a 330hp Jacobs; the D17A and D17R with 350hp and 450hp Wright Whirlwinds respectively and the D17S with the Pratt & Whitney R-985 Wasp Junior.

424 Staggerwings of all marks had been built when the USA entered World War 2 and the D17S was then manufactured for the communications role as the UC-43 (207 built for the Army) and GB-1 (63 for the Navy). The type was also supplied to Britain under Lease-Lend. After the war it was returned to the civil market but only 20 G17S aircraft were built.

About 100 Staggerwings remain active, mainly in the USA, but two are currently based in Britain; Phillip Wolf bases G-BDGK at Redhill and Robert Lamplough keeps his camouflaged N18V at Duxford.

Beechcraft Model 18 USA

Photo: A Beechcraft C-45 preserved in prewar USAAC markings by the Confederate Air Force, Harlingen, Texas.
Data: C-45

Powerplant: Two 450hp Pratt & Whitney R-985-AN-3 or -B5 radials
Span: 47ft 7in
Length: 33ft 11.5in
Height: 9ft 2.5in
Wing area: 349sq ft

The original Model 18 light transport was flown in January 1937 as an executive twin but it was the selection of the type for the USAAC as a military transport which really established the design. The prewar civil models were the 18, A18 and B18 whilst the initial military version was the C-45, 5,204 of which were eventually delivered to the US

forces. In addition to its role as a light transport the type was selected for navigational training as the AT-7 and in 1941 a further redesign produced the AT-11 Kansan in which the forward fuselage was remodelled to provide a weapons bay and accommodation for a trainee bombardier. A total of 1,582 Kansans was built between 1941 and 1943, 36 of which were completed as AT-11A navigational trainers.

After the war the Model 18 was built in several versions, the last of which was the H18 Super-Liner which appeared in 1964, production eventually coming to a halt some years later after a record-breaking run of over 30 years.

Model 18s of all variants are to be found all over the world in considerable numbers, a Model E18S, G-ASUG, being preserved at the Royal Scottish Museum's Museum of Flight at East Fortune, near Edinburgh.

Boeing F4B-4 and P-12E

USA

Span: 30ft
Length: 20ft 4.75in
Height: 9ft 9in
Wing area: 227sq ft

The F4B and P-12 single-seat fighters were the most successful aircraft built for the US military in the inter-war period, a total of 586 being built, a figure which was not exceeded by any other military type until the outbreak of World War 2. The basic design stemmed from the experimental Models 83 and 89 which were built as private ventures and which first flew in 1928. Both aircraft were delivered to the US Navy in August 1928 and received the designation XF4B-1, after being successfully evaluated a production order was placed for 27 aircraft and the first F4B-1 (Boeing Model 99) was delivered on 6 May 1929.

The US Army Air Corps was so impressed by the Navy fighter that it took the unprecedented step of ordering a batch without bothering to carry out its own evaluation and nine aircraft were ordered as P-12s (Boeing Model 102) plus one modified aircraft which was known as the P-12A.

Subsequent developments were as follows: F4B-2 (42 built), F4B-3 (21 built), F4B-4 (74 built), P-12B (90 built), P-12C (96 built), P-12D (35 built), P-12E (110 built), P-12F (25 built). The type was also delivered to Spain and Brazil and five civil versions were built as the Boeing Model 100.

Five variants of the basic design are known to survive, one F4B-4, two P-12Es and two Model 100s, all are in the USA with the exception of one which is in the Royal Thai Air Force Museum at Bangkok.

Photo: Boeing P-12E, serial 32-17, still flying with Ed Maloney's Planes of Fame Museum, Chino Airport, California, formates with the Museum's P-26A Peashooter.
Data: F4B-3

Powerplant: One 550hp Pratt & Whitney R-1340D Wasp

Boeing P-26A Peashooter

USA

Photo: Ed Maloney's P-26A, 33-123/N3378G, airborne over Chino.

Powerplant: One 600hp Pratt & Whitney R-1340-27
Span: 27ft 11.5in
Length: 23ft 10in
Height: 10ft 5in
Wing area: 149sq ft

The P-26 was designed in 1931 and incorporated several very advanced features, it was the first monoplane fighter to see service with the Army Air Corps and also the first all-metal fighter to be built. Three experimental Model 248s were evaluated before the initial contract was placed in January 1933 for 111 of an improved version known as the P-26A. These were being delivered by the end of 1933 and entered service with pursuit squadrons both in Hawaii and in the Panama Canal Zone.

The P-26B introduced a fuel-injected powerplant

and the P-26C retained the standard engine but featured revised control systems. All P-26Cs were retrospectively modified to P-26B standard. The P-26 was also sold to China (11 aircraft) and Spain (one) whilst a number were transferred to the Philippine Army in 1941. Two aircraft from a batch of seven which were sold to the Guatemalan Military Air Corps in 1942-43 were returned to the USA in 1957-58. One is now exhibited in the National Air & Space Museum, Washington, DC, and the other is flying with Ed Maloney's Planes of Fame Museum at Chino Airport, California.

Boeing 247D   USA

Photo: The Science Museum's Boeing 247D, N18E, at Wroughton.

Powerplants: Two 550hp Pratt & Whitney R-1340-S1H1-G Wasp
Span: 74ft
Length: 51ft 7in
Height: 12ft 6in
Wing area: 836sq ft

The Model 247 all-metal low wing twin-engined airliner was first flown in February 1933 and was built to fulfil a specification issued by United Air Lines. This it handsomely did and production aircraft started to enter service with United late that year. 75 of these 10-passenger airliners were built, the last 13 of which were fitted with geared engines and featured other improvements which caused them to be designated 247Ds, several earlier 247s were brought up to D standard later in their lives.

Probably the best-known 247 was NR257Y, a 247D which was flown by Rosco Turner and Clyde Pangbourne to come third in the 1934 MacRobertson race to Australia, later registered NC13369 this historic aircraft is now restored to its Turner/Pangbourne configuration in the National Air & Space Museum, Washington, DC.

Several examples remain in flying condition but the most notable flight made by any in recent years must have been the Trans-Atlantic delivery flight of N18E which arrived at the Science Museum's Wroughton airfield in August 1982 having been flown from the Wings & Wheels Museum at Orlando, Florida.

Breguet XIX Grand Raid & Super Bidon   France

Photo: *Point d'Interrogation* on show at the Paris Air Show in 1971.

Powerplant: One 650hp Hispano-Suiza 12 Nb
Span: 60ft
Length: 34ft 2in
Empty weight: 4,827lb
Loaded weight: 14,133lb

The Breguet XIX Grand Raid was a large, military general purpose aircraft, two of which still survive, one in the Musee de l'Air at Chalais Meudon, Paris, and another CASA-built example in the Spanish Air Force Museum at Cuatro Vientos, Madrid. The Bidon was, however, a special development of the earlier type which was intended specifically as a long-range record breaker. Design and construction of the Bidon was supported by French perfumier M Francis Coty who anonymously provided £10,000 towards the cost in order that the aircraft might make an attempted non-stop flight from Paris to New York.

After an abortive start on the Atlantic attempt in July 1929 the Bidon was named *Point d'Interrogation* (*Question Mark*) and departed Le Bourget on 27 September 1929 on an attempt to break the World Long Distance Record. This it did when it landed in Northern Manchuria, China, 4,913 miles away after 51hr and 19min in the air. The aircraft then set several more distance records before going back into the shops for a new engine and more fuel tanks to be fitted.

It was ready the following autumn and on 1 September 1930 left Le Bourget, landing at New York's Curtiss Field after 37hr and 17min in the air. After a goodwill tour of American cities the aircraft was shipped back to France and eventually retired to the Musee de l'Air where it is now displayed in the new museum at Le Bourget, scene of its triumphant return on 25 October 1930.

Bucker Bu131 Jungmann   Germany

Photo: Although painted in prewar German markings G-BECU is a Spanish-built Jungmann owned by Amercian Gerry Chisum, a C-130 pilot with Air Alaska.
Data: Bu131B

Powerplant: One 105hp Hirth HM504A
Span: 24ft 3in
Length: 21ft 8in

Height: 7ft 5in
Wing area: 145sq ft

The Bu131 was first flown in 1934 and the initial production model was the Bu131A with the 80hp Hirth HM 60R engine. Large numbers of these two-seat aerobatic trainers were built for the Luftsportverband before the more powerful Bu131B (105hp Hirth HM 504) was introduced in 1936. The

outstanding flying qualities of the Jungmann meant that it was, and still is, an extremely popular aerobatic mount and manufacturing licences were taken out for it in Switzerland, Czechoslovakia and Spain. The Spanish CASA concern built 150 aircraft initially and returned the type to production in 1956, building a further 50. The Spanish aircraft are now beginning to come on to the private market, joining Swiss-built aircraft that have been enthusiastically flown by private owners world-wide over the past 15 years.

Bucker Bu133 Jungmeister

Germany

Photo: Bu133C Jungmeister G-AXMT.

Data: Bu133C

Powerplant: One 160hp Siemens Sh14A-4 radial
Span: 21ft 7.5in
Length: 19ft 4in
Height: 7ft 4.5in
Wing area: 130sq ft

The Jungmeister was introduced in 1935 as a single-seat, advanced aerobatic biplane, the prototype of which was fitted with a 140hp Hirth HM6 inline motor. Production versions of this superb little aeroplane were fitted with either the Hirth (Bu133B) or Siemens Sh14A-4 (Bu133C) but the vast majority were of the latter type. As with the Jungmann before it the Jungmeister was also built under licence in Switzerland and Spain. The Swiss Air Force finally retired its last Jungmeisters in the mid-1960s and several came on to the British civil register, others are flying throughout Europe and North America — in the latter country some have been re-engined with Warner radials or modern flat-fours.

Caproni Ca100 Caproncine

Italy

Photo: I-GTAB is preserved in the Caproni Museum at Vizzola Tichino.

Powerplant: One 135hp Colombo S63
Span: 27ft 5in
Length: 24ft
Height: 9ft
Wing area: 262.5sq ft

The CA100 was first produced in 1929 and was originally based on the de Havilland Moth airframe. It bears a passing resemblance to the Moth but is easily distinguished by virtue of the overhanging lower wings which protrude well on either side of the uppers. The fin and rudder is also of a revised shape. Powered by the 135hp Colombo S63 four-cylinder engine, five CA100s survive, including two float planes. Production is believed to have ended in 1936.

Caudron C635 Simoun

France

Photo: Albert Prost's immaculate Caudron Simoun, F-AZAM

Powerplant: One 220hp Renault Bengali 6Q-09
Span: 34ft 1in
Length: 28ft 6in
Height: 7ft 4in
Wing area: 172.16sq ft

The Simoun appeared at the 1934 Paris Salon as the C620 and was subsequently built in large numbers, the final version being the C635 which was powered by the Renault 6Q-09 engine of 220hp. Of wooden construction the cabin provides accommodation for four plus baggage, the type is therefore broadly comparable to the contemporary Percival Gull (qv). At least two Simouns are known to exist: F-ANRO is exhibited at the Le Bourget premises of the Musee de l'Air, it is actually CS-ADG; another has been restored to fly as F-AZAM by Albert Prost and Abel Mouls, it was originally delivered to the USA for the use of French Embassy staff in 1937 and was brought back to France in 1972 for use in a film.

Cessna 165 Airmaster   USA

Photo: Cessna 165 Airmaster, N25483.

Powerplant: One 165hp Warner Super Scarab
Span: 34ft 2in
Length: 24ft 8in
Height: 7ft
Wing area: 181sq ft

The original Airmaster was the C-34 of 1934, it was a development of the one-off C-3 which had been built the previous year for publisher Marcellus Murdock and was reputed to be the most efficient light aircraft in its class. The C-34 put Cessna back into the light aircraft business and was followed three years later by the improved C-37. Ninety C-34/37 Airmasters were built and several remain active, including the prototype.

1938 saw the introduction of the C-38 which had a modified undercarriage but only 15 were built before production gave way to the C-145 with revised flaps. The 165, powered by the 165hp Warner Super Scarab, appeared in 1939 and remained in production until 1942. 41 C-145s and 42 C-165s were built and several remain active in the USA. One model C-145, NC19495, has been brought to the UK by Ron Souch who will be restoring it to fly as G-AFOH.

CFM Tummelisa

Sweden

Photo: The sole surviving CFM Tummelisa, Fv656.
Data: Not available

The Tummelisa was a single-seat fighter trainer, designed to meet a requirement of the Swedish Army Air Force Flying School, and which first appeared in 1919. It was powered by the 90hp Thulin engine and a total of 30 was built by Kjellson

and von Porat at Malmen. In Swedish Army service the Tummelisa was designated 01 and was in use between 1926 and 1934. One example was maintained in flying condition by the Swedish Air Force Museum until the mid-1960s but it is now believed to be no longer airworthy. It is on show in the museum at Malmslatt, Linkoping.

Chilton DW1

UK

Photo: G-AFGH is now Lycoming-powered and owned by M. L. & G. L. Joseph.
Data: Original DW1

Powerplant: One 32hp Carden Ford
Span: 24ft
Length: 18ft
Height: 4ft 10in
Wing area: 77sq ft

The first DW1 was built in 1937 by two graduates of the de Havilland Technical School, the Hon Andrew Dalrymple and A. R. Ward. It was a tiny, all-wood, single-seat monoplane powered by a 32hp Carden Ford engine and its performance on such low power was nothing less than sensational with a top speed of 112mph. The prototype, G-AESZ, and the first two

production aircraft, G-AFGH and 'GI, were powered by the Carden Ford but the fourth machine was fitted with the 44hp Train 4T air-cooled unit as the DW1A, G-AFSV, which won the 1939 Folkestone Trophy Race at an average speed of 126mph.

All four Chiltons, together with the jigs and drawings plus the unfinished DW2, survived the war and were taken over by the College of Aeronautical Engineering Ltd at Redhill. The prototype was written-off in 1953 but the other three survive, G-AFGH having been rebuilt with the fuselage of the DW2 in 1951. G-AFGH is now flying with a 55hp Lycoming 0-145-A2, G-AFGI is undergoing restoration with John McDonald at Booker and G-AFSV is owned by Roy Nerou of Coventry who is also having a second aircraft built from scratch, to be registered G-BDLV.

Cierva Autogiro series

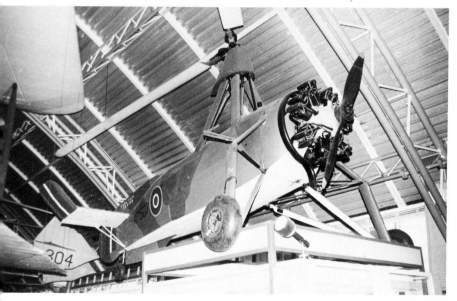

Photo: C8L Mk II, G-EBYY and C30A,
G-ACWP/AP507; Paris and the Science Museum.

Data: C30A

Powerplant: One 140hp Armstrong Siddeley Genet
Major IA

Rotor diameter: 37ft

Length: 19ft 8.5in

Height: 11ft 1in

Senor Don Juan de la Cierva, Spanish inventor of the
first practical autogiro, brought his C6A to England in
1925 where it was demonstrated at Farnborough by
Frank Courtney in October of that year. It was based
on a redundant Avro 504K fuselage and it was
probably this fact which led to the long association
between Cierva and Avro, the latter company
building most of his designs under licence. Of the
many different Cierva designs which were produced
between the wars four different types are known to
survive.

The earliest is the C8L Mk II, G-EBYY, which was
built in 1928 from Avro 504N components. It was
flown in the 1928 King's Cup Air Race and then

made a 3,000-mile tour of the British Isles before leaving Croydon on 18 September 1928 for Le Bourget, it thus became the first rotating-wing aircraft to cross the Channel. It was later flown to Berlin via Brussels and returned via Amsterdam on 4 October to be displayed at the Musee de l'Air, Chalais Meudon, where it remains today.

The first Cierva to attain anything like production status was the C19 which was produced in four main versions, the Mks I-IV, between 1929 and 1932. One example of a Mk IV is preserved at the Spanish Air Force Museum, this is EC-AIM, a Mk IVP production version which was supplied new in December 1932 as G-ABXH.

With the relative success of the open cockpit, two-seat C19, Cierva turned his attention to the single-seat and cabin two-seat market. The single seater was little more than an autogiro version of the Comper Swift known as the C25 and built by Comper while the cabin version was based on the DH Puss Moth and was built by de Havilland as the C24. This latter machine, G-ABLM, passed into the hands of the Science Museum and is today exhibited at the Mosquito Aircraft Museum, Salisbury Hall.

The most successful variant of all was the C30 which was put into production by Avro as the C30A in 1934; civil and export production accounted for 66 machines with a further 12 built for the RAF as Army Co-operation aircraft. The type was licence-built in France as the Le.O. C301 (175hp Salmson 9NE) and also in Germany where Focke Wulf built 40 powered by the Siemens engine, French production having amounted to 25. Several C30As survive both in the UK and on the Continent and one is even preserved in Argentina (LV-FBL).

Comper Swift UK

Photo: CLA7 Swift G-ABUU is owned and flown by John Pothecary

Powerplant: One 75hp Pobjoy R
Span: 24ft
Length: 17ft 8.5in
Height: 5ft 3.5in
Wing area: 90sq ft

The Swift was designed by Flt Lt Nicholas Comper as a logical progression of the Cranwell Light Aeroplane series of sporting types which he had been associated with during the 1920s. The prototype was built at Hooton Park during 1929 and was powered by the unreliable 35hp ABC Scorpion engine. The next few machines had the 50hp Salmson radial but it was the little Pobjoy radials which eventually became standard on the type. The first Pobjoy P was fitted in 1930 and the production 75hp R was available the following year. Subsequent developments included the Niagara and Cataract radials which were fitted by several owners to increase the power of their Swifts and three special aircraft were fitted with DH Gipsy III and Major engines of 120 and 130hp respectively.

The Swift was a popular mount of sporting pilots during the early 1930s and several long-distance flights were made, notable amongst which was C. A. Butler's flight from England to Australia made in G-ABRE during November 1931.

Four Swifts survive in the UK, all Pobjoy-powered, a fifth survives in Argentina and a Gipsy Swift is still flying in Australia.

Consolidated PT-1 Trusty USA

Photo: PT-1, serial 26-233, is preserved by the US Air Force Museum, Wright-Patterson AFB, Ohio.

Powerplant: One 180hp Wright E (Hispano-Suiza)

Span: 34ft 9.5in
Length: 27ft 8in
Height: 9ft 6in
Wing area: 296sq ft

The PT-1 was a redesign of the Dayton-Wright TW-3 which was adapted to have the cockpits in tandem instead of side by side, one prototype was accepted in 1923 and 221 production aircraft were ordered in four batches during 1925. The PT-1 featured a welded fuselage of chrome-molybdenum steel tube which bestowed great strength upon it, so much so that the type acquired the nickname Trusty. The type was exceptionally stable and easy to fly and was said to have bred overconfidence in some students, an undesirable trait for pilots who were to go on to fly far more powerful and lethal machines, and it gave birth to a whole series of PT and NY for the AAC and Navy, the last being the Y1PT-12/BT-7 for the Army and NY-3 for the Navy.

Several PT-1s and variants survive in the USA.

Curtiss NC-4   USA

Photo: Aircraft NC-4 is today preserved in the US Naval Aviation Museum at Pensacola, Florida.

Span: 126ft
Length: 68ft 2in
Height: 24ft 5in
Wing area: 2,441sq ft

The Model NC was a joint venture between the US Navy and Curtiss (hence the designation) and which was the brainchild of Rear Admiral David W. Taylor, Chief of the Navy's Bureau of Construction & Repair. The NC was designed to be delivered *by air* direct from the USA to France and thus to beat the increased threat of German U-boats which were attacking shipping in the North Atlantic.

The war ended soon after the completion of NC-1 and the need for delivery by air was forgotten but another use was soon found for the giant boats — an attempt at the *Daily Mail's* £10,000 prize for the first aircraft to successfully cross the Atlantic.

Of the three aircraft of the special Seaplane Division One it fell to NC-4 to become the first aircraft to complete the Atlantic crossing, albeit in stages from Newfoundland via the Azores, Portugal and Spain, arriving at Plymouth on 31 May 1919. This historic aeroplane is today preserved at the Naval Aviation Museum, Pensacola, Florida.

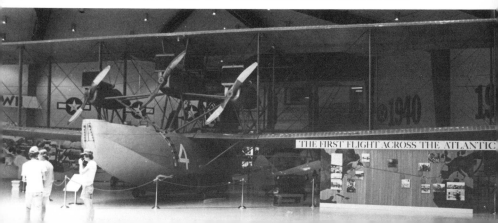

Curtiss Hawk (biplane series)

Photo: 32-240 is a P-6E Hawk preserved in the US Air Force Museum, Dayton, Ohio.
Data: P-6E

Span: 31ft 6in
Length: 22ft 7in
Height: 8ft 11in
Wing area: 252sq ft

The Hawk series originated as a private venture by the Curtiss company in 1922 when it was keen to find a military customer for its products. It ushered into America the era of steel tube construction, although the wing structure was initially of wood, and was in production in various forms from 1923-1938. The name Hawk was a company name which

was never officially adopted by the US military and today four Hawks of various models survive.

P-6E 32-240 is displayed by the US Air Force Museum at Wright-Paterson AFB, Dayton, Ohio; Al Williams' famous civilian Hawk 1A *Gulfhawk*, N982V, is on display at the US Marine Corps Museum at Quantico, Virginia; export Model 35 Hawk II D-316, originally acquired by the German Air Ministry for dive-bombing experiments, is today in store with the museum of Aircraft & Astronautics at Krakow, Poland and, finally, an export Model 68B Hawk III — one of 24 delivered to Thailand between August 1935 and February 1936 — is preserved by the Royal Thai Air Force Museum at Don Muang AFB Bangkok, Thailand.

Curtiss Model 42 R3C-2 Racer

USA

Photo: The most successful of the Model 42 racers was A6979 which is exhibited in the NASM at Washington DC, USA.

Span: 22ft
Length: 22ft
Height: 10ft 4in
Wing area: 144sq ft

This aircraft was built in two versions, the -1 landplane and -2 seaplane, for the 1925 racing season. Three were completed and issued with US Navy serials A6978, A6979 and A7054, the first and

last being delivered to the Navy whilst '79 went to the US Army.

A6979 was completed as a -1 landplane and as such won the 1925 Pulitzer race at 248.99mph, it was later converted to a -2 and flown by Army Lt James H. Doolittle it set up a new seaplane record of 245.7mph to win the 1925 Schneider Trophy on 26 October. The following year it came second in the same event in the hands of USMC Lt Christian Schill It is today preserved by the National Air & Space Museum of the Smithsonian Institution, Washington DC.

Curtiss Model 50 Robin

USA

Photo: This OX-5 powered Robin was seen at Flabob, California, by R. G. Moulton.
Data: Robin B

Span: 41ft
Length: 25ft 8.5in
Height: 7ft 9.5in
Wing area: 223sq ft

The three-seat Robin was conceived at Curtiss' Garden City facility in 1927 and made a successful maiden flight on 7 August the following year. Production was assigned to the newly-acquired St Louis plant of the Curtiss-Robertson Division and its initially low selling price was achieved by the use of cheap war-surplus OX-5 engines. Production reached a peak of 17 per week by mid-1929 and the Robin became the most successful US light aircraft of its day.

The designation varied with the engine fitted, some 325 Robin and Robin Bs being built together with some 300 Curtiss Challenger-powered Cs. Other powerplants included the short-lived Curtiss Crusader, the Warner Scarab and the Wright Whirlwind, bringing total production of all variants to 769. Several Robins of various models remain active in the USA.

Curtiss Model 58A XF9C-2 Sparrowhawk

USA

Photo: The XF9C-2 is seen here at Silver Hill, Maryland after its last rebuild in 1974.

Span: 25ft 6in
Length: 19ft 5in
Height: 7ft 3in
Wing area: 172.8sq ft

Although originally designed to fulfil the US Navy's Spec 96 of 10 May 1930 for a single-seat shipboard fighter the Sparrowhawk gained fame as a parasite fighter with the airships *Acron* and *Macon*. The surviving example was built with Curtiss funds as a private venture and registered X986M but was later bought by the US Navy for the sum of $29,953 and assigned serial number 9264. After the loss of the *Macon* the aircraft was stripped of its Skyhook and sent to NAS Anacostia before being donated to the Smithsonian Institution in 1939. It has since been completely refurbished twice and is now displayed at the National Air & Space Museum, Washington, DC.

Curtiss P-36A Hawk

USA

Photo: The last P-36A known to exist is preserved in the US Air Force Museum, Dayton, Ohio.

Span: 37ft 3.5in
Length: 28ft 6in
Height: 11ft 1in
Wing area: 236sq ft

Originally developed as the Curtiss entry for the US Army pursuit aircraft competition intended for 1935 the Model 75 was largely the work of designer Donovan A. Berlin. Although it lost the contest 227 were eventually delivered to the US Army, 753 were exported and at least 25 were locally-built under licence in foreign countries. Export Model 75s were delivered to France, Norway and Holland, some even finding their way to Finland via Germany. After the fall of France some of the French aircraft found their way into RAF service as Mohawks. One P-36A, serial 38-001, is preserved at the US Air Force Museum, Wright-Paterson AFB, Dayton, Ohio in the colourful 1939 'War Games' markings of the 27th Pursuit Squadron.

De Havilland DH51 UK

Photo: The sole surviving DH51 flying from Old Warden.

Powerplant: One 120hp Airdisco
Span: 37ft
Length: 26ft 6in
Height: 9ft 9in
Wing area: 325sq ft

The unnamed DH51 was conceived as a practical and cheap three-seat touring machine, the prototype flying on 1 July 1924. The structure of the large, two bay biplane was typically de Havilland with the traditional plywood-covered fuselage for ease of rigging and maintenance and the cost was kept low by fitting the war-surplus 90hp RAF 1A engine. Although performance was encouraging the Air Ministry refused to grant a Certificate of Airworthiness because the engine had only single ignition, the cost of converting to dual with an associated Type Test was prohibitive so the decision was made to fit the 120hp Airdisco motor. This unit gave a considerable boost to the performance but also to the price and as a result only two more were constructed.

The third and last DH51 was built in 1925 as G-EBIR and shipped to Kenya for Lord John Carberry, here it had a long and distinguished career, first as G-KAA and later as VP-KAA. It had bouts of semi-dereliction but was restored to fly in the mid-1950s and was eventually donated to the Shuttleworth Collection, flying back to the UK in an RAF Blackburn Beverley in July 1965. After some time on static display the airframe was refurbished by Hawker Siddeley apprentices at Chester and the engine by Rolls-Royce at Leavesden, its first flight as G-EBIR being made at Old Warden on 15 March 1973.

De Havilland DH53 Humming Bird

UK

Photo: The restored prototype, G-EBHX, flying at Old Warden.

Powerplant: One 26hp Blackburne Tomtit
Span: 30ft 1in
Length: 19ft 8in
Height: 7ft 3in
Wing area: 125sq ft

Although bearing a later type number the Humming Bird was actually produced *before* the large DH51, having been constructed to compete in the 1923 Lympne Light Aeroplane Trials. Construction followed traditional de Havilland lines — on a much smaller scale than before — and the Humming Bird can claim to be the first true light aeroplane to have been built by de Havilland.

Although the DH53 did not win any prizes in the trials it was obviously the most practical aeroplane there and early in 1924 a batch of 12 was laid down at Stag Lane, eight for the RAF, three to Australia and one to Aero in Prague. One other was built to a Russian order almost a year later and in the 1960s

another was built by S. N. Green of Calgary, Alberta, registered CF-OVE it was powered by a 40hp Continental A-40 and made its first flight on 7 May 1967.

The little Humming Birds were not really practical as means of transport but many soldiered on after RAF service as pioneers of the 'ultra light' movement. The last two of the RAF order were built for experimental hooking flights on the airship R-33 and one of these is believed to have donated parts to the Martin Monoplane G-AEYY, the wings and tail surfaces of which are being incorporated into a 'new' Humming Bird to carry the serial J7326.

The original prototype passed through a succession of owners to be recovered from a Kentish shed and restored for the Shuttleworth Collection in 1960. Following a serious accident it was rebuilt again in the early 1970s by Peter Franklin but it is now undergoing yet another rebuild following a further accident at Old Warden. In addition to three mentioned above an anonymous example, thought to be c/n 118, was sighted in an annexe of Perth Technical College, Western Australia, in 1972.

De Havilland DH60 Moth

UK

Photo: Cliff Lovell's American-built DH60M Gipsy Moth G-AAMY.
Data: DH60G

Powerplant: One 100hp de Havilland Gipsy I
Span: 30ft
Length: 23ft 11in
Height: 8ft 9.5in
Wing area: 243sq ft

With the experience gained from the construction of the DH51 and DH53 Capt Geoffrey de Havilland realised that neither would ever become the ideal

private owner's aeroplane and therefore decided to break completely with contemporary thought and produced the DH60 Moth. Basically a scaled-down DH51 with single-bay folding wings the Moth was powered by a four-cylinder aircooled engine based on half of the V-8 Airdisco, this 60hp unit was the first Cirrus engine; the combination of airframe and engine flew as a prototype on 22 February 1925 and was immediately accepted as the standard for light aeroplanes — a standard which was to last for several decades.

The first Moths were built for the Air Ministry supported flying clubs but private owners soon

caught on to the new type and it became the design on which the de Havilland company's fortunes were founded. Subsequent developments centred mainly on increasing the power of the engine and the 60hp Cirrus I gave way to the 85hp Cirrus II, 90hp Cirrus III and 105hp Cirrus Hermes I. A small batch was constructed for the RAF and they were fitted with 75hp Armstrong Siddeley Genet I radials

Various airframe improvements were incorporated between 1925 and 1928 which included lowering the engine to give a better view forward, increasing the span and decreasing the gap, and the fitting of a split-axle undercarriage. The final production versions were known as the DH60X Moth and series production came to an end with G-AABL in September 1928 although several 'one-off' examples were to be constructed to special orders.

Production ceased in favour of the new DH60G, the immortal Gipsy Moth. Moth orders had reached such a peak that the Aircraft Disposal Company (ADC) was in danger of running out of war-surplus components with which to assemble more Cirrus engines, the only solution was for de Havilland to build its own and this finally emerged as the 100hp DH Gipsy I of 1928. With the Gipsy engine installed

the Moth became an even larger success and sales were boosted by the racing and record-breaking achievements of Amy Johnson, Francis Chichester and others. At £650 ex-works the Gipsy Moth was extremely popular and by the end of 1929 production was running at almost three a day at Stag Lane with licences granted to Morane-Saulnier in France and the Curtiss-operated Moth Aircraft Corporation of America.

The wooden Gipsy Moth continued in production in the UK until 1934, a total of 595 having been built compared with some 400 of the Cirrus-powered version. A metal-fuselaged version of the Gipsy Moth, the DH60M, was introduced in 1928 and several hundred were constructed for both British and overseas customers.

Today several Moths and Gipsy Moths survive world-wide and a handful are maintained in flying condition; examples surviving in the UK are G-EBLV, G-EBWD, G-AAAH, G-AAWO, G-ABAG, G-ABEV, G-ABYA and G-ATBL. Of these 'EBLV, 'EBWD, 'ABEV and 'ATBL are all regularly flown and an American-built DH60M, N585M, has recently been imported and is now flying as G-AAMY.

De Havilland DH80A Puss Moth   UK

Photo: Puss Moth G-AAZP was operated for many years by the de Havilland Sports & Social Club at Chester, it is now privately owned.

Powerplant: One 120hp DH Gipsy III or one 130hp DH Gipsy Major
Span: 36ft 9in
Length: 25ft
Height: 7ft
Wing area: 222sq ft

Developed from the unnamed, all-wood, DH80 the Puss Moth first flew in early 1930 in response to demands from private owners who were now venturing further afield and who wanted the comfort and warmth of a cabin for their passengers and for themselves. The Puss Moth was built with contemporary de Havilland thoughts on light aeroplane design very much in mind, the fuselage

was of welded steel tube — as on the DH60M — and the power was provided by the new Gipsy III engine of 120hp. This engine was important as it was the first to have been persuaded to run successfully upsidedown, thus giving a smooth line to the nose and a view with no interruptions from cylinder heads and valve gear.

The three-seat Puss Moth was an immediate success, despite early crashes which were traced to wing-flutter and a total of 259 was built at Stag Lane with a further 25 at the Canadian subsidiary. It was widely used as a private aircraft and as an air taxi and several were used for long-distance record-breaking, notably Jim Mollison's G-ABXY *The Heart's Content* with which he flew the Atlantic from east to west in August 1932. Production ended in 1934 and several Puss Moths survive today including G-AAZP, G-ABDW, G-ABLS and G-AEOA in the UK, all but 'BDW being in flying trim.

De Havilland DH82A Tiger Moth UK

Photo: Tiger Moth G-AYUX/PG651, owned and flown by Peter Harris.

Powerplant: One 130hp DH Gipsy Major 1
Span: 29ft 4in
Length: 23ft 11in
Height: 8ft 9.5in
Wing area: 239sq ft

Flown initially on 26 October 1931 the Tiger Moth was the ultimate development of the DH60 series and was to become the standard elementary trainer of the RAF for many years. The airframe was a strengthened DH60M fuselage to which was fitted the inverted DH Gipsy Major of 130hp and swept-back wings of a modified section to improve stalling and spinning characteristics. Early versions were powered by the 120hp Gipsy III and featured a fabric covered rear fuselage decking; the familiar DH82A

was built to Spec T26/33 and the initial order was for 50 aircraft.

From 1937 onwards production capacity outstripped military orders and the type was delivered to many overseas air forces and to flying clubs and schools within the UK, one of the largest fleets being that of the Brooklands School of Flying, but with the threat of war increased orders were placed for RAF use.

By 1940 factory space at Hatfield was required for the Mosquito so Tiger Moth production was transferred to the Morris Motors factory at Cowley near Oxford, here the Tiger was built on a true production line system and by August 1945 3,214 aircraft had been built to add to the 3,065 which had been constructed at Hatfield. Total production exceeded 8,000 when licence production in Australia, Canada, New Zealand, Portugal, Sweden and Norway was taken into account and it is hardly surprising that today the Tiger Moth is the most numerous de Havilland type extant.

After the war the Tiger soldiered on with the RAF until 1955 when the final examples were replaced by Chipmunks, ex-RAF aircraft had started to be released for civilian sale from 1946 but by 1950 the market was flooded with them and the Tiger was the standard flying club trainer throughout the 1950s and into the 1960s.

With the introduction of modern American types in the early 1960s the Tiger rapidly disappeared from the flying club scene and it was not until the 'vintage boom' of the late 1960s and early 1970s that it started to acquire its current sought-after status once again. There are over 100 Tiger Moths in the UK today and many more in the USA, Canada and Australia, most are in private hands but one or two are operated by flying clubs, the only club to be solely equipped with the type being the Cambridge Flying Group where it is still possible to be trained from scratch on the Tiger Moth.

De Havilland DH83 Fox Moth   UK

Photo: Tony Haig-Thomas piloting his immaculate Fox Moth G-ACEJ, destroyed by fire in July 1982.

Powerplant: One 130hp DH Gipsy Major
Span: 30ft 10.75in
Length: 25ft 9in
Height: 8ft 9.5in
Wing area: 261.5sq ft

The Fox Moth was designed by Arthur Hagg to utilise the wings, undercarriage, empennage and engine of the Tiger Moth — then in volume production for the RAF — married to a new wooden fuselage capable of carrying four passengers and a pilot. The passengers were accommodated in a comfortable enclosed cabin while the pilot was seated high above them and behind them with an excellent view in all directions except beneath him. It was an instant success with the many small airlines, air taxis and bush flying concerns which were flourishing in the early 1930s and 98 of them were built prior to the outbreak of World War 2.

After the war a demand from Canadian bush pilots caused the Canadian branch of the de Havilland company to put a slightly updated version — using many war surplus DH82C parts — into production as the DH83C Fox Moth. It differed mainly in the installation of the 145hp Gipsy Major 1C engine and its modified cabin which only accommodated three passengers but had a stengthened floor and an outsize freight door for handling bulky items. Fifty two DH83Cs were built.

Today a small number are known to survive including G-ACCB, derelict with the Midland Air Museum, Coventry; ZK-ADI, flying in the USA; and several DH83Cs including G-AOJH with John Lewery at Bournemouth.

De Havilland DH84 Dragon UK

Photo: G-ACIT is a Dragon 1 exhibited by the Historic Aircraft Museum Southend.

Powerplants: Two 130hp DH Gipsy Major
Span: 47ft 4in
Length: 34ft 6in
Height: 10ft 1in
Wing area: 376sq ft

The Dragon was laid out as a design for the Iraqi Air Force but was put into production at the request of Edward Hillman who wanted a small, twin engined airliner with the same operating costs as his Fox Moths with which he could inaugurate cut-price cross-Channel flights.

Hillman ordered four Dragons 'off the drawing board' and the first, G-ACAN, was flown to his aerodrome at Maylands in December 1932 where it was named 'Maylands' by Amy Mollison. Once the Dragons entered service they were found to be cheaper to run than the Fox Moth, having a cruising speed of 109mph with six passengers — each of whom was allowed up to 45lb of baggage — and with a petrol consumption of only 13gal/hr!

Orders flowed in for the type and a production line was established at Stag Lane where 115 were built during the next three years, most going to small airline companies but some being completed as DH84M military versions for Iraq, Denmark and Portugal. From the 63rd machine various modifications were incorporated to produce the Dragon 2, these were outwardly distinguished from the Mk 1 by their individually-framed windows and faired undercarriage struts.

Production ceased in 1935 in favour of the enlarged Dragon Rapide but an urgent need for a radio and navigation trainer in Australia during World War 2 was met by shipping all the surviving Dragon jigs and drawings to the Australian de Havilland subsidiary at Bankstown where 87 were built for the RAAF between October 1942 and June 1943. The Dragon was preferred to the Dominie as the Gipsy Major was in production at Melbourne for Australian Tiger Moths.

After the war a few Dragons survived, mainly as pleasure-flying aircraft, and two are currently displayed in the UK; G-ACIT with the Historic Aircraft Museum, Southend, and VH-SNB with the Museum of Flight, East Fortune. A third, EI-AFK is painted to represent the first aircraft of Aer Lingus, EI-ABI, and is displayed with the Irish Aviation Museum at Dublin Airport, Eire. Others are known to survive in the USA and Australia.

De Havilland DH85 Leopard Moth UK

Photo: G-ACLL is powered by a 145hp DH Gipsy Major 10 and finished to represent Capt Geoffrey de Havilland's personal aircraft, G-ACHD.

Powerplant: One 130hp DH Gipsy Major 1
Span: 37ft 6in
Length: 24ft 6in
Height: 8ft 9in
Wing area: 206sq ft

Designed as a successor to the Puss Moth, to which

it bears a passing remembrance, the Leopard Moth was a totally different aeroplane which made its first flight on 27 May 1933. Whereas the Puss Moth had featured a welded steel tube fuselage the Leopard returned to the plywood structure favoured by the earlier Moths, the wings were tapered on both leading and trailing edges and the moving of the undercarriage anchorage from the cabin roof to the rear of the engine mount allowed the door to open wider.

A considerable saving in weight was gained by

abandoning the metal fuselage and this was reflected in the performance of the new type which had a top speed 9mph up on its predecessor with the same payload. Production was started at Stag Lane but the old aerodrome closed down in January 1934 and the later aircraft were built at Hatfield, 132 being sold before production ceased after three years.

The Leopard Moth was a highly favoured private owner's machine which also saw service as an air taxi, several were used for long-distance flights and

one broke the Australia-England record in the spring of 1934. 44 were impressed for military service during World War 2, most of them serving as crew taxis with the Air Transport Auxiliary, but very few survived to see civilian life again. Today there are seven registered in the UK, two of which were brought back from Switzerland in recent years, others are known to exist world-wide and one is flying in Canada.

De Havilland DH87 Hornet Moth UK

Photo: G-ADLY is owned by A. Wood and is based at Audley End, Essex, it was originally Sir W. Lindsay-Everard's 'The Leicestershire Foxhound II'.
Data: DH87B

Powerplant: One 130hp DH Gipsy Major 1 or 1F
Span: 31ft 11in
Length: 24ft 11.5in
Height: 6ft 7in
Wing area: 244.5sq ft

With the demise of the Gipsy Moth in 1934 there was no longer a two-seater in the de Havilland range of light aeroplanes and the DH87 originated in that year as an experimental type to discover the practicalities of building a two-seat cabin replacement for the earlier machine. Any aeroplane designed to replace the Gipsy Moth would have to be

outstanding and the new type incorporated many new features; the rear fuselage was of wooden construction in the manner of the Leopard Moth, the forward fuselage was of welded tube, and the wings were tapered as in the large DH86 airliner.

Production commenced in August 1935 but it soon become apparent that the sharply tapered wings of the production DH87A gave it a sharp wing drop at the stall and a new wing was designed to eliminate this problem. With the new square-tipped wing the Hornet Moth became the DH87B and was set for a bright future in private and club flying.

The last Hornet Moth was built in 1937 so at the outbreak of war most were relatively new and ideal for military communications duties. 24 survived impressment to fly again in the UK and today the Hornet Moth is still the most numerous of the civilian Moths with 14 on the British register.

De Havilland DH88 Comet UK

Photo: The immortal Comet G-ACSS, *Grosvenor House*, at Old Warden before its restoration started.

Powerplant: Two 230hp DH Gipsy Six R
Span: 44ft
Length: 29ft
Height: 10ft
Wing area: 212.5sq ft

In 1933 it was announced that the Australian philanthropist, Sir MacPherson Robertson, had put up £15,000 in prize money for a 12,300-mile air race from England to Australia to commemorate the centenary of the founding of the State of Victoria in 1834. The de Havilland directors were determined that the winning aircraft would be British — and preferably of DH origin — and announced their intention to build a 200mph racer for a nominal price of only £5,000.

Orders had to be placed by February 1934 and with only nine months before the race construction started on three Comets. They were built in great secrecy at the old Stag Lane factory, the first aircraft making its maiden flight after transportation to Hatfield on 8 September 1934, just six weeks before the race.

Registered G-ACSP, 'CSR and 'CSS, the three Comets started the race on 20 October 1934 from the new aerodrome at Mildenhall. G-ACSP was flown by Jim & Amy Mollison but withdrew at Allahabad; 'SR was flown by Ken Waller and Owen Cathcart-Jones who reached the finish at Melbourne after 108hr and 13min flying time, they collected films of the finish and immediately set off home, arriving at Lympne on 2 November to set up a new out and back record; but 'CSS, flown by C. W. A. Scott and Tom Campbell Black, had got to Melbourne ahead of everyone else in a time of just under 71hr, winning the speed prize for England and de Havilland.

With the race over the Comets were disposed of, 'SP to Portugal, 'SR to France and 'SS to the Royal Aircraft Establishment. Two others were then built, one for France and another as G-ADEF 'Boomerang' to the order of Cyril Nicholson.

The Comets soon faded into obscurity, only 'CSS surviving in the UK to be rebuilt for Ken Waller by Essex Aero Ltd at Gravesend, it was used to break the England-New Zealand return trip in March 1938, flown by Arthur Clouston and Victor Ricketts, but it was then stripped down and stored at Gravesend for 13 years before coming out of obscurity to be restored for the 1951 Festival of Britain. After 15 years with the de Havilland engine factory at Leavesden this historic aeroplane was handed over to the Shuttleworth Collection where it is nearing the end of a lengthy rebuild to flying condition.

De Havilland DH89A Dragon Rapide UK

Photo: Dragon Rapide G-AGTM is finished in Royal Navy colours as NF875

Powerplants: Two 200hp DH Gipsy Six Srs 1 or Gipsy Queen 3
Span: 48ft
Length: 34ft 6in
Height: 10ft 3in
Wing area: 336sq ft

The Rapide was conceived as an enlarged, faster derivative of the Dragon but actually owed more to the four-engined DH86 airliner which had been built to the requirements of QANTAS. Powered by two Gipsy Six engines it was initially seen as the Dragon Six but the name was soon changed to Dragon Rapide, the prototype being sold in Switzerland and the first production machines being delivered once again to Hillmans Airways at Romford.

The elegant Rapide was ordered by many of the small internal airlines, one of the largest fleets being

that of Railway Air Services, and as with the Dragon a military version known as the DH89M was produced for the Spanish Government, the RAF rejecting it in favour of the Avro Anson.

By 1937 various improvements had been incorporated into the airframe which necessitated a change in designation to DH89A, the major change was the installation of small trailing edge flaps outboard of the engine nacelles and many early aircraft were brought up to this standard at overhaul.

With the outbreak of war many Rapides were impressed and production at Hatfield was increased to meet the demand. The purely military aircraft were known as the DH89B Dominie, the Mk 1 being a navigation and W/T trainer whilst the Mk 2 was for communications. After the war many war-surplus

Dominies were converted for civilian use as Dragon Rapides. With space at Hatfield required for Mosquito production the Dominie production line was transferred to Brush Coachworks Ltd at Loughborough where a further 346 were built between 1943 and 1945. The last 100 Dominies were delivered to the DH Repair Unit at Witney and furnished to civilian standards.

Rapides were the mainstay of many small charter and joyriding concerns throughout the postwar years and several carried on into the 1970s as jump ships for parachuting clubs, these have now been withdrawn and of the 20 Dragon Rapides in the UK at present seven are airworthy and several more are being restored by John Pierce.

De Havilland DH90 Dragonfly   UK

Photo: Dragonfly G-AEDU is finished in red and white and is currently based at Old Warden with the new De Havilland Flying Centre.

Powerplants: Two 130hp DH Gipsy Major 1
Span: 43ft
Length: 31ft 8in
Height: 9ft 2in
Wing area: 256sq ft

The Dragonfly prototype flew on 12 August 1935 and was a five-seat light or excutive transport powered by a pair of 130hp Gipsy Majors. In this

respect is resembled the Dragon but in construction it was totally different, the wings were sharply tapered as on the Rapide and the fuselage was a wooden monocoque of extremely advanced design. 66 production Dragonflies were built during the next three years, mainly as executive transports, and two are known to survive today.

G-AEDU has been rebuilt to fly for Tony Haig-Thomas and Martin Barraclough, it is the former ZS-CTR and CR-AAB; and N2034, ex G-AEDT and VH-AAD, is flying in the USA having been sold to the Tallmantz collection of California in 1964.

De Havilland DH94 Moth Minor

UK

Photo: G-AFNG is a coupe Moth Minor owned by Tony Haig-Thomas.

Powerplant: One 80hp DH Gipsy Minor
Span: 36ft 7in
Length: 24ft 5in
Height: 6ft 4in
Wing area: 162sq ft

The Moth Minor is notable as being the last in the long line of Moths and the design with which Capt Geoffrey de Havilland returned to his original 'Moth' concept of 1925 but with the benefit of some 12 years experience in the light aeroplane field.

The prototype was flown at Hatfield on 22 June 1937, 'D. H.' himself was at the controls and power was believed to have been provided by the experimental 80hp Gipsy IV engine which had been fitted to the Swallow Moth in 1931. The Moth Minor was seen to be an elegant low wing monoplane with tandem open cockpits, built along traiditional de Havilland lines with folding wings and power provided in production aircraft by the 80hp de Havilland Gipsy Minor.

Development trials took up most of 1938 and the type entered production in 1938-39, eight a week being manufactured by June 1939. It is clear that if the war had not intervened the Moth Minor would have followed the example of the Gipsy Moth and would have become one of the most popular of the Moths. A special batch of development aircraft were built alongside the production machines to test various ideas including various types of tricycle undercarriages and coupe cabin tops. Over 100 production aircraft had been built by September 1939 but early in 1940 the type was abandoned and the jigs and drawings, together with all the finished and unfinished airframes, were shipped to Australia where production was resumed as a trainer for the Royal Australian Air Force.

Today five Moth Minors survive in the UK, three in flying trim with Bob Ogden, Tony Haig-Thomas and the Strathallan Collection; one is under reconstruction with B. Welford, and a fifth is in store. Others are known to survive in Australia, New Zealand and North America and one is in store in France.

Dewoitine D26 and D27

Switzerland

Photo: Bob Willies landing his Jacobs-powered D26, G-BBMI/U-282.
Data: D26

Powerplant: One 250hp Hispano 9QA or one 300hp Jacobs R-755-A2
Span: 33ft 9in
Length: 21ft 6in
Height: 9ft 1in
Wing area: 188sq ft

Frenchman Emile Dewoitine wound up his French company and moved to Switzerland in 1927. Here he produced the D27 parasol monoplane fighter

which was evaluated by the Swiss Air Force in 1928 and ordered into production. Construction was undertaken by EKW (Swiss Federal Workshops) and the Hispano-Suiza powerplant was licence-built by the Swiss Locomotive and Machine Works. A total of 66 D27s were eventually built and were in front-line service until 1940 when the survivors were transferred to flying schools. Scrapping commenced in 1944 and today only one aircraft, serial J-257, has survived and is preserved in the Swiss Museum of Transport & Communications at Lucerne.

Concurrently with the D27 a single-seat trainer version, the D26, was in production and a total of 11 was built. Nine of these aircraft were powered by the

250hp Hispano 9QA radial (licence-built Wright Whirlwind) and the remaining two had the more powerful 300hp Whirlwind for use as combat trainers. In 1948 the survivors were passed on to the Swiss Aero Club where they were used as glider tugs and some re-engined with the 300hp Jacobs R-755-A2 radial. At least three D26s survive, U-288 is preserved at the Swiss Air Force Museum at Dubendorf, U-282 is registered as G-BBMI and flies from Duxford airfield, Cambridgeshire, and U-290 is registered F-AZBF and flies with the Salis Collection at La Ferte-Alais, France.

Dewoitine D520

France

Photo: No 862 is the only flyable D520, seen here at La Ferte-Alais, June 1982.

Powerplant: One 1,000hp Hispano-Suiza 12 Y 51
Span: 33ft 5.75in
Length: 28ft 8.75in
Height: 8ft 6in
Wing area: 150sq ft

The D520 was the last of a line of Dewoitine fighters which had begun with the D500. It was intended to replace the Morane Saulnier MS406 (qv) and was first flown on 2 October 1938. The design was a great advance on its immediate predecessor, the D510, and Dewoitine claimed that it could be built in half the time taken previously. With the German occupation of France in 1940 the Dewoitines were ordered for second-line duties with the Luftwaffe but it is believed that few were delivered because of delaying tactics adopted by the workers and on the liberation of the factory at Toulouse several D520s were taken over by the French Forces and used against the retreating German army.

The D520s were used by the postwar Armee de l'Air and at least one was not retired until as late as 1953. Three D520s are held by the Musee de l'Air: No 408 is undergoing restoration, No 603 is at Luxeuil, and No 862 (ex-Luxeuil) has been restored to flying condition.

Douglas DWC World Cruiser

USA

Photo: DWC 'Chicago' in the old NASM building, Washington, D.C.

Powerplant: One 400hp Liberty.
Span: 50ft
Length: 35ft 2.5in
Max speed: 104mph
Cruising speed: 90mph

In the spring of 1923 the US Air Service began to show considerable interest in a round-the-world flight by a formation of military aircraft. No existing type was suitable and the Douglas company put forward a modification of its DT-2 in July of that year. This aircraft had provision for interchangeable wheel or float undercarriages and was initially designated D-WC, later simplified to DWC.

Four aircraft were built for the flight and bore the names *Seattle*, *Chicago*, *Boston* and *New Orleans*. They left Lake Washington on 4 April 1924 and the two survivors returned on 28 September at the end of the first aerial circumnavigation of the world.

DWC-1 *Seattle* crashed in Alaska and its remains were recovered for the Transportation Museum of Alaska but DWC-2 *Chicago* is preserved at the National Air & Space Museum, Washington, DC, whilst DWC-3 *New Orleans* is on show at the US Air Force Museum, Wright-Paterson AFB, Dayton, Ohio.

Douglas DC-2   USA

Photo: DC-2, VH-CDZ, is undergoing restoration to airworthy condition by the Australian Wing of the Confederate Air Force.
Data: Douglas DC-2

Powerplants: Two 710hp Wright Cyclones
Span: 85ft
Length: 62ft
Cruising speed: 191mph

Making its maiden flight on 11 May 1934 the DC-2 was the production version of the DC-1 prototype which had been built to a TWA specification to compete with the Boeing 247D operated by United Air Lines. Three main commercial versions and eight

military transport models were built by Douglas and various production licences were also negotiated. 131 were sold by Douglas and a small number were built under licence in Japan by the Nakajima concern.

Several DC-2s exist today in the US and Australia but the most famous of them all is without doubt c/n 1354 *Hanssin Jukka* which was operated by the Finnish Air Force against the Russians in both the Winter and Continuation Wars of 1940-41. Armed with one machine gun in a dorsal turret and with bomb racks under the centre-section it bombed at least one Russian airfield. It is today preserved as a coffee-bar in the centre of Hameenlinna, Finland.

Douglas DC-3   USA

Photo: Douglas DC-3A, EI-AYO, landing at Wroughton after its ferry flight from Shannon.

Powerplants: Two 1,200hp Pratt & Whitney R-1830-90C
Span: 95ft
Length: 64ft 5in
Height: 16ft 11in
Wing area: 987sq ft

17 December 1935 was the 32nd anniversary of the Wright Brothers' first flight at Kitty Hawk and the day on which the prototype of the world's most successful transport aeroplane took to the air. A stretched version of the DC-2, the DC-3 initially flew as the 'DST' or Douglas Sleeper Transport but it was to become known under a variety of names including 'Dakota', 'Skytrain', 'Gooney Bird' and many others.

800 were built as civil machines before

production was switched to the military after its selection as the standard transport type for the Allies in World War 2, 10,125 being delivered up until 1945. Hundreds are still in service worldwide in both civil and military guise and several are still operated commercially in the UK by Eastern Air Transport of Kirmington. Preserved examples in the UK include two C-47s — at Cosford and Aldershot — and a rare prewar DC-3A with the Science Museum Reserve Collection at Wroughton, Wilts.

Douglas B-18A Bolo   USA

Photo: This modified Bolo is exhibited with the US Air Force Museum at Dayton, Ohio.
Data: Douglas B-18A Bolo

Powerplants: Two 1,000hp Wright Cyclones
Span: 90ft
Length: 56ft 9in
Height: 15ft 1in
Max speed: 214mph

Basically built around the wings, engines, undercarriage and empennage of the DC-2 the Bolo was built to a 1934 Air Corps bomber requirement to replace the Martin B-10. 217 B-18As were purchased in three batches under Contract AC9977,

the most significant difference between the B-18A and the earlier B-18 being in the modified bomb-aimer's position in a newly-stepped nose.

Although obsolete at the outbreak of war the Bolos were the most numerous US bombers stationed outside the continental US at the time of the Japanese attack on Pearl Harbor, where many were destroyed on the ground. The Bolos were soon relegated to coastal and anti-submarine patrols and ended the war as trainers. At least four B-18As survive today: 37-469 and 39-025 both with the US Air Force Museum at Wright-Paterson AFB, Dayton, Ohio; and 37-505 and 38-593 with the Tuscon Air Museum Foundation, Arizona. Of the four only -593 is on display to the public.

English Electric Wren   UK

Photo: Wren No 4, c/n 3, still flying with the Shuttleworth Collection.

Powerplant: One 398cc ABC
Span: 37ft
Length: 24ft 3in
Wing area: 145sq ft
Max speed: 50mph

The single-seat Wren ultra-light was designed by W. O. Manning and a total of three was built, J6973

was delivered to the Air Ministry in 1921 and two others were built for the 1923 Light Aeroplane Trials at Lympne. The two Lympne trials machines survived in storage for many years and were acquired in the mid-1950s by the English Electric Company who rebuilt a flyable aircraft from the best parts of the two. This machine flew again at Warton in January 1957 and was then presented to the Shuttleworth Collection where it is maintained in airworthy condition.

Ercoupe 415C
USA

Photo: SE-BFX is an Ercoupe 415D previously registered NC3788H.

Powerplant: One 90hp Continental C90-16F
Span: 30ft
Length: 20ft 2in
Height: 6ft 3in
Wing area: 142.6sq ft

The Ercoupe made its maiden flight as a single-finned prototype, the Erco 310, in October 1937 and development continued to produce the two-control, non-spinning 415C early in 1940. Some 112 were built before the outbreak of war put an end to production and the type re-entered production in 1946. The Ercoupe design has passed through various hands since then and has been known as the Forney Aircoupe and Alon A-2. Some 5,500 were built, some with conventional controls, and the type is in widespread use in the USA. A small number are active in the UK and Europe.

Fairchild Model 24
USA

Photo: The only prewar Model 24 in Europe is Paul Skogstadt's Ranger powered D-ECAF.
Data: Model 24W

Powerplant: One 165hp Warner R-500 Super Scarab
Span: 36ft 4in
Length: 23ft 9in
Height: 7ft 7.5in
Wing area: 193.3sq ft

The Model 24 was basically a cabin derivative of the earlier Model 22 and the first two-seat Model 24-C8 appeared in April 1932 with power supplied by a 95hp American Cirrus. Only 10 were sold before the advent of the C8A which featured the 125hp Warner Scarab, 25 of which were sold following its introduction in 1933. The first three-seat Model 24 was the C8C which appeared in 1934 and which was powered by the 165hp Warner Scarab, production now took an upturn and 125 were built between 1934 and 1935. An improved model, the C8E, which featured a long-chord cowling was produced in 1936 and 50 were built. The C8D and C8F were versions of the basic design powered by Ranger in-line engines, only 11 C8Ss were built before production was switched to the C8F of 1936 and finally the C8H of 1937, production of these versions totalling 40 and 25 respectively.

The first four seat version was the Model 24G of 1937, which was Warner-powered, 100 of these were built before the refined 24J was introduced the following year, 40 being eventually built. Alongside the four-seat Warner models came the Ranger powered 24K of 1938, 60 of which were sold before the 24R appeared in 1939. 60 more 24Rs were built during 1939-1940 before production was taken over as the UC-61K, 306 of which were built for the AAC but delivered to the RAF under Lend-Lease. The Warner-powered 24W was produced alongside its Ranger-powered stablemate and 135 had been sold commercially before 1941 when all production was switched to military contracts, 675 being built as UC-61s for the USAAF and RAF. In RAF service the 24W was known as the Argus I or II and the 24R as the Argus III.

Both Warner and Ranger-powered varieties continued in production until 1947 with approximately 150 of each model being built as Model 24R-46 or 24W-46. The Model 24 is still fairly common the USA but is comparatively rare in Europe.

Fairey IIID   UK

Photo: Portuguese IIID No 17 *Santa Cruz* exhibited at Lisbon.

Powerplant: One 450hp Napier Lion IIB, V or VA, or one 375hp Rolls-Royce Eagle VIII
Span: 46ft 1.25in
Length: 36ft
Height: 13ft
Wing area: 500sq ft

The Fairey IIID was a direct development of the two experimental Fairey biplanes of 1917. The manufacturers progressed through various modifications of the basic design before coming up with the Napier Lion powered IIID which was in production for the RAF and FAA from 1920 to 1925. The early examples were powered by the Rolls-Royce Eagle VIII of 375hp but the Lion was standardised in the second production batch (N9567-N9578) and the only other aircraft fitted with the Eagle were six machines serialled N9630-N9635.

As a general purpose aircraft with the RAF it was used as a bomber or for spotting and reconnaissance duties, the highlight of its land-based career being the historic formation flight from England to South Africa and back between November 1925 and June 1926. The aircraft was extensively used by the Fleet Air Arm both with wheels for deck-landings and as a twin-float seaplane.

207 IIIDs were built before production ceased in 1926 in favour of the much-improved IIIF which was to serve with the RAF and FAA for the next decade. The IIID was delivered to various overseas customers and one example survives in Portugal. This Eagle-powered aircraft, c/n F402, serial 17, was one of three long-range specials ordered by Portugal in 1921 for a flight from Lisbon to Rio de Janeiro. The other two aircraft were wrecked during the attempt but No 17 made it to Rio, arriving on 17 June 1922, and is now preserved in the Museu de Marinha at Lisbon.

Fairey Swordfish   UK

Photo: The last airworthy Swordfish is LS326 which is based at Yeovilton with the Fleet Air Arm Historic Aircraft Flight.

Powerplant: One 690hp Bristol Pegasus IIIM3 or 750hp Pegasus XXX
Span: 45ft 6in
Length: 36ft 4in
Height: 12ft 10in
Wing area: 607sq ft

The Swordfish symbolises FAA operations during World War 2 which is rather unusual as it was considered almost obsolete at the outbreak! In fact the Swordfish remained fully operational until the end of the European war while its erstwhile successor — the Albacore — was withdrawn from front line squadrons in November 1943.

The Swordfish's remarkable longevity was due to its superb handling qualities, it was a real pilot's aeroplane which would do just about anything that was asked of it, qualities which were essential for wartime carrier operations.

The Swordfish prototype, known as the TSRII (Torpedo-Spotter-Reconnaissance) flew on 17 April 1934 and the first contract for 86 aircraft was placed in April 1935. By 1940, when Fairey transferred production to Blackburns at Brough, some 692 had been delivered, peak production from the Hayes factory having been during 1937 with 201 delivered. The Swordfish I remained in production until 1943 when the Mk II appeared, this version incorporating a strengthened lower wing to allow the carriage of underwing rocket projectiles. The final British version was the Mk III which mounted a Mk X ASV radar scanner between the undercarriage legs whilst the Mk IV was a Canadian development with enclosed cockpits. The last of 2,391 built was a Mk III built at Brough in December 1944.

Six Swordfish are preserved in the UK, one in flying condition, and a number of Canadian built Mk IVs survive in North America.

FIAT G5bis   Italy

Photo: The only remaining G5bis is I-BFFI at Vigna di Valle.

Powerplant: One 200hp FIAT A70S radial
Span: 34ft 1.5in
Length: 25ft 9in
Height: 7ft 11.75in
Wing area: 186sq ft

The G5 was a tandem two-seat tourer and aerobatic trainer which was designed by Ing Gabrielli and which first appeared in 1933, powered by a 140hp FIAT A54 radial. The aircraft was of mixed construction, with a welded steel tube fuselage on which the fabric covering was supported by an aluminium framework, and plywood-covered wings. Progressive refinement resulted in the 1934 model, the G5bis, which was powered by the 200hp FIAT A70S radial.

One example of the G5bis has survived and is preserved in the Italian Air Force Museum at Vigna di Valle to the north-west of Rome.

FIAT C29 Italy

Powerplant: One 1,000hp FIAT AS5
Span: 21ft 8in
Length: 17ft 10.5in
Height: 9ft 0.25in
Wing area: 86.1sq ft

Following the Italian defeat in the 1927 Schneider trophy competition a High Speed School (Scuola d'Alta Velocita) was established at Lake Garda and a new aircraft designed to equip it. This was the C29, the first of which made its maiden flight in the hands of Francesco Angello in June 1929. This first aircraft was serialled MM129 but it only had a very short life, being lost in a landing accident on the lake on 16 July 1929.

A second aircraft, MM130, was then sent to the lake. This differed from the first in that it had a larger fin but this too was lost when it dived into the water just after take-off on 17 August 1929. Parts of MM130 were salvaged and used to construct a third aircraft, MM130bis which was shipped to Calshot for the 1929 Schneider contest but not used.

The third C29, MM130bis, survives in the Italian Air Force Museum at Vigna di Valle.

FIAT C32/Hispano HA132L Chirri Italy & Spain

Photo: MM 4566 is displayed at Vigna di Valle but is thought to be a Spanish-built Chirri.

Powerplant: One 600hp FIAT A30 RAbis
Span: 31ft 2in
Length: 24ft 5.375in
Height: 8ft 11in
Wing area: 237.8sq ft

The CR32 was a refinement of the CR30 and was probably the most successful Italian fighter of the inter-war period. It first flew in 1933 and was still in limited service 10 years later, having seen service on both sides in the Spanish Civil War and in World War 2. In addition to home use the CR32 was exported to Austria, China, Hungary, Paraguay and Venezuela and a licence to build the later CR32quater was assigned to Hispano Aviacion in 1938 where it became the standard fighter of the Spanish Air Force.

Developments included the CR32bis of 1935 which featured heavier armament and the ability to carry bombs under the fuselage, and the CR32ter and quater versions which appeared in 1936. At the outbreak of war the CR32 formed more than 25% of the fighter strength of the Italian Air Force, some Austrian machines were taken over by the Luftwaffe and the type remained in service for a considerable time. In Spain the Chirri was still being used as an aerobatic trainer as late as 1954 and one FIAT built example was still flying as late as 1956, being displayed at Fiumicino that year.

Two CR32s survive, both believed to be Hispano-built Chirris; 'MM4566' is displayed at the Italian Air Force Museum, Vigna di Valle, and '31-2' is with the Spanish Air Force Museum at Cuatro Vientos, Madrid.

Fleet 16B Finch II   Canada

Photo: Finch II 4510 is maintained by the Canadian National Aeronautical Collection at Rockcliffe, Ontario.

Powerplant: One 125hp Kinner B-5
Span: 28ft
Length: 21ft 8in
Height: 7ft 9in
Wing Area: 194sq ft

The origins of the Finch lie in the Fleet 1 of 1928 which was named after Maj Reuben Fleet, founder of Consolidated Aircraft. The Fleet 1 entered production as the Consolidated Husky Junior, it was powered by a 125hp Kinner radial. From 1929 the aircraft was built by the Fleet Aircraft Division of Consolidated which had been created especially for that purpose. Further developments of the basic design were the

Model 2 (100hp Kinner), the Fleet 7 primary trainer, the Fleet 9 advanced trainer, the Fleet 10 primary military trainer and the Fleet 11 advanced military trainer. Some 600 Fleets were built by Consolidated before production ended in 1935, the Division was acquired by Brewster four years later but production was not resumed.

Manufacturing rights to the Fleet designs were acquired by Fleet Aircraft of Canada and a further 600 aircraft were built both for the home market and for export. The Models 10 and 11 were built for the RCAF and the final version was the 16B Finch II, 400 of which were delivered to the RCAF between 1939 and 1941. Although originally built with open cockpits a sliding canopy was soon found to be necessary because of the severity of the Canadian winters. Fleets of various models are still to be found in fair numbers throughout the USA and Canada.

Focke Wulf Fw44 Stieglitz   Germany

Photo: OY-DVW is an Fw44J based at Stauning with the Dansk Veteranflysamling.
Data: Fw44J

Powerplant: One 150hp Siemens Sh14a radial
Span: 29ft 6in
Length: 23ft 11in
Height: 8ft 10in
Wing area: 215sq ft

The first Stieglitz was flown in 1932 and it was to become one of the most successful of primary trainers. The initial models were the Fw44B and 44C

with the 150hp Siemens Sh14a radial or 135hp Argus As8 inline respectively, the radial-powered version being produced in far greater numbers than the inline. Minor changes created the Fw44D and E but the most popular of all the Stieglitz versions was the Fw44J. The type was built in substantial numbers for the Luftwaffe and licence production was undertaken in Sweden, Brazil and Argentina. 500 were built in Argentina, commencing in 1938, and a large number were still in use there during the early 1960s. The type is fairly common throughout Germany and Scandinavia and a fair number are maintained in flying condition.

Fokker CVD and CVE

Holland

Photo: This Swedish CVE/S6B was still airworthy in the early 1960s.
Data: Swiss-built CVE

Powerplant: One 650hp Hispano-Suiza HS-61-Nb
Span: 15.3m
Length: 9.5m
Height: 3.6m
Wing area: 39.3sq m

The Fokker CV was a two-seat general reconnaissance and bombing biplane which first appeared in 1925. It was used by the Netherlands Air Force and was also built under licence in both Sweden and Switzerland. The Swedish aircraft were known as the S6 and were powered by the air-cooled SFA-built Bristol Mercury VI radial engine. Dutch versions had the Rolls-Royce Kestrel and Swiss machines were fitted with the Hispano-Suiza HS-61-Nb of 650hp.

In both Swedish and Swiss service the Fokker CVE had a long and useful life, the Swedish aircraft were withdrawn in 1945 and the Swiss machines, withdrawn from front-line units in 1940, soldiered on until 1954 in the target-towing role.

Four examples survive: CVD '618' is on show in the Aviodome museum at Schipol, Amsterdam; CVD '349' is with the Dutch Air Force Museum at Soesterberg AFB; Swedish-built CVE/S6B, Fv386, is preserved at the Swedish Air Force Museum, Linkoping; and Swiss-built CVE, C-331, is preserved at the Swiss Air Force Museum at Dubendorf.

Fokker FVII and FVIIB/3m
Holland

Photo: Fokker FVIIA, HB-LBO, in pride of place in the Swiss Museum of Transport & Communications at Lucerne.
Data: FVIIA

Powerplant: Various including the 450hp Gnome-Rhone Jupiter 9AB
Span: 63ft 3.75in
Length: 47ft 10.75in
Height: 12ft 9in
Wing area: 635sq ft

The Fokker FVIIA appeared in 1925 as a high wing, single-engined monoplane with accommodation for eight passengers and two crew. It was built at Amsterdam and powered by the 450hp Gnome-Rhone Jupiter 9AB radial. The exceptionally clean airframe gave the Fokker monoplane a superb performance and it was used for many long-distance flights. A three-engined version, the FVIIA/3m was produced concurrently and formed the equipment of many European airlines including Sabena and KLM.

A more powerful and enlarged derivative was the FVIIB/3m which had the span increased to over 71ft. This was just as successful as its predecessors and was again used for many record flights. Probably the most famous Fokker of all is the FVIIB/3m, VH-USU, *Southern Cross* in which Sir Charles Kingsford Smith made his early record breaking flights, this historic aeroplane was stored throughout the last war and restored to fly postwar for a film about 'Smithy's' life. It is now exhibited in a glass-fronted hangar at Brisbane, Australia. Several aircraft, both single and three-engined, survive in museums.

Ford Tri-Motor
USA

Photo: Ford 5-AT-B N9863 was used by American Airlines for promotional work in the 1960s it is now preserved by the National Air & Space Museum, Washington, DC.
Data: Ford 5-AT

Powerplants: Three 425hp Pratt & Whitney Wasp C or 450hp Wright Whirlwind
Span: 77ft 10in
Length: 49ft 10in
Height: 13ft 8in
Wing area: 835sq ft

The Tri-Motor, or 'Tin Goose' to give it its more popular name, was one of the most important American transport aircraft ever built as it was the foundation of many of that country's national airlines. Conceived by W. B. Stout the Model 4-AT was based on the Fokker FVII/3m, one of which had been acquired by Henry Ford, which was re-engineered by Tom Towle using the patent Junkers method of all-metal construction.

The first 4-AT was produced in 1926 and had accommodation for 11 passengers, it was available in two versions — the 4-AT-B with three 235hp Wright Whirlwinds or the 4-AT-E with three 300hp Whirlwinds. A larger development, the 5-AT was introduced in 1928. This aircraft had an enlarged wing, accommodation for up to 13 passengers and was powered by three 420hp Pratt & Whitney Wasps or three 450hp Wright Whirlwinds. A hybrid known as the 6-AT was basically a 4-AT-E fitted with the larger wing of the 5-AT. 199 Tri-Motors were built and in 1966 an updated version known as the Bushmaster 2000 was constructed but the type never entered production. Several original aircraft still exist and at least one is still operated by Scenic Airways on pleasure flights from Reno, Nevada.

Foster Wikner Wicko GM1   UK

Photo: Foster Wikner Wicko GM1 G-AFJB, painted as DR613.

Powerplant: One 130hp DH Gipsy Major
Span: 34ft 6in
Length: 23ft 3in
Height: 6ft 7in
Wing area: 153sq ft

The Wicko two-seat, aerobatic monoplane was designed by Australian Geoffrey N. Wikner who had arrived in the UK during 1934. The prototype was powered by the 'Wicko F' powerplant, a converted Ford V-8 car engine, and was flown from Hillman's aerodrome at Stapleford Tawney in 1936. The design was faultless but performance was poor because of the weight of the watercooled engine so the decision was taken to re-engine the prototype with the 90hp Blackburn Cirrus Minor I.

This engine was later discarded and the airframe redesigned around the 130hp de Havilland Gipsy Major I in which form the aircraft was known as the GM1. Nine production aircraft were built at Eastleigh, Southampton, before the outbreak of war put a stop to further construction. Several were impressed for communications use under the name Warferry, two of which survived to fly as civil aircraft once more. Of these G-AFJB is preserved by owner Ken Woolley at Berkeswell, Warwickshire.

Funk B

USA

Photo: This Model B is in the colours of Gulf Oil and was photographed at Old Rhinebeck, NY.
Data: B75L

Powerplant: One 75hp Lycoming GO-145
Span: 35ft
Length: 20ft 1in
Height: 6ft 1in
Wing area: 169sq ft

The first Funk B was built by Joe and Howard Funk in the rear of a Kansas poultry shop in 1937 and was interesting as it was powered by a 60hp Ford-B car engine. In this respect it was remarkably similar to the contemporary Foster Wikner Wicko (qv). Production started at Akron, Ohio in 1938 and 60 were sold during 1939-1940, to be followed by a further 60 B75L models in 1941-1942, the latter powered by a 75hp Lycoming. Production was resumed at Coffeyville, Kansas, in 1947-1948 and 217 B85Cs were built, powered by the 85hp Continental. A considerable number of Funks are still flying in the USA.

General Aircraft Monospar

UK

Photo: Piet Van Asch's ST-25, ZK-AFF, still airworthy in New Zealand.
Data: ST-25

Powerplants: Two 95hp Pobjoy Niagara III
Span: 40ft 2in
Height: 7ft 10in
Wing area: 217sq ft

The Monospar light twin series was the result of a patented form of wing structure which was the brainchild of Swiss engineer H. J. Stieger, the first full-scale aircraft to be built according to the principle being the ST-3 of 1931. Following flight trials a new company, General Aircraft Ltd, was set up at Croydon to build aircraft based on the monospar principle and the ST-4 was sold in considerable numbers both at home and overseas.

Technical development continued and the company moved to larger premises at the London Air Park, Hanworth, where the final version, the ST-25, was built. Today at least three Monospars are known to survive: ST-12, VH-UTH, is being rebuilt to static display standard at the Newark Air Museum, Nottinghamshire; ST-25, OY-DAZ, is preserved at the Danmarks Flyvemuseum, Egeskov; and ST-25, ZK-AFF, is still flying at Hastings, New Zealand.

General Aircraft GAL 42 Cygnet

UK

Photo: The only surviving Cygnet II is G-AGBN.

Powerplant: One 150hp Blackburn Cirrus Major II
Span: 34ft 6in
Length: 23ft 3in
Height: 7ft
Wing area: 179sq ft

Although initially designed and built by C. W. Aircraft Ltd in 1937 the design and producton rights of the Cygnet were taken over by General Aircraft Ltd at Hanworth who set about turning the all-metal design into a fool-proof aeroplane suitable for mass-production.

This they succeeded in doing and a considerable number of production aircraft were envisaged when the outbreak of war put paid to their plans. Only nine examples were built between 1940-1941, five of which were impressed into the RAF as trainers for Douglas Boston crews converting to tricycle undercarriages.

Four survived the war and were disposed of on the civilian market, three of them flying again, but today only G-AGBN remains, restored in wartime camouflage and exhibited by the Scottish Museum of Flight, East Fortune.

Gloster Gauntlet

UK

Photo: The World's sole surviving Gloster Gauntlet, GT-400, ex K5271

Powerplant: One 645hp Bristol Mercury VIS2
Span: 32ft 9.5in
Length: 26ft 2in
Height: 10ft 4in
Wing area: 315sq ft

The Gauntlet is notable as the last of the classic open biplane fighters to equip the Royal Air Force, entering service with No 19 Sqn, Duxford, in May 1935 as a replacement for the Bristol Bulldog. It was a development of the Gloster SS18 which had flown in 1928 and which was progressively refined via the SS19 and SS19B into the Gauntlet, initial orders for which ran to 24 but which were soon followed by orders for a further 204.

By 1937 the Gauntlet equipped no less than 14 squadrons of Fighter Command but its heyday was short-lived and replacement in the form of Gladiators and Hurricanes appeared the following year. Nevertheless, there were still 26 Gauntlets on strength in 1939.

Considerable numbers of Gauntlets were shipped to the South African Air Force and 24 of these found their way into the Finnish Air Force, which operated the type until they were retired in 1945 and put into store. The 10 survivors were disposed of as scrap in 1950 but 20 years later one was discovered in a derelict condition by a Mr Hintikka, a vintage car enthusiast. By 1975 he had acquired the remains of the aircraft, K5271, and subsequently obtained parts of several other aircraft. The Gauntlet was then inspected by W/O Kalevi Eskonmaa of the Finnish Air Force Technical School at Halli who decided that it was capable of restoration to flying condition! Work started in 1976 and five years later the restored Gauntlet, painted in its Finnish colours as GT-400 but with the civil registration OH-XGT, took to the air on the power of an Alvis Leonides 127 taken from a Percival Pembroke, on 10 May 1982.

Gloster Gladiator

UK

Powerplant: One 840hp Bristol Mercury IX
Span: 32ft 3in
Length: 27ft 5in
Height: 10ft 4in
Wing area: 323sq ft

The Gladiator was the last in a long line of Gloster biplane fighters which had included the Grebe, Gamecock and Gauntlet. The prototype was known as the SS37 and was flown in September 1934 as a private venture which conformed to Air Ministry Spec F7/30. The official trials were successful and the Gladiator was ordered in July 1935, the initial contract being for 23 machines with a further 180 ordered the following September. The total built when production finally ceased in April 1940 was over 480 for the RAF whilst several overseas air forces also ordered the type.

The Gladiator was the last of the RAF's classic biplane fighters and was also the first RAF fighter to feature an enclosed cockpit — although many pilots preferred to fly them with the hoods open. They entered service with No 72 Sqn in January 1937 and were used offensively in the Battle of France and with No 247 Sqn during the Battle of Britain. The Gladiator was really outclassed by the outbreak of war but its wartime exploits are legion, the best remembered operations being those of No 263 Sqn off frozen Norwegian lakes and the defence of Malta by the immortal *Faith*, *Hope* and *Charity* trio of Sea Gladiators.

One Gladiator remains in flying condition, L8032/ G-AMRK, with the Shuttleworth Collection and others are preserved at the Royal Air Force Museum, Hendon and the Swedish Air Force Museum, Linkoping. Several frames were recovered from the bottom of a Norwegian lake and are undergoing various forms of restoration and the fuselage of Sea Gladiator N5520 *Faith* is exhibited at the National War Museum of Malta, Fort St Elmo, Valletta.

Granville Brothers Gee Bee Series USA

Data: Model A

Powerplant: One 100hp Kinner radial
Span: 29ft 2.5in
Length: 20ft 8in
Wing area: 185sq ft

The Granville Brothers entered the lightplane business in 1929 with an attractive little two-seat biplane known as the Model A. Ten were built at Boston before the Tate family became interested in the concern and provided the finance to set up a factory at Springfield, Mass, where the brothers concentrated on their fast and furious little 'flying barrel' racers. One of the Model As survives, N901K, which is part of the Bradley Air Museum, Conn, but of the racers only one original survives, the large two seat 'QED' which is preserved as XB-AKM at Santa Lucia, Mexico.

A replica of the most famous Gee Bee, the Model Z, has recently been built and flown in California.

Great Lakes 2T-1 Sport

USA

Photo: NC304Y is a 2T-1A photographed at Old Rhinebeck, NY.

Powerplant: One 100hp ACE Cirrus
Span: 26ft 8in
Length: 20ft 4in
Wing area: 187.6sq ft

The 2T-1 series was designed by Charles W. Meyers and substantial numbers were built by the Great Lakes Aircraft Corporation of Cleveland, Ohio, between 1929 and 1932. Three main versions were built, differing in their powerplants: the 2T-1 had the 85hp American Cirrus, the 2T-1A had the 100hp American Cirrus, and the 2T-1E had the 95hp American Cirrus Hi-Drive (also known as the Ensign).

Production ceased in 1936 but the aircraft was so well thought of that many were re-engined with more modern powerplants to keep them airworthy and in the 1970s the company was reorganised at Wichita, Kansas, and the type put back into production for a short time. Production has now been suspended temporarily. A scaled-down version for homebuilders is known as the Baby Great Lakes. One Great Lakes biplane, a 2T-1A powered by a Warner Scarab radial, has been imported to the UK as G-BIIZ and is based at Booker with the Hon Patrick Lindsay.

Grumman G-22 and G-23

USA

Photo: Can Car G-23 c/n 101, N2803J, restored as an FF-1 at the Naval Aviation Museum, Pensacola, Florida.
Data: G-23/FF-1

Powerplant: One 750hp Wright R-1820F
Span: 34ft 6in
Length: 24ft 6in
Height: 11ft 11in
Wing area: 310sq ft

The G-22 was a special 'one-off' aircraft built to the order of Maj Al Williams for the use of the Gulf Oil Co. Registered NR1050 it was delivered to Williams at Roosevelt Field, New York, on 1 December 1936 and was then flown extensively on promotional tours across the US. It was shipped to Europe and flown throughout 1938 by Williams and others, including Ernst Udet, then head of the Luftwaffe. In 1948 the Gulfhawk II was withdrawn from active flying and presented to the National Air & Space Museum. It features the 28ft 6in span upperwing of an F2F

married to the fuselage of an F3F and is powered by a 1,000hp Wright Cyclone R-1820-G1.

The G-23 was a Canadian-built version of the FF-1 fighter, 15 of which were built by Canadian Car & Foundry for the RCAF from 1938 in order to keep the Fort Williams plant operating while Hurricane production was set up. In Canadian service the type was known as the Goblin. Grumman built some 24 fuselages, Brewster built 24 wing sets and the type was also ordered by Spain (via Turkey) for use in the Civil War. In Spanish service the type was known as the R-6 Delfin and eight of the 40 delivered survived until the mid-1950s only to be scrapped!

One Canadian-built G-23 Goblin, c/n 101, was discovered at Managua, Nicaragua, by J. R. Sirmons in 1962. It was rebuilt with improvised parts and flown back to the US where it was overhauled by Grumman and presented to the Naval Aviation Museum at Pensacola where it is painted to represent an FF-1 of Fighting Squadron VF-5B 'The Red Rippers' which used the type on board the USS *Lexington* from 1933-1935.

Handley Page Gugnunc

UK

Photo: Cugnunc G-AACN following assembly at Wroughton.

Powerplant: One 155hp Armstrong Siddeley Mongoose II
Span: 40ft
Length: 26ft 9in
Max speed: 112.5mph
Min speed: 33.5mph

The Gugnunc was built in 1929 as a competitor in the Guggenheim Air Safety Competition which was held in the USA. It was a two-seat biplane, powered by a 155hp Armstrong Siddeley Mongoose II radial and it featured a number of Handley Page patented safety devices — such as the automatic slot — which gave it remarkable slow flying characteristics.

The Gugnunc was runner-up in the competition and was transferred to the Royal Aircraft Establishment in December 1930 as K1908. It was flown at the Hendon Air Pageant in a crazy flying routine — for which it was ideally suited — and eventually passed into the hands of the Science Museum. It came out of storage very briefly for the 1951 'Fifty Years of Flying' exhibition and in 1979 was assembled at the new Science Museum store at Wroughton, Wiltshire.

Hawker Cygnet

Photo: G-EBMB as exhibited in the RAF Museum, Hendon.

Powerplant: One 32hp Bristol Cherub III
Span: 28ft
Length: 20ft 3in
Wing area: 165sq ft
Max speed: 65mph

The Cygnet two-seat ultra-light biplane was designed by Sidney Camm for the 1924 Lympne Light Aeroplane Trials, for which event two aircraft were constructed, G-EBJH and G-EBMB. Both aircraft were re-engined with Bristol Cherub IIIs for the 1926 trials, which were won by 'BMB with 'BJH second.

'BJH was written off in a take-off crash in August 1927 but 'BMB was put into store at Brooklands to re-emerge in 1949 when it was restored to flying condition by Hawkers at their Langley factory. It then joined their 'Vintage Circus' which included a Tomtit, Hart and Hurricane, and was flown at various displays throughout the 1950s.

Retired from display work, the sole survivor was presented to the RAF Museum in 1972 alongside the Hart and Hurricane and is now the centrepiece of the Sidney Camm Hall. Luckily the drawings of the Cygnet still survive in the British Aerospace archive at Kingston and several reproductions are currently under construction both in the UK and Australia.

Hawker Danecock

Photo: Aircraft 158 suspended in the Arsenal Museum, Copenhagen.

Powerplant: One 385hp Armstrong Siddeley Jaguar IV
Span: 32ft 7in
Length: 26ft 1.25in
Max speed: 145mph

The Danecock was a modified version of the Hawker Woodcock, the first single-seat fighter to be produced by the H. G. Hawker Engineering Co Ltd. Three were ordered by the Danish Navy in 1925 as land-based fighters intended for the defence of Copenhagen Naval Station.

Powered by the 385hp Armstrong Siddeley Jaguar IV instead of the Woodcock's Bristol Jupiter IV the Danecock also differed from the standard aircraft in that the wings were of unequal span and armament consisted of two 7.7mm Madsen machine guns which were mounted on the forward fuselage sides. The three British-built Danecocks were delivered by February 1926 and were serialled 151, 152, and 153 but a licence to build the type was acquired and the Naval Dockyard built a further seven during 1927 and five in 1928. The locally

roduced aircraft were known as the LB II and were located serials 154-165.

The Danecocks served until replaced by Hawker imrods in 1934-35 and were last used in 1936. ne four survivors were placed in store but on the utbreak of war three were broken up and one

retained as a museum exhibit. Having survived the German occupation No 158 was restored by the Main Workshops of The Royal Danish Air Force at Vaerloese and is currently displayed at the Royal Danish Arsenal Museum in the centre of Copenhagen.

Hawker Tomtit

UK

Powerplant: One 150hp Armstrong Siddeley ongoose IIIC
Span: 28ft 6in
Length: 23ft 8in
eight: 8ft 4in
Wing area: 238sq ft

e Tomtit appeared in 1928 in response to an RAF quirement for a Mongoose-powered replacement the Avro 504N. It was one of two types selected small-scale production and evaluation, the other ing the Avro Trainer which was eventually lected as the Tutor.

The Tomtit was of fabric covered all-metal nstruction, it possessed excellent flying qualities d had two features which were new to elementary iners, Handley Page automatic slots and full blind-ng instrumentation in the rear cockpit.

Thirty-six Tomtits were built between 1928 and 31, 25 for the RAF, four for the Royal New aland Air Force, and five as private aircraft istered to Hawkers as development machines. e RAF aircraft served until 1935, mainly at the ntral Flying School, Wittering and No 3 FTS at antham, and following their retirement a number peared on the civil register.

One of these machines was G-AFTA which was wn throughout the war as the private mount of

Spitfire test pilot Alex Henshaw. After the war it passed into the ownership of Hawker test pilot Neville Duke and was bought back by Hawkers in 1950 and painted in their house colours of blue and gold. With the disbanding of the Hawker vintage collection the Tomtit was, thankfully, presented to the Shuttleworth Collection where it is maintained in pristine flying condition as K1786.

Hawker Hart and variants

UK

Photo: Hart II G-ABMR painted as 'J9941' is now exhibited at the RAF Museum in non-flying condition.
Data: Hart II

Powerplant: One 560hp Rolls-Royce Kestrel IIIS
Span: 37ft 3in
Length: 29ft 4in
Height: 10ft 5in
Wing area: 348sq ft

The Hart was designed to Spec 12/26, the prototype flying in June 1928, and after competitive trials against the Fairey Fox II and Avro Antelope it was selected as the standard bomber of the Royal Air Force. The initial batch of pre-production aircraft was built in 1929 and the first aircraft were delivered to No 33 Sqn at Eastchurch in January 1930.

Some 460 Harts were built for the RAF and a further 500 were built as trainers, several overseas air forces selecting the type during the 1930s too. It was fast and manoeuvrable, as shown by the inability of Siskin fighters to catch the Harts in the 1930 Air Exercises, and formed the equipment of seven home-based regular squadrons between 1930-1936, Auxiliary Air Force units operating the type from 1933-1938.

From 1936 the Hart was replaced in the front-line squadrons by the Hawker Hind but continued to serve in India until 1939. 528 Hinds were built between 1934 and 1938, this being little more than a developed Hart with a fully blown Kestrel V and

various airframe refinements. It was essentially a stop-gap type which bridged the gap until the more modern Battles and Blenheims entered service, it had left front-line units by 1938 but continued with the Auxiliary squadrons for another year.

The Hart was such a remarkably successful design that a whole family of derivatives sprang from it; these included the Demon two-seat fighter of 1931, the Audax army co-operation type of 1931, the Hardy general purpose type of 1934 and the Hector army co-operation type of 1936. All these variants were visually very similar with the exception of the Hector which was powered by the 24-cylinder Napier Dagger instead of the V-12 Rolls-Royce Kestrel.

Several examples of the Hart family survive; Hart II G-ABMR is preserved in the Royal Air Force Museum alongside a Hart Trainer, K4972, and an Afghan Hind, K4762?; another ex-Afghan Hind has been restored to fly by the Shuttleworth Collection and is registered G-AENP; an ex-RNZAF Hind is under restoration at Western Springs, Auckland; another derelict Hind is with the Canadian National Aeronautical Collection; a Hartbees is exhibited at Saxonwold, South Africa; and a Mercury-engined Hart is displayed at the Swedish Air Force Museum, Linkoping. Two Demons, one of which is A1-8, are under reconstruction at the RAAF base at Point Cook, one is for the RAAF Museum and the other to fly with owner J. McDonald.

Howard DGA-15P

USA

Photo: Red and black Howard DGA-15P seen at Horn Point, Maryland.

Powerplant: One 450hp Pratt & Whitney Wasp Junior

Span: 38ft
Length: 25ft 8in
Height: 9ft 5in
Wing area: 185.5sq ft

Following his success in the 1935 Bendix and Thompson Trophy races Ben O. Howard produced commercial versions of his winning 'Mr Mulligan'. The custom-built DGAs were said to be the fastest four-seaters on the market in 1937-38, they were certainly the most expensive. Four versions were available: DGA-8 (320hp Jacobs), DGA-9 (285hp Jacobs), DGA-11 (450hp Pratt & Whitney) and

DGA-12 (300hp Jacobs).

Thirty-one aircraft were sold before the introduction of the DGA-15P in early 1940, 40 of which were sold commercially before the type entered series production for the US Navy as the GH ambulance and NH-1 trainer. 525 were built of which about 50 remain in flying condition.

Junkers F13 Germany

Photo: F13 CH-59 served with the Swiss airline Ad Astra in the 1920s.

Powerplant: One 385hp Junkers L5
Span: 58ft 3in
Length: 31ft 6in
All up weight: 5,960lb

With the end of World War 1 the Junkers factory turned its attention to the commercial market and on 25 June 1919 the first J13 — later to become the F13 — made its maiden flight. The F13 was one of the most significant transport aircraft of its day and laid the foundations which were to develop into the

well-known Junkers products of World War 2.

Before production was finally terminated in 1932 322 F13s were built. The early models had accommodation for two crew in an open cockpit and four passengers in the cabin, later models had an enclosed cockpit. Construction was of all-metal, the familiar Junkers corrugated skinning being very much in evidence.

At least four F13s are known to survive: 'D-3866' is with the Deutches Museum, Munich; CH-59 is with the Kozlekedesi Museum, Budapest; SE-ACC is with Tekniska Museet, Stockholm; and an unmarked example is with the Musee de l'Air, Le Bourget.

Junkers Ju52/3m Germany

Photo: CASA-built C352, G-BECL, is based at Blackbushe, Hants.

Powerplants: Three 830hp BMW 132A radials
Span: 95ft 10in
Length: 62ft
Height: 14ft 10in
Wing area: 1,190sq ft

The Ju52 originally appeared in October 1930 as a single-engined, all metal transport. The seventh aircraft was modified to take a trio of Pratt and Whitney Hornets and flown in April 1931, the results being so encouraging that all subsequent aircraft were completed as tri-motors.

The Ju52/3m was extensively built during the 1930s for both civil and military use and was exported widely. At the outbreak of World War 2 it was the standard Luftwaffe transport aircraft and was to continue in this role until 1945.

3,234 examples were built in Germany, 2,804 of them during the war years, and the type was also built by the German-controlled Amiot plant in France — where production continued postwar as the AAC1 for the Armee de l'Air — and a further 100 were licence-built in Spain by CASA as the C352-L.

A few genuine German-built examples have survived, notably three which were delivered to the Swiss Air Force in 1939, but the majority of those seen today are Spanish-built examples which differ from German and French aircraft by virtue of their ENMA Beta B-4 engines.

Klemm L25 Germany

Photo: R. S. Russell's Kilkerran-based G-AAUP *Clementine.*

Powerplant: One 45hp Salmson AD9
Span: 42ft 7.5in
Length: 25ft 7in
Height: 6ft 11in
Wing area: 215sq ft

The L25 appeared in 1927 as the first product of Leichtflugzeubau Klemm and was a two-seat, low wing monoplane of all-wood construction which was powered by the 45hp Salmson AD9 radial. The aeroplane had remarkable slow-flying characteristics and was reputed to be virtually stall and spin-proof, it was therefore an ideal trainer for even the most inept of student pilots. The aeroplane proved to be remarkably popular and was developed throughout the late 1920s and early 1930s. Licences to build the type were acquired in several countries including the UK where it was eventually developed into the BA Swallow 2 (qv). Three genuine Klemm-built L25s are registered in the UK but one is currently based in Germany and another is only a fuselage, this leaves the Prestwick/Kilkerran-based G-AAUP as the only flying example in the country.

Klemm L35D   Germany

Photo: Klemm L35 D-ECCI was based at Rotterdam in 1978.

Powerplant: One 100hp Hirth HM504A-2 or 80hp Hirth HM60R.
Span: 34ft 1in
Length: 24ft 7in
Height: 6ft 8in
Wing area: 163.5sq ft

The L35 appeared in 1935 as a successor to the earlier L25 from which it differed primarily in its method of construction, the new aircraft having a welded steel tube fuselage and ply-covered wooden wings. The prototype was powered by an 80hp Hirth in-line but production versions were also fitted with the 100hp Hirth HM504A-2. The type was built in large numbers both for civilian flying clubs and as a basic trainer for the Luftwaffe. The L35D was a licence-built version which was manufactured in Sweden as a trainer for the Royal Swedish Air Force between 1941 and 1942, several of these were sold on the civil market on their retirement from military service and a number found their way back to Germany. The L35 is still flown in small numbers.

Lockheed Vega   USA

Photo: Wiley Post's *Winnie Mae* in the NASM, Washington, DC.
Data: 5-C

Powerplants: One 450hp Pratt & Whitney Wasp SC-1
Span: 41ft
Length: 27ft 6in
Height: 9ft
Wing area: 279sq ft

The Vega was one of the most significant aircraft built in the USA and served as the foundation of the Lockheed Company. The prototype Model 1 Vega was flown by Eddie Bellande on 4 July 1927 and the type went into service with American, Braniff, Northwest, TWA and Western Airlines as well as being used for record-breaking flights by Amelia Earhart and Wiley Post (both of whose Vegas survive with the National Air & Space Museum, Washington, DC). The Model 2D Vega differed from the original in

95

having the 220hp Wright Whirlwind replaced by a 300hp Pratt & Whitney Wasp Junior. The Models 5 and 5-C had five and seven seats respectively and were powered by the uprated 450hp Wasp SC-1.

In all 118 Vegas were built with wooden fuselages and a further 10 had a Dural fuselage and were known as DL-1s. An additional 31 aircraft were built using Vega tooling and jigs, these were known

as the Sirius, Explorer, Air Express and Altair and all were low or mid-wing monoplanes.

Several Vegas survive in the USA in addition to the two NASM machines; these are NR199E/N965Y at the Henry Ford Museum, NC12288 with the Air Power Museum at Ottumwa, and a flying example restored as a copy of Wiley Post's *Winnie Mae* NC-105-W.

Lockheed 9-C Orion   USA

Photo: Doolittle's *Shellightning* now masquerades as 'CH-167' at Lucerne, Switzerland.

Powerplant: One 750hp Wright Cyclone
Span: 42ft 10in
Length: 27ft 6in
Wing area: 294sq ft

The Orion was a low-wing derivative of the Vega which was designed by Richard von Hake and introduced in 1931. Also known as the Sirius and Altair 9 the Orion featured a retractable undercarriage and could carry six passengers at over 200mph on the power of its 650hp Wright Cyclone.

The Orion was used by a number of airlines including Varney and American, who had six each, Pan American, Continental, TWA and Swissair. The sole surviving Orion is the one-off 9-C which featured a Dural fuselage and was built for racing by Jimmy Doolittle with the name *Shellightning*. Registered N12222 it was restored to fly by Tallmantz Aviation with a 735hp Cyclone and passed on to David Johnson of Peterborough, New Hampshire. It then lapsed into a poor state and was finally acquired by Swissair who shipped it to Lucerne and restored it to display standard in the Transport Museum in Swissair markings as 'CH-167'.

Lockheed 10 and 12 Electra　　　　　USA

Photo: CF-TCA was the first aircraft of Trans Canada Air Lines, it is now preserved by the National Aeronautical Collection at Uplands Airport, Ottawa.
Data: Model 10A

Powerplants: Two 400hp Pratt & Whitney Wasp Junior SB
Span: 55ft
Length: 38ft 7in
Height: 10ft 1in
Wing area: 458.3sq ft

The Model 10 Electra first flew in 1934, it was powered by a pair of 400hp Wasp Juniors, had accommodation for two crew and 10 passengers, and was the forerunner of a long line of famous Lockheed twins. The Electra was the type that put the bankrupt Lockheed Corporation back on its feet and 148 were built, the last in 1941. The principal production version was the Wasp Junior-powered 10A but other models included the 10B (440hp Wright Whirlwind), and the 10C and 10E with Wasp Juniors.

A scaled-down version with accommodation for only six passengers appeared in 1936 as the Lockheed 12. This was aimed principally at the corporate market and 114 Electra Juniors were delivered up to 1942 when production ended. A military development, the 212A, was fitted with a dorsal turret and supplied to the Netherlands East Indies and other countries.

Substantial numbers of both types survive throughout North America, one of which, NC5171N, a Model 10B, was acquired by the Science Museum from the Wings & Wheels Museum at Orlando, Florida, and made its Trans-Atlantic delivery flight to Fairoaks, Surrey, arriving on 17 June 1982. It was later ferried to its new home at Wroughton, Wiltshire, arriving on 21 June 1982.

Luscombe Phantom and Silvaire　　　　　USA

Photo: Joe Illiffe's White Waltham-based Model 8F Silvaire.
Data: Model 8A-2 Silvaire

Powerplant: One 65hp Continental A-65
Span: 35ft
Length: 20ft
Height: 5ft 10in
Wing area: 140sq ft

The Phantom first flew in May 1934 and was essentially an all-metal derivative of the Monocoupe D-145. It was a side by side two-seater powered by the 145hp Warner Super Scarab and at the time of its introduction was revolutionary for its stressed-skin construction. Approximately 25 Phantoms were built, the last in 1941, but the design was refined via the Luscombe 4 into the Luscombe 8 which appeared in late 1937.

The 8 was powered by a 50hp Continental A-50 but this was soon replaced by the 65hp Continental or Lycoming in the Models 8A and 8B which appeared in March 1939. The 8C and 8D both featured the 75hp Continental A-75 and a total of 1,200 Silvaires of all models had been built when production was shelved in 1942. Postwar, production was resumed with the Models 8E and 8F and after passing through numerous hands the last versions of the design were built in 1960. A four-seat postwar development known as the Model 11A Sedan was built in small numbers.

Several thousand Silvaires of all models remain in existence, mainly in the USA but there are some in Europe and one Model 8F is registered in the UK as G-AFYD.

Macchi M7   Italy

Photo: The sole surviving Macchi M7, Fv 945 in the Swedish Air Force Museum.
Data: Not available

The Societa Anonima Nieuport Macchi was founded in 1912 at Varese, Italy, initially to build Nieuport designs under licence. This it did throughout World War 1, 1,375 aircraft being built in 1918 alone, and some of these were flying boats of indigenous

design. After the Armistice development along both lines continued and the M7 pusher-engined racing flying-boat was one of the company's first success stories. Powered by an Isotta-Fraschini V-12 engine of 250hp the M7 was entered in the 1921 Schneider Trophy contest and was flown to victory by Lt Giovanni de Briganti at a record speed of 177.8mph. One example of the M7, delivered to Sweden in 1920, has survived in the Swedish Air Force Museum at Linkoping.

Macchi M39, M67 and MC72 Racers   Italy

Photo: The MC72, fastest seaplane ever built.
Data: MC72

Powerplant: One FIAT AS6 boosted to 3,100hp
Span: 31ft 1in
Length: 27ft 3.6in
Height: 10ft 9.875in
Wing area: 161.4sq ft

The Schneider Trophy was a hard-fought contest and

of great national importance, the Macchi racers figuring prominently in all the races from 1921-1929. Three of the Macchi floatplanes still survive, two of them in excellent condition. The M39 was built in 1926 for that year's contest and was by far the fastest aircraft present. Three were constructed, powered by the 850hp FIAT AS2 V-12 engine, and they came in in first and third places at 246.5 and 218mph respectively. One of the three, MM76, is preserved in beautiful condition at Vigna di Valle.

The M67 was built for the 1929 contest and was powered by the 1,400hp Isotta-Fraschini Asso 18-cylinder 'W' type engine driving a three-bladed airscrew. Two aircraft were entered but both were forced to retire and the badly damaged remains of one of them, MM105, is stored at Vigna di Valle for eventual reconstruction.

The MC72 was built for the 1931 contest but was not ready in time, if it had been the outcome might have been rather different for when the aircraft was eventually ready one of them succeeded in smashing the S6B's World Air Speed Record. The attempt was made by WO Francesco Angell on 10 April 1933 and the new record was 423.8mph. The following year the same pilot pushed the record to 440.68mph, a figure which still stands as the fastest ever seaplane. This historic machine survived wartime storage at Desenzano and now has pride of place in the Italian Air Force Museum at Vigna di Valle.

Martin B-10   USA

Photo: The Martin B-10 in the US Air Force Museum.

Powerplants: Two 775hp Wright Cyclone R-1820
Span: 70ft 6in
Length: 44ft 9in
Height: 15ft 5in

The B-10 was America's first all-metal monoplane bomber to be produced in any quantity and featured such innovations as internal bomb stowage, rectractable undercarriage, a rotating gun turret and enclosed cockpits. It was so advanced that at the time of its introduction into the AAC it was 50% faster than contemporary biplane bombers and as fast as most fighters. The Air Corps placed orders for 121 B-10s between 1933 and 1936, the largest bomber contract since World War 1, and ordered a further 32 as B-12s with Pratt & Whitney engines rather than Wright Cyclones.

In 1934 Gen Henry H. 'Hap' Arnold led a formation of 10 B-10s on a 7,360-mile flight from Washington DC to Fairbanks, Alaska, and back. Although obsolete and replaced in US service by B-17s and B-18s at the outbreak of World War 2 export versions of the B-10 were flown by China and the Netherlands East Indies against the Japanese.

One export version of the B-10 was discovered in a training school in Argentina, having been delivered new to the Argentine in 1938, and was donated to the US Air Force Museum in 1971. Following restoration by the 96th Maintenance Sqn (Mobile), Air Force Reserve, at Kelly AFB, Texas, in 1973-1976 the aircraft was painted in the markings of one of the Alaskan flight aircraft and put on display at Wright-Patterson AFB, Ohio.

Mignet HM14 Pou-du-Ciel   France

Photo: A genuine prewar Flea preserved by the Lincolnshire Aviation Museum.

Powerplant: Various but including the 25hp Scott A2S Flying Squirrel
Span: 22ft
Length: 13ft
Height: 5ft 6in
Wing area: 140sq ft

Mignet's little 'Flying Flea' was the phenomenon of the mid-1930s, at a time when the man in the street was yearning to follow in the footsteps of Amy Johnson, Jim Mollison, et al, the Pou du Ciel offered the chance of building your own aeroplane. Easy to construct and powered by a motor cycle or car engine the Flea craze swept Europe and well over 100 were registered in Britain alone in less than a

year. Many hundreds more were certainly started but abandoned when ominous reports of the little biplane's handling qualities began to circulate. In Mignet's hands the Flea could do no wrong but few amateur constructors were ignorant of the weight and balance problems associated with the design. In certain circumstances the aircraft could get into an uncontrolled dive from which there was no escape and the Flea was banned.

Mignet solved the problem quite simply but by then confidence was lost, war was on the horizon and the Flea was forgotten. Many were stored in attics and barns to re-surface in the 1960s when the first Aircraft Preservation Societies were forming and a number of modern aircraft have been built to the original plans. One Volkswagen-powered HM293 is airworthy and based at the Historic Aircraft Museum, Southend.

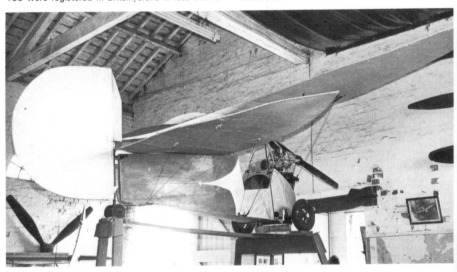

Miles Hawk Major and Hawk Speed Six   UK

Photo: The sole surviving Hawk Speed Six, G-ADGP, based at Old Warden.
Data: Hawk Major

Powerplant: One 130hp DH Gipsy Major
Span: 33ft
Length: 24ft
Height: 6ft 8in
Wing area: 169sq ft

The Miles Hawk low wing monoplane first appeared in 1933 and proved immediately popular as it was both easy to fly and cheap because of the availability of cheap Cirrus IIIA engines with which to power it. With the end of the cheap engine stocks it was

decided to fit the 130hp DH Gipsy Major and generally clean up the airframe to produce the Hawk Major of 1934. This aeroplane was deservedly popular and sold in large numbers, particularly to sporting pilots of the day, and it was logical that an even more powerful single seater should be developed.

The first single-seater to appear with the 200hp DH Gipsy Six was G-ACTE, initially known as the Gipsy Six Hawk but later renamed Hawk Speed Six. Two further Speed Sixes were built, G-ADOD and G-ADGP which were flown by Miss Ruth Fontes and her brother Luis Fontes in the 1935 King's Cup Air Race. The first two had relatively short lives but 'DGP was flown for many years postwar by Ron Paine who

now tends it for new owner Roger Reeves, it is based at Old Warden.

One Hawk Major, G-ADMW is preserved in store by the RAF Museum in its impressment markings as DG590, and two Hawk Majors are flying in Canada whilst a third, CC-FBB is preserved at Santiago, Chile.

Miles M3A Falcon Major   UK

Photo: Falcon Major G-AEEG is notable as it won the 1979 King's Cup Air Race!

Powerplant: One 130hp DH Gipsy Major
Span: 35ft
Length: 25ft
Height: 6ft 6in
Wing area: 174.3sq ft

With the success of the two seat Hawk series behind him F. G. Miles designed the M3 Falcon which was basically a three-seat cabin development of the earlier type. The prototype flew in 1934 and the first production M3A followed in January 1935, this differed in having a raked forward windscreen and seating for four. Ten production Falcon Majors were followed by the three-seat M3B and four-seat M3C Falcon Sixes which were fitted with the 200hp DH Gipsy Six. The M3D was similarly powered but had an increased all up weight of 2,650lb.

At least three Falcons are known to survive, G-AEEG is maintained by Phillip Mann at Biggin Hill; another Falcon Major, VH-AAT, is flying at Casey Airfield, Berwick, Victoria, Australia; and a Falcon Six is believed to be stored at Zaragosa, Spain.

Miles M11A Whitney Straight   UK

Photo: G-AFGK was the last airworthy Whitney Straight in the UK until sold to an American buyer.

Powerplant: One 130hp DH Gipsy Major 1
Span: 35ft 8in
Length: 25ft
Height: 6ft 6in
Wing area: 178sq ft

The Whitney Straight was designed to the specification of Mr Whitney Straight who wanted a modern but docile two-seater with which to equip his chain of flying clubs. The aircraft was first flown in the spring of 1936 and production deliveries started soon afterward and 50 had been built by the time that production was halted by the outbreak of war. 31 were sold on the home market the remainder being exported to Australia, New Zealand and several European countries. The Whitney Straight had an uneventful career and was notable mainly for extreme ease of handling, three survived in the UK for many years but the last airworthy survivor was sold in the United States leaving only G-AERV in store in Northern Ireland and G-AEUJ which is currently being rebuilt to fly for Bob Mitchell.

Miles M14A Magister   UK

Photo: P6382 is still flying with the Shuttleworth Collection.

Powerplant: One 130hp DH Gipsy Major 1
Span: 33ft 10in
Length: 25ft 3in
Height: 6ft 8in
Wing area: 172sq ft

The Magister appeared in 1937 as the ultimate development of the Miles Hawk series. It was a direct development of the Hawk Trainer, several versions of which had been built, and was developed to fulfil Spec T40/36. A few civil aircraft were built prewar as Hawk Trainer IIIs, but the vast majority were completed as Magisters for the RAF, production ending after 1,203. The Magister was significant as it was the first monoplane trainer in RAF service and the first to be fitted with flaps, as such it ushered in the new generation of monoplanes then being ordered.

With the Magister being declared obsolete after World War 2 many reverted to civil use where they were known as Hawk Trainer IIIs and settled down to a long life as an instructional and sporting aircraft which finally came to an end in the early 1960s when their wooden structures were declared unfit for the issue of Public Transport Certificates of Airworthiness. Today only two Maggies are known to be in flying trim, P6382 at the Shuttleworth Collection and R1914 with the Strathallan Aircraft Collection, several others are preserved in non-flying condition.

Miles M17 Monarch   UK

Photo: Monarch G-AFLW was rebuilt by Rex Coates.

Powerplant: One 130hp DH Gipsy Major
Span: 35ft 7in
Length: 25ft 11.75in
Height: 8ft 9.25in
Wing area: 180sq ft

The Monarch was basically an enlarged three-seat Whitney Straight which incorporated many standard Magister components — such as the wings — for ease of production and cheapness. It was flown for the first time on 21 February 1938 and 10 production examples were built before the war put a stop to further production. Six were built to British orders and the type was all set to follow the Hawk as another success story when the war intervened. An interesting feature of the design was the so-called 'glide control' which interconnected the throttle and flaps and gave a much greater degree of control during the approach than had previously been possible.

Three Monarchs are known to have survived, G-AFLW is in flying condition with Neil Jensen at Biggin Hill whilst both G-AFJU and G-AFRZ/G-AIDE are believed to be under restoration to flying condition.

Miles M18 Mk 2

UK

Photo: The surviving M18, G-AHKY, after its restoration by Rex Coates.

Powerplant: One 150hp Blackburn Cirrus Major III
Span: 31ft
Length: 24ft 10in
Height: 9ft 4in
Wing area: 183sq ft

The un-named M18 was intended as a replacement for the Magister and design work commenced in 1938 under the direction of a young Swiss stressman named Walter G. Capley. Although four prototypes were eventually built, all of them differing in detail, and despite very favourable comments the M18 never entered production — even though the Air Ministry ordered it twice, both orders being almost immediately reversed.

The first three M18s survived the war, the original being scrapped in 1947 and the third crashing on 25 May 1950. The second aircraft was registered G-AHKY in 1946 and went on to have a long and successful racing career in the hands of H. B. Iles, winning the 1956 Goodyear Trophy, the 1957 Osram Cup and finally the 1961 King's Cup. It was rebuilt in the early 1970s by Rex Coates and is now part of the Scottish Aircraft Collection Trust, Perth.

Morane Saulnier MS230

France

Photo: One of a number of MS317s still used as glider tugs is F-BGKX.
Data: MS230

Powerplant: One 230hp Salmson 9 ABb

Span: 35ft 2in
Length: 22ft 9in
Height: 8ft 11in
Wing area: 212sq ft

The MS230 was one of a trio of parasol winged trainers which appeared from the Morane Saulnier concern during 1930, the others being the MS181 single-seater and the MS315 which was basically a lighter version of the MS230. The MS230 was built in greater numbers than the other two, some 1,100 being constructed in France, Belgium and Portugal, and a small number were even built after the war during 1948-1949. The MS181 was mainly built for the flying schools of the Cie Francais d'Aviation whilst the MS315 was built to the tune of some 300 prewar machines. The latter type re-entered production after the war, the engine being changed to the 220hp Continental W-670-6A as used in the Stearman PT-13 series (qv), in this form it was known as the MS317.

Today examples of all types survive, the most numerous being the MS317 which is still used as a glider tug by some French clubs. Examples of the other types are flying, one MS230 being registered in the UK as G-AVEB, and a second as G-BJCL.

Morane Saulnier MS406 C1 France

Photo: J-277 in the Musee de l'Air, Paris, where it represents an MS406 C1.
Data: D-3801

Powerplant: One 1,000hp licence-built Hispano-Suiza HS-51 12Y
Span: 34ft 10in
Length: 26ft 3in
Height: 10ft 6in
Wing area: 193.75sq ft

The prototype MS405 fighter appeared at the 1936 Paris Salon and an order for 16 aircraft was placed for the Armee de l'Air, these comprised three 405s, the fourth was a 406 and the rest up to the 11th were 405s. The 12th aircraft was of simplified design and the 13th was intended for high-speed parachute dropping. Large scale production of the MS406C commenced in 1938 and, together with the Curtiss Hawk, it became the standard French fighter aircraft, its pilots fighting a valiant battle against the advancing Germans until the capitulation in 1940. Some 406Cs were taken over by the Luftwaffe for second-line duties.

In 1939 two aircraft were purchased by the Swiss Air Force and after an evaluation the type was put into production by the EKW as the D-3800. Eight pre-production (O series) aircraft were delivered before the full-production series commenced delivery in January 1940. 74 aircraft were built, plus two which were assembled from spare parts, and they remained in service until 1954. During the production of the D-3800, which were powered by the 860hp Hispano-Suiza HS-77-Ycrs engine, the design of the 1,000hp HS-51 12Y was finalised and this engine powered further aircraft which were known as the D-3801. A total of 207 aircraft were delivered, including 17 which were built up from spare parts in 1947-1948 and the type remained in service, latterly as a target tug, until 1959. Two D-3801s have been preserved, J-276 is with the Museum of Transport & Communications at Lucerne whilst J-277 is with the Musee de l'Air at Le Bourget where it has been painted as an MS406 C1 and all Swiss identity plates removed!

Northrop Alpha, Delta and Gamma

USA

Photo: Northrop Alpha NC-11Y restored in TWA colours at the National Air & Space Museum, Washington, DC.
Data: Not available

Following his design of the Lockheed Vega in 1927, John K. Northrop left to form his own company at Burbank where his first product was the Alpha which entered series production in 1931 with financial backing from Boeing. The Alpha was an all-metal low wing monoplane, powered by a Pratt & Whitney Wasp, and which cruised at 140mph with three passengers and up to 465lb of mail or cargo. The Alpha was used commercially by Transcontinental & Western Air Inc (TWA), 13 of them being used to carry the mail from San Francisco to New York in an elapsed time of just over 23hrs. One Alpha, NC-11Y,

has survived and was acquired by the National Air & Space Museum in 1975. It was taken to Kansas City where volunteers at TWA's maintenance base restored it to near flying condition, it is now displayed in the NASM, Washington, DC.

Following the Alpha Northrop produced the Gamma, one of which, NR12269 *Polar Star*, is also preserved by the NASM, and the Delta. The Delta was an eight-seat faster airliner developed from the Gamma mailplane which first appeared in 1933. Eleven were built, mainly for corporate use, but one was delivered to the US Navy under the designation RT-1. The Delta was also produced in Canada for the RCAF and the derelict remains of RCAF 673 have been recovered for the Canadian National Aeronautical Collection.

Parnall Elf II

UK

Photo: The Shuttleworth Collection's Parnall Elf II.

Powerplant: One 120hp ADC Hermes III
Span: 31ft 3.5in
Length: 22ft 10.5in
All up weight: 1,700lb
Cruise speed: 103mph

Following moderate success with his Parnall Pixie monoplanes in the Lympne Trials, 1923-1926, Harold Bolas designed the Elf biplane, three of which were built at Yate between 1928 and 1932. It was an attractive two-seat machine which in its Mk I form was powered by the 105hp ADC Hermes I. Only one was built before the Mk II appeared, powered by the 120hp Hermes II and differing from the Mk I by virtue of its horn-balanced rudder. Two Mk IIs, G-AAIN and 'IO, were built and then production ceased. The first of these survived the war and surfaced again for the 'Fifty Years of Flying' exhibition at Hendon, after which it was acquired by the Shuttleworth Collection. It has now been restored to full flying condition after a lengthy rebuild.

Percival Gull

Photo: Jean Batten's Gull Six, G-ADPR, at Old Warden.
Data: Gull Six

Powerplant: One 200hp DH Gipsy Six
Span: 36ft 2in
Length: 24ft 9in
Height: 7ft 4.5in
Wing area: 169sq ft

The Gull appeared in 1932 as a three-seat, cantilever monoplane which was initially powered by the 130hp Cirrus Hermes IV. It was one of the cleanest and most efficient aircraft ever produced and was immediately successful as a long range record breaker and racing aircraft as well as in its designed role as a fast luxury tourer.

The first batch of 24 production Gulls was subcontracted to the Parnall factory at Yate but in 1934 the Percival Aircraft Co Ltd set up its own works at Gravesend and started production of a revised version powered by the 200hp DH Gipsy Six and known as the Gull Six. 22 Gulls were built at Gravesend before the company moved in 1936 to Luton Airport, production eventually giving way to the four-seat Vega Gull which appeared in 1935.

Gulls were used by many famous pilots of the 1930s to set records, including Amy Mollison, Sir Charles Kingsford Smith, Charles Gardner, the Duchess of Bedford and by designer Edgar Percival himself but the most memorable flights are those made by Jean Batten in Gull Six G-ADPR. This historic aircraft survived wartime impressment to be bought back by the manufacturers and was eventually presented to the Shuttleworth Collection in 1961, it is now being rebuilt to flying condition.

At least four other Gulls are known to survive; G-ACGR, being rebuilt to static condition at the Brussels Air Museum; G-AERD, being repaired following a take-off accident and owned by Cliff Lovell; VH-CCM, believed to be flying from Archerfield, Australia; and VH-UTP, discovered in a semi-derelict condition but under rebuild in Queensland by John Hill and Donald McG. Johnston.

Percival Mew Gull UK

Photo: Tom Storey and Martin Barraclough's rebuilt Mew Gull, G-AEXF.
Data: Type E2

Powerplant: One 200hp Gipsy Six
Span: 24ft
Length: 20ft 3in
Height: 6ft 10in
Wing area: 88sq ft

The remarkable Mew Gull appeared as a prototype in March 1934, it was powered by a 165hp Napier Javelin IA at first but was fitted with a revised undercarriage and 200hp Gipsy Six for racing. Its short life came to an end during the Coupe Michelin in October 1935 when the pilot, Compte Guy de Chateubrun, bailed out when he became lost in fog.

The next aircraft was the Type E2, also registered G-ACND, which featured an entirely new and far more shapely fuselage married to similar wings and tail surfaces. Again powered by the 200hp Gipsy Six it was raced with some success by Edgar Percival and others. Three production Type E2 Mew Gulls were then built, G-AEKL for Air Publicity Ltd, ZS-AHM for Maj A. M. Miller, and ZS-AHO for Capt S. S. Halse. All three were intended to race in the 1936 Schlesinger Race to South Africa but 'EKL was

damaged at Liverpool in a fatal accident before the race, 'AHM retired at Belgrade and 'AHO was damaged in a forced landing at Gwelo, Southern Rhodesia. The sixth and last Mew Gull was a total redesign, G-AFAA, the Type E3H. Built as the personal mount of Edgar Percival, it featured a slimmer fuselage and smaller wing than its predecessors.

The most famous Mew Gull of all was, however, Miller's ZS-AHM. Flown back to the UK it was registered G-AEXF on sale to Alex Henshaw and following a series of modifications which were carried out by Jack Cross of Essex Aero it took the 1938 King's Cup at the record speed of 236.25mph and then broke the out-and-back record to the Cape in February 1939, a record which still stands after over 40 years. 'EXF was rediscovered in 1950 and flew in races throughout the 1950s and early 1960s in the hands of Hugh Scrope, Peter Clifford, Nat Somers and others. It was finally grounded after a forced landing in August 1965 and passed into the hands of so-called 'preservationists' who allowed it to disintegrate to almost nothing. The derelict remains were finally bought by Tom Storey and Martin Barraclough and totally rebuilt to flying condition, the 'new' Mew Gull flying again in 1978.

Percival Q6 UK

Photo: G-AFFD photographed at Redhill at the time of its acquisition by the Midland Air Museum Ltd.

Powerplant: Two 205hp DH Gipsy Six Srs II
Span: 46ft 8in
Length: 32ft 3in
Height: 9ft 9in
Wing area: 278sq ft

The Percival Type Q was the company's first twin engined design and was intended to be its entry into the light airliner and executive market which had

been dominated by types such as the de Havilland Dragon Rapide and Dragonfly. Initially two versions were proposed, the Q4 with two Gipsy Majors had accommodation for a pilot and up to four passengers but it was only the Gipsy Six-powered Q6 which entered production.

First deliveries were in 1938 and the type was moderately popular with private owners and with companies requiring executive transports, a few were sold as airliners, notably to Western Airways which operated G-AFIX in 1939 and G-AHOM in 1946. Seven were built for the RAF as

communications aircraft with the name Petrel and all but one of the civil machines were impressed for similar duties.

Several survived the war to fly again but the sole survivor today is the first production aircraft, G-AFFD, delivered new to Sir Phillip Sassoon in March 1938 it was eventually acquired by the Midland Air Museum Ltd and stored at Duxford but in 1980 was sold to a private owner in the Isle of Man who hopes to restore it to flying condition.

Percival Proctor   UK

Photo: Proctor II Z7197 (ex-G-AKZN) is stored at Swinderby for the RAF Museum.
Data: Proctor I

Powerplant: One 210hp DH Gipsy Queen 2
Span: 39ft 6in
Length: 25ft 10in
Height: 7ft 3in
Wing area: 197sq ft

The Proctor I was the standard Vega Gull built to Air Ministry requirements with three seats instead of four and with slightly revised cockpit windows. The first aircraft was flown at Luton in October 1939 and was followed by 246 production aircraft. The Proctors II and III with both radio trainers and 196 and 436 of each were delivered, the majority being built under contract by F. Hills & Sons Ltd of Manchester. The Mks II and III were used by both the RAF and Fleet Air Arm, the FAA versions featuring a wing-mounted dinghy installed in the wing root.

The final military Proctor was the Mk IV which appeared as a prototype in 1943. It was designed to fulfil Spec T9/41 and was originally named Preceptor, it differed from earlier Marks in having a deeper and wider fuselage to accommodate operational-type wireless equipment. Many later had the W/T equipment removed and were used as communications aircraft.

The Mk IV continued in production for a short time postwar as the civilian Mk V, the Mk VI being a straightforward seaplane derivative fitted with twin floats. Many surplus Proctors were sold on the civilian market and the type was popular with flying clubs, charter operators and sporting pilots in much the same way as its Gull and Vega Gull ancestors had been in prewar days.

Fifteen Proctors of various Marks survive in the UK of which four are still airworthy, these are Proctor I G-AIWA/R7524 with Neil Jensen at Redhill, Proctor III G-ALJF with J. F. Moore and Susan Saggers at Biggin Hill, Proctor III G-AOGE with R. J. Sewell at Booker, and Proctor IV G-ANXR/RM221 with Bob Batt at Southend. At least two others are under reconstruction to fly again.

Piper Cub

USA

Photo: Jack Benson's Cub was built as an L-4H with the serial 44-79649, a fact revealed by the extended rear windows of the military version.
Data: J-3C-65

Powerplant: One 65hp Continental A-65-8
Span: 35ft 2.05in
Length: 22ft 4.5in
Height: 6ft 8in
Wing area: 178.5sq ft

The Piper Cub appeared in February 1931 and was initially known as the Taylor E-2 Cub, 157 of which had been built by 1935 when the F-2 was introduced. This model differed from the original in having an enclosed cockpit. 200 F-2 Cubs were then built before production was switched to the improved J-2 in 1936, 1,200 of which were delivered in the following two years.

C. G. Taylor and W. T. Piper parted company in 1935 and subsequent Taylor designs were built as Taylorcraft (qv) but in 1938 the re-named Piper Aircraft Corp brought out the J-3 Cub which was initially powered by the 40hp Continental A-40-4 and later by 50hp units built by Continental, Lycoming and Franklin. 737 Cubs were built in 1938, 1,806 in 1939 and 3,016 in 1940 in which year the J-3C-65 Cub Trainer appeared with the 65hp Continental 0-170-3. Production was then transferred to military contracts as the L-4 Grasshopper, 5,673 of which were built.

Civilian production of the Cub Trainer resumed after the war as the Cub Special which was refined into the PA-11 of 1947 and finally the PA-18 Super Cub. The Super Cub remains in production and at the time of its appearance 14,125 civil Clubs had been built in addition to the L-4s previously mentioned.

Pitcairn Mailwing

USA

Photo: Eastern Air Transport PA-5 Mailwing, NC2895, exhibited in the National Air & Space Museum, Washington, DC.
Data: PA-75

Powerplant: One 250hp Wright J-6 Whirlwind
Span: 33ft
Length: 22ft 10.5in
Height: 9ft 3in
Wing area: 252sq ft

As its name implies the Mailwing was a single-seat biplane intended for mail-carrying on the US Mail routes along the Eastern seaboard of the USA. The PA-5 was introduced in 1927 and developments of

the type included the PA-6, PA-7 and PA-8 Super Mailwings which were all powered by the 300hp Wright Whirlwind. Thirty Mailwings and approximately 90 Super Mailwings were built and the type was extensively used by Eastern Air Transport Inc, forerunners of today's Eastern Air Lines. A two-seat derivative, the PA-7S Sport Mailwing, flew in 1930 and was used as a company demonstrator, a small number were then laid down as high performance sporting aircraft.

At least five Mailwings of various types survive, some of which are maintained in flying condition, one of the flyers being at the Shannon Air Museum in Fredericksburg, Virginia.

Polikarpov Po2   USSR

Photo: An unidentified Po2 in Russian markings which is exhibited in the Armeemuseum der DDR, Dresden.

Powerplant: One 125hp M-11D radial
Span: 37ft 5in
Length: 26ft 9.5in
Height: 9ft 11in
Wing area: 415sq ft

The Po2 tandem two-seat biplane was designed by N. N. Polikarpov in 1924 and flew for the first time three years later as the U-2. The aircraft was very widely used for flying clubs, agricultural and ambulance duties as well as serving with the Red Air Force throughout World War 2 for liaison, communication, observation and night intrusion (!) roles. Production within the USSR ceased in 1944 but the design was built under licence in Poland from 1948 with the designation CSS-13, for agricultural flying, and CSS-S-13 for air ambulance work. Very large numbers of Po2s still served in the countries of the Communist bloc into the 1960s and the type is still seen occasionally.

Polikarpov I-16   USSR

Powerplant: One 1,000hp Shvetson M-62
Span: 29ft 6.5in
Length: 19ft 6in
Max speed: 326mph

The I-16 was designed concurrently with the I-15 but represented a major advance on contemporary Russian fighters as it was a low wing monoplane with a fully retractable undercarriage. In this respect it was the first aircraft in its class to enter service with any air force in the world. The prototype made its first flight on 31 December 1933 and the first production examples began to arrive on the squadrons late in 1934. As with the I-15 the little monoplane was dispatched to Spain where by the end of September 1936 over 100 were in service and proving their superiority over the Heinkel He51 and FIAT CR32s of the Nationalist forces.

The I-16 was shown to be outclassed by the Bf109 by the end of the Spanish conflict and the type proved to be obsolescent by the outbreak of World War 2. One example of the I-16 survives in Finland, this being an I-16UTI which was a two-seat trainer version of the Type 10 model with reduced fuel capacity to compensate for the extra pilot. It is preserved at Rissala Air Force Base.

Polikarpov I-153

USSR

Photo: The only remaining I-153 is aircraft No 9 exhibited at Le Bourget.

Powerplant: One Shvetson M-63 radial of 1,100hp
Span: 32ft 9.75in
Length: 20ft 5in
Height: 9ft 7in

The I-153 was the final development of a line of fighters which had first appeared as the I-5 of 1930. The I-153 appeared in 1938 and differed from its immediate predecessor, the I-15 in having the 1,000hp Shvetsov M-62R engine, a rectractable undercarriage, and a gull-type centre-section to the upperwings as on the early I-15 aircraft. The I-153 was essentially a stop-gap design which was produced to counter the Japanese Ki-27 fighters which were proving to be superior to the I-15s in service in the east of the country and which were involved in border skirmishes along the frontiers with Manchuria and Mongolia. Production continued until 1940, by which time the 1,100hp M-63 engine had been standardised, and remained in Soviet service until 1944. The I-153 was also supplied to Nationalist China and some aircraft were captured by the Germans, sold to Finland, and used *against* the Soviet forces in 1942. One I-153 survives, exhibited in the Musee de l'Air, Paris.

Rearwin Sportster and Cloudster

USA

Photo: 8135T Cloudster G-BGAV is now flying from Biggin Hill in its original Pan Am colours of white and dark blue.
Data: Model 8135T

Powerplant: One 120hp Ken Royce 7G
Span: 34ft 1.75in
Length: 21ft 6in
Height: 7ft 4in
Wing area: 161.8sq ft

The Sportster two-seat cabin monoplane first appeared in 1935 and was essentially a combination of the best features of two earlier models, the Model 3000 Junior and Model 6000 Speedster. The initial version was the Model 7000 with the 70hp Le Blond radial but alternative powerplants produced the Models 8500 (85hp Le Blond) and 9000 (90hp Warner Scarab Junior). A luxury development of the Sportster appeared in 1938 as the 9000L (90hp Le

Blond) or 9000KR (90hp Ken Royce 5G). These final versions differed visually from their predecessors by virtue of their long-chord cowlings and rounded rear fuselages. 260 Sportsters of all types were delivered up until 1941 and 12 were built under licence in Sweden.

The Cloudster appeared as the two-seat 8090 in April 1939, this model was powered by the 90hp Ken Royce and was swiftly followed by the Model 8125 with the 120hp Ken Royce. The Model 8135, three-seater, became the major production version in 1940 and this was built in some numbers — including a batch of 25 special two-seat instrument trainers for Pan American which were known as the Model 8135T. A total of 125 Cloudsters was built before production ceased.

One Model 8500 Sportster, one Model 9000L Sportster and one Model 8135T Cloudster are owned by Phillip Mann and based at Biggin Hill, Kent, several others survive in the USA.

Robinson Redwing II UK

Photo: John Pothecary with his Redwing II, G-ABNX.

Powerplant: One 80hp Armstrong Siddeley Genet IIA
Span: 30ft 6in
Length: 22ft 8in
Height: 8ft 7in
Wing area: 250sq ft

The Redwing appeared at the height of the new-found popularity of light aeroplanes, the summer of 1930, and was a side-by-side two seater powered by a 75hp ABC Hornet with a generous wing area to give admirable slow speed handling. The prototype

was known as the Redwing I and was followed by the production Redwing II which differed by virtue of its 80hp Armstrong Siddeley Genet IIA radial. Ten Redwings had been built at Croydon before the company moved to Blue Barns Aerodrome near Colchester in March 1932 but only two more Redwings were built, one of which was the sole Mk III sesquiplane, G-ABRL, which reverted to Mk II standard in 1934.

Today one Redwing II, G-ABNX, is still in existence and is regularly flown by owner John Pothecary who rebuilt it during 1959-1962 and has maintained it in flying condition ever since. It is based at John's private airfield in Surrey.

Ryan M-1, Brougham and NYP   USA

Photo: Lindbergh's Ryan NYP *Spirit of St Louis* in the NASM, Washington DC
Data: B-5 Brougham

Powerplant: One 300hp Wright J-6-9 Whirlwind
Span: 42ft 4in
Length: 28ft 3in
Wing area: 224sq ft

The first M-1 mailplane was built in 1926 for use on T. Claude Ryan's air line routes from San Diego, California. Designed to carry a pilot, two passengers and mail in open cockpits beneath the parasol wing the M-1 was powered by a variety of engines but the most popular were the Wright-Hispano A-150 and the Wright Whirlwind J-4B. With the latter unit the M-1 had quite a respectable performance and led to the Hisso-powered M-2 of 1926-27. The M-2 was still an open cockpit aeroplane and in an effort to improve passenger comfort an enclosed cabin version known as the Bluebird was built. This was written-off and cannibalised to build another M-2 but the seeds had been sown and several M-1 and M-2s were converted 'in the field' to have rudimentary cabin windows as the M-1C and M-2C. One M-1C, c/n 23, regn 2532, was exhibited in the San Diego

Aerospace Museum but its present status is uncertain following a fire at the museum which destroyed many exhibits.

The logical development of the Bluebird was the Ryan B1 Brougham of 1927, the prototype of which was under construction when Ryan received the order for Lindbergh's New York-Paris special. All attention was focused on the NYP and the outcome is well-known. The first Brougham was completed in time for Lindbergh's return to the US and the type was sold in considerable numbers as a result of the publicity surrounding the flight. The last of 142 was delivered in 1928.

The NYP was based on the B1, the most noticeable changes being the redesigned nose which housed fuel and oil tanks and the increased-span wing which was not simply lengthened but was strengthened internally by spacing the ribs closer than normal. The NYP has been an exhibit at the NASM, Washington, DC, since 1928 but several flying replicas have been built. Three were converted from Broughams in 1955 by Tallmantz Aviation for film use and one was built from scratch by the EAA to celebrate the 50th anniversary of Lindbergh's feat in 1978. It is now on show at the EAA Museum, Hales Corner, Wisconsin.

Ryan S-T Sport Trainer and variants   USA

Photo: Ryan PT-22 Recruit, 41-15721, displayed in the US Air Force Museum as a memorial to the late Chief Warrant Officer Romano, donated by his widow and son in 1969.
Data: PT-22

Powerplant: One 160hp Kinner R-540-1
Span: 30ft 1in
Length: 22ft 5in
Height: 6ft 10in
Wing area: 134.25sq ft

Following the reorganisation of his company T. Claude Ryan re-entered the manufacturing business in 1934 with the S-T Sport Trainer, a two-seat single-seater, powered by a 95hp Menasco and featuring a monocoque all-metal fuselage married to fabric-covered wings of mixed wood and aluminium construction. A swift change to the 125hp Menasco C4 Pirate resulted in the STA, 71 of which were built between 1935 and 1940. The addition of the 150hp Manasco C4S supercharged engine gave rise to the STA-Special, 11 of which were built between 1936

and 1939 and these in turn led to the STM military trainer which was eventually ordered by a number of overseas air forces before the first XPT-16 prototype was delivered to the Air Corps in 1939 to pave the way for some 1,500 Ryan trainers which were built during World War 2. In US service the aircraft was known as the PT-20, PT-20A and PT-22, the main differences lying in the powerplant (Menasco or Kinner) and in minor structural alterations. Nearly 100 PTs of various types remain airworthy in the US together with a small number of prewar STAs, and a solitary PT-22, N1344, is based at Halfpenny Green near Birmingham with owner Hilliary Mitchell.

Seversky P-35A   USA

Photo: '41-17449' was delivered to Sweden as an EP-106 but was donated to the USAF Museum by the Swedish Government in 1971. It is painted to represent the aircraft flown by Lt Boyd 'Buzz' Wagner, CO of the 17th Pursuit Sqn.
Data: P-35A

Powerplant: One 1,050hp Pratt & Whitney R-1830
Span: 36ft
Length: 26ft 10in
Height: 9ft 9in

The P-35 was the first 'modern' fighter to enter service with the US Army Air Corps. 77 were purchased between 1937 and 1938 and they featured all-metal construction, retractable undercarriage and fully-enclosed cockpits. Of the 77 acquired 75 were assigned to the 1st Pursuit Group at Selfridge Field, Michigan.

The P-35 was also exported, 20 being delivered to the Imperial Japanese Navy where they became the only American-built aircraft to be operated by the Japanese during World War 2! Sweden also bought a batch of 60 improved versions known as the EP-106 and a second batch of 60 was taken over by the US Army in 1940 and designated P-35A. Most of these were assigned to the 17th and 20th Pursuit Squadrons in the Philippines where they were all lost in action against the Japanese.

Four P-35 variants are known to survive: 36-404 is a P-35 with the USAF Museum at Dayton, Ohio; the Museum also displays an EP-106, c/n 282-11, which is painted as P-35A '41-17449'; another EP-106, Fv 2134, is preserved by the Swedish Air Force Museum at Linkoping; and Ed Maloney has an AT-12/2-PA in flying condition at Chino Airport, California.

Short S16 Scion UK

Photo: Connellan Airways' unique DH Gipsy Minor-powered Scion 2.
Data: Scion 1

Powerplants: Two 85hp Pobjoy Niagara I or II
Span: 42ft
Length: 31ft 6in
Height: 10ft 4.5in
Wing area: 255.3sq ft

The Scion was a departure from the norm as it was a small, twin-engined feeder liner quite unlike Short's normal large flying boats. The prototype, G-ACJI, was flown from Gravesend in August 1933 and four production Mk 1s appeared from the seaplane works in 1933-34. Experience with the prototype and Mk 1s led to an improved 1935 model known as the Scion 2 which differed structurally in the cabin glazing and engine mountings, 12 were built at Rochester Airport before pre-occupation with the Empire and military contracts led to the transfer of Scion production to Pobjoy Airmotors & Aircraft Ltd. The Pobjoy-built Scions were known as the S16/1 and total production amounted to six aircraft.

At least three Scions are known to have survived the war to fly again, G-AEZF, the last Scion built, finally lapsed into dereliction at Southend in the 1960s but G-ACUX/VH-UUP was maintained in flying condition by Marshall Airways of Sydney for many years and is today preserved by the Ulster Folk & Transport Museum following its sale by the Strathallan Collection and Scion 2 VH-UTV was re-engined with DH Gipsy Minors and flew with Connellan Airways at Alice Springs until acquired by Cliff Douglas for his Chewing Gum Field Air Museum, Queensland.

Spartan Arrow UK

Photo: Sole surviving Spartan Arrow is Raymond Blain's G-ABWP.

Powerplant: One 105hp Cirrus Hermes II
Span: 30ft 7in
Length: 25ft
Height: 9ft 6in
Wing area: 251sq ft

Yet another of the range of two-seat light biplanes that was available on the British market in the 1930s was the Spartan Arrow, a development of the Simmonds Spartan which had first appeared in 1928. The Simmonds Spartan had been unique as it featured wings of symmetrical aerofoil section which allowed one spare to be fitted in any of the four possible positions. A similar degree of interchangeability was possessed by the tailplane, fin, rudder and elevators.

The Arrow appeared in 1930 and had abandoned the symmetrical section in favour of a Clark YH but an ingenious system of detachable wingtips still gave some degree of interchange.

The Arrow never gained the popularity of such immortals as the Moth and Avian, probably because of a lack of secure finance in a limited market, but one Arrow has survived. G-ABWP was recently restored to fly for its owner, Raymond Blain, and has been based at both Long Marston and Barton. A larger derivative, the Spartan Three-seater, was also built and one survives in a derelict state in Eire.

Stampe SV-4   Belgium

Photo: G-AZGC is a French-built SV-4C owned by the Hon Patrick Lindsay.
Data: SV-4C

Powerplant: One 140hp Renault 4 Pei
Span: 27ft 6in
Length: 22ft 10in
Height: 9ft 1in
Wing area: 194.3sq ft

The SV-4 was designed by J. Stampe and M. Vertongen and first flew on the power of a 120hp DH Gipsy III in 1933. As such it was a contemporary of the de Havilland Tiger Moth but differed from it in both the wooden fuselage structure (the Tiger was of welded steel tube) and the ailerons on all wings (the Tiger having them on the lower wings only). The major production version in prewar years was the SV-4B, with the 130hp Gipsy Major, which was built both for the Belgian Air Force and for civilian use.

After World War 2 the original Stampe et Vertongen concern merged with Aeronautiques G. Renard to form Stampe et Renard SA which maintained the prewar aircraft and returned the design to production in 1947, 65 being built for the Belgian Air Force. Meanwhile in France the SNCA du Nord built a further 700 SV-4Cs (140hp Renault 4 Pei) for both civilian and military use.

The Stampe outclassed the Tiger Moth aerobatically and was a favoured mount of many pilots throughout the 1950s and 1960s. It is now obsolescent for competition aerobatics but is still in widespread use in private and club hands.

Stearman 75 USA

Powerplant: (Standard aircraft) one 220hp
Continental R-670-5
Span: 32ft 2in
Length: 24ft 9in
Height: 9ft 8in
Wing area: 297.4sq ft

Lloyd Stearman entered the aviation world via the
Laird Airplane Company of Witchita, Kansas, in
1921. He rose to become chief engineer of the
revamped Swallow Aircraft Company in 1923 and
then moved with Walter Beech to found the Travel
Air Manufacturing Co in partnership with Clyde
Cessna. Here he designed the Travel Air 2000/3000/
4000 series of 1925-1929 before leaving in 1926 to
found Stearman Aircraft Inc at Venice, California.

At Venice Stearman produced the Models C-1
and C-2 before offers of finance tempted him back to
Wichita where the C-3MB mailplane was produced
in 1927. Two years later Stearman Aircraft Inc
became part of the United Aircraft & Transport
Corporation and subsequent developments included
the C3R Business Sportster of 1929-1933, the

Stearman 4E Speedmail series of 1929-1931 and
the Stearman 6L Cloudboy of 1931.

The Cloudboy was significant as it was the first
Stearman intended for training and four were
delivered to the Army Air Corps as YPT-9s in 1931.
The experimental Model 70 of 1933 led to the X75
which was eventually selected as the new Primary
Trainer for the Army Air Corps as the PT-13 in July
1935. Although the PT-13/PT-17/N2S series is
almost universally known as the Stearman this name
is not strictly accurate as Boeing had pulled out of
the United group in 1934 taking Stearman with it as
a wholly-owned subsidiary. Between 1935 and
1944 the Stearman was produced in greater
numbers than any other biplane in history, 10,346
were manufactured and the last one was bought
back by Boeing, used for communications duties for
13 years, and finally presented to the USAF Museum
in 1958.

The Stearman was also known as the Kaydet but
the name was only officially used in connection with
those aircraft delivered to the RCAF under Lend-
Lease agreements. The Stearman is one of the most
widely operated vintage aircraft in the World and
hundreds are still flying.

Stinson Reliant USA

Photo: F-BBCS is an SR10C Reliant and is regularly
flown with the Salis Collection at La Ferte-Alais,
south of Paris
Data: V-77

Powerplant: One 290hp Lycoming R-680-E3B
Span: 41ft 10.5in
Length: 29ft 4.25in
Height: 8ft 7in
Wing area: 258.5 sq ft

The first Reliant was the SR5 of 1934 which was
powered by the 215hp Lycoming R-680 radial and
which had accommodation for four persons.
Development of the basic design resulted in the SR6
and SR7 before the five-seat SR8 was introduced in
1936. The somewhat confusing system of suffix
letters which was introduced with this model
enabled the particular combination of powerplant
and propeller to be identified.

The SR9 appeared in 1937 to be followed by the

SR10 in 1938, this model continued in production for the next two years when Stinson was taken over by Vultee Aircraft and the designation was amended to V-77, 500 of which were produced for the Royal

Navy under Lend-Lease agreements. The Reliant is a popular aircraft in the USA but only one is known to survive in flying condition in Europe.

Supermarine S6A and S6B

UK

Photo: S6B S1595 in the Science Museum, London.
Data: S6B

Powerplant: One 2,300hp Rolls-Royce R
Span: 30ft
Length: 28ft 10in
Height: 12ft 3in
Wing area: 145sq ft

With Britain's victory in the 1927 Schneider Trophy it fell to R. J. Mitchell of Supermarines to design a successor to his victorious S5 seaplane. This emerged as the S6, two of which were constructed for the 1929 contest which was held at Calshot, Hampshire. N247 was flown by Flg Off H. R. D. Waghorn to average 328.63 mph and win the trophy for Britain whilst the second aircraft, N248, was flown by Flg Off R. L. R. Atcherley to set up two new World Air Speed Records over 50 and 100km.

On 12 September 1929 N247 was used by Sqn

Ldr A. H. Orlebar, AFC to raise the Absolute World Air Speed Record to 357.7mph. The S6s later went back to the works where they were readied for the 1931 contest with larger floats and more powerful engines, in which form they were known as S6As. The main contestants for 1931 being the even more advanced S6Bs, S1595 and S1596.

S1595 regained the trophy for Great Britain for a third and final time on 12 September 1931, the pilot was Flt Lt J. N. Boothman and on 29 September the other S6B, with its engine boosted to give 2,600hp, was flown by Flt Lt G. H. Stainforth to a new World Air Speed Record of 407.5mph, the S6B was thus the first aircraft in the world to exceed 400mph.

Two aircraft have survived, S6A N248 — which for many years masqueraded as 'S1596' — is exhibited in the R. J. Mitchell Hall, Southampton, and S6B S1595 is on show at the Science Museum, London, along with the Schneider Trophy which it won outright.

Supermarine Walrus

UK

Photo: Supermarine Seagull V, A2-4, Battle of Britain Museum, Hendon.

Powerplant: One 620hp Bristol Pegasus IIM2 or 775hp Pegasus VI
Span: 45ft 10in
Length: 37ft 7in
Height: 15ft 3in
Wing area: 610sq ft

The Walrus was the final development of the long line of Seagull amphibians and was built as a private venture known as the Seagull V. The prototype flew in June 1933 and was adopted by the Australian Government who ordered a batch under the name Seagull V. It was not until May 1935 that an RAF contract was placed for the type and with it came the official name Walrus, to distinguish the type from the old Seagull IIIs which had served with No 440 Flight of the Fleet Air Arm in the 1920s.

The initial Air Ministry contract was for 12 Walrus Is but the following year additional orders for a further 204 aircraft were placed. Most of the Mk Is saw service with the Fleet Air Arm where they were catapulted from the decks of warships and then winched back on board.

In RAF service the Walrus is best remembered as a wartime Air-Sea Rescue aircraft but the majority of the ASR Walruses were wooden-hulled Mk 2s built by Saro, this version being preferred as it was less likely to detonate any magnetic mines. Production came to an end in 1944 after 741 had been built 453 of which were by Saro at East Cowes. Two Walruses are preserved in the UK; L2301 (ex-G-AIZG) is exhibited at the Fleet Air Arm Museum, Yeovilton, and A2-4 (an ex-Australian Seagull V) is on show at the Battle of Britain Museum, Hendon.

Supermarine Stranraer

UK & Canada

Photo: Stranraer CF-BXO restored to its former RCAF markings as '920'.

Powerplant: (Standard) two 875hp Bristol Pegasus X, (CF-BXO) two Wright Cyclone GR-1820-G202A
Span: 85ft
Length: 54ft 10in
Height: 21ft 9in
Wing area: 1,457sq ft

The Stranraer is significant as it was R. J. Mitchell's last flying boat design, it appeared in 1935 and was initially known as the Southampton V but the designation was swiftly changed as the type had little in common with its predecessor.

Twenty-three Stranraers were ordered for the RAF as general reconnaissance boats and the first entered service with No 228 Sqn at Pembroke Dock in 1936. The type was also adopted for use by the Royal Canadian Air Force and licence-production was undertaken by Canadian Vickers at Montreal. On the outbreak of war the Stranraer was obsolete, having been replaced by the Sunderland, but 15 remained on strength with Nos 201 and 209 Sqns and remained in use until superseded by Sunderlands and Lerwicks respectively during 1940.

One Canadian built Stranraer was used extensively postwar as CF-BXO and when finally withdrawn from flying in the late 1960s it was

cquired by the RAF Museum and flown to the UK nside a Belfast freighter. It now has pride of place in the RAF Museum at Hendon but differs from a

standard aircraft in that its two Bristol Pegasus X radials have been replaced by two Wright Cyclones!

Taylorcraft Models A, B and D   USA

Photo: Taylorcraft BC-12D N36298 photographed at Horn Point, Maryland.
Data: BC-12D Twosome

Powerplant: One 65hp Continental A65
Span: 36ft
Length: 22ft
Height: 6ft 8in
Wing area: 183.5sq ft

C. G. Taylor, designer of the Cub, left W. T. Piper in 1935 and formed the Taylorcraft Aviation Company the following year. The first product of the new company was the side-by-side Taylorcraft Model A, production of which was taken over the following year by the Taylor-Young Airplane Company.

Taylor-Young changed its name to Taylorcraft Aviation Corporation and brought out the revised Model B in 1939. In its initial form it was powered by 50hp Continental, Franklin or Lycoming engines but in 1940 the Continental A65 became standard alongside the Franklin 4AC-176 and Lycoming

0-145-B2. With these engines the model designation became BC, BF or BL as appropriate. Other variants were the BT which was intended solely for training and the B-12 luxury model of 1941, as most of these had Continentals they were known as BC-12s. Production resumed as the strengthened BC-12D Twosome at the end of 1945 and the type has recently been put back into production at the original Taylorcraft factory. Some 6,000 Model Bs of various types were built and the type is very common in the USA. One BC-12D, G-BIGK ex N96002, has been imported into the UK by Cliff Lovell.

The Model D was introduced in 1941 as a tandem two-seater but only a small number were built before production was taken over for military contracts as the O-57A and L-2A, some 2,000 of which were manufactured.

The Model C designation was reserved for British-built Plus C aircraft built under licence by Taylorcraft Aeroplanes (England) Ltd at Leicester, (qv).

Tipsy B, Trainer and Belfair

Photo: Tipsy Trainer 1 G-AISB was assembled postwar and is owned by R. E. Barker.
Data: Trainer 1

Powerplant: One 62hp Walter Mikron 2
Span: 31ft 2in
Length: 21ft 8in
Height: 5ft 8in
Wing area: 129sq ft

The Tipsy B was a two-seater designed by E. O. Tips, the prototype of which was built in Belgium as OO-DON and exhibited at Heathrow in May 1937. Licence production of the British version started at Hanworth later that year and the first British aircraft was exhibited at Heathrow in May 1938. Because of numerous structural refinements needed to suit

British airworthiness requirements the British version was redesignated Tipsy Trainer, a slightly heavier model becoming the Tipsy Trainer 1.

Fifteen Tipsys had been constructed by the outbreak of war, 10 of which survived to be joined by a final three postwar aircraft which were erected in new premises on the Slough Trading Estate. In it country of origin the Tipsy B returned to limited production at Gosselies where seven were constructed with the type name Belfair. The Belfair featured a fully-enclosed cabin and the last three were sold in an incomplete state to D. Heaton who had them completed at Sherburn-in-Elmet, Yorkshire as G-AOXO, G-APIE and G-APOD in 1957.

Seven Tipsy Trainers and three Belfairs survive in the UK at the present time, four of which are airworthy.

Travel Air Model R 'Mystery Ship'

Photo: Texaco No 13 as displayed in the Chicago Museum of Science & Technology.
Data: NR-1313

Powerplant: One 450hp Wright Whirlwind R-975
Span: 30ft 9in
Length: 21ft 6in
Max speed: 235mph
Cruising speed: 150mph

The Model R was designed in their own time by Herb Rawdon and Walter Burnham, Walter Beech became interested and two were built for the 1929 National Air Races. One of them was flown by Doug Davis to win the Thompson Trophy and considerable publicity ensued as the 'Mystery Ship' — as it was dubbed by the popular press — was considerably faster than contemporary US fighters. A total of five Model Rs was eventually built of which two survive. The two aircraft still extant are NR-613K and NR-1313; the former was initially powered by a 120hp Chevrolair and flown by Doug Davis in the 1929 Nationals after which it was re-engined with a Wright Whirlwind and sold to Pancho Barnes. It finally ended up in derelict condition with the Tallmantz Collection but was brought back by 'Pancho' at the Tallmantz auction of 1968. Following her death the aircraft passed to her son, Bill Barnes, who is restoring it to fly at Fox Field, Lancaster, California. The other survivor was built for Frank Hawkes as 'Texaco No 13' and flown by him in the 1930 Thompson Trophy and was then used to break the East-West coast-to-coast record, flying from Long Island to Los Angeles in 14hr, 50min and 43sec on 6 August 1930. Following a colourful career 'Texaco No 13' was rebuilt to static condition and is exhibited at the Chicago Museum of Science & Technology.

A replica Model R has been built and flown by Jim Younkin and two others are said to be under construction.

Travel Air 2000 and 4000 USA

Photo: Travel Air D-4000, N425.
Data: D-4000

Powerplant: One 220hp Wright R-760 Whirlwind
Span: 34ft 8in
Length: 24ft 2in
Height: 8ft 11in
Wing area: 297sq ft

The Travel Air Manufacturing Company was formed by Walter Beech and Clyde Cessna in February 1925, its first product being the three-seat Model 2000 which was powered by the Curtiss OX-5 war surplus engine. Some 600 Model 2000s were built before the introduction of the improved Travel Air 4000 in 1926. This model featured the 220hp Wright Whirlwind but was otherwise the same as the earlier aircraft. Variants included the A-4000 (150hp Axelson), B-4000 (220hp Wright), C-4000 (185hp Challenger), D-4000 (220hp Wright), K-4000 (100hp Kinner) and W-4000 (125hp Warner). Some 600 Model 4000s were built of which about 50 remain airworthy, some converted to crop-dusters. The final derivative of the basic 4000 was the 4D of 1929, intended for the sporting pilot only about 25 were built, two of which remain airworthy.

Valtion Viima 2

Photo: Phillip Mann's Biggin Hill-based Viima 2, G-BAAY.

Powerplant: One 150hp Siemens Sh14A
Span: 34ft 5in
Length: 25ft 10in
Height: 9ft 10in
Wing area: 297sq ft

The first Viima two-seat training biplane was flown in 1935 with a second prototype appearing the following year. It was adopted as a standard trainer by the Finnish Air Force that year and a further 23 were then built. These served for many years an when retired the survivors were sold to flying club and private owners. One of them was converted t take the Cirrus Major 3 engine, in which form it wa known as the Viima 2B, but the remainder wer fitted with the 150hp Siemens Sh14A radial. Or Viima 2, G-BAAY, was bought by Phillip Mann an based at Biggin Hill for several years before bein sold in 1982. Its Finnish Air Force colours and seria 'VI-3' were then removed and the aircraft extensivel rebuilt to convert it to Focke Wulf Stiegli configuration, in which guise it now masquerades a 'Wk Nr 1003'.

Waco Biplane

Photo: Waco 10.

Powerplant: 90hp Curtiss OX5
Span: 30ft 6in
Length: 23ft 5in
Wing area: 288sq ft

The Waco biplanes were in production from 1919 to 1942, first by the Advance Aircraft Company and from 1929 by the Waco Aircraft Company of Troy, Ohio. The company was founded by E. J. Junkin and C. J. Brukner but business was slow until the advent of the popular three-seat Waco 9 of 1925, some 350 of which were built. The Waco 10 was essentially an updated Waco 9 which was developed by Charles W. Meyers and which went into production in 1927, it continued in production f the next three years by the end of which time it h been re-designated the Waco O series.

The three-letter designations were introduce with the RNF in 1930 and though at first sight the seem confusing they are straightforward enough: th first letter identifies the engine, the second the bas airframe, and the third is a type-grouping. Beari this in mind the major Waco models produced ov the next 12 years were the DSO (1928), A (1928), RNF (1930), QDC (1931), QCF (1931), U (1933), YKC (1934), YOC (1935), UMF (193 ZGC-7 (1937), YKS-7 (1937), UPF-7 (193 AVN-8 (1938) and SRE Aristocrat (193 Considerable numbers of all Waco variants rema airworthy in the USA.

Westland Wapiti

UK

Photo: The world's only surviving Wapiti 'K183' at Palam, New Delhi.
Data: Wapiti IIA

Powerplant: One 550hp Bristol Jupiter VIIIF or XFa
Span: 46ft 5in
Length: 32ft 6in
Height: 11ft 10in
Wing area: 468sq ft

The Wapiti was conceived as a two-seat General Purpose type which incorporated as many DH9A components as was possible as a cost-saving measure. The prototype flew in early 1927 and production Wapitis entered service shortly afterwards, to give long and faithful service both at home and over the deserts of Iraq and the North-West Frontier of India. The Mk I featured the 420hp Bristol Jupiter VI, wooden wings and a wooden rear

fuselage but the Mk II introduced all-metal fuselage construction and an ungeared 460hp Jupiter VI. In 1931 the Mk IIA with 550hp Jupiter VIII appeared to be followed by a batch of 35 Mk Vs. The final RAF version was the Mk VI, a dual control trainer, 16 of which were constructed during 1932. Total RAF production came to 517 aircraft, the last one coming off the line in August 1932.

The last Wapitis in service in the UK were withdrawn from Auxiliary Squadrons in 1937 but about 80 were still in service with the RAF in India at the outbreak of war. One of these was discovered in a derelict state in the 1960s and has been restored to static display condition — using many non-standard components — at the Indian Air Force Museum at Palam, New Delhi. It carries the incomplete serial 'K183'.

Westland Widgeon III

UK

Photo: The world's sole surviving airworthy Widgeon is Joe Drage's VH-UHU.

Powerplant: One 90hp ADC Cirrus III or alternative
Span: 36ft 4.5in
Length: 23ft 5.25in
Height: 8ft 5in
Wing area: 200sq ft

The Widgeon I was built as a two-seat parasol wing monoplane for the 1924 Lympne Light Aeroplane Competition. It crashed during the qualifying heats and was subsequently rebuilt as the Widgeon II with a more powerful Armstrong Siddeley Genet I and with a smaller rudder. The production version, known as the Widgeon III was a fully-revised design with plywood covered fuselage and constant-chord wings, the prototype of which flew in April 1927.

The Widgeon III was an attractive little aeroplane and was popular because it was free of the rigging problems associated with contemporary light biplanes but pressure of work on the Wapiti contract meant that production ceased after less than 30 had been built, the last in 1929.

Two Widgeons survive, both in Australia. VH-UGI is stored at Bankstown, NSW, where it was part of the Marshall Airways collection and VH-UHU is still flown as part of Drage's Historical Aircraft Museum, Wodonga, Victoria. The crashed remains of a third Widgeon, G-AUKA, are held at the Central Australian Aviation Museum, Alice Springs.

Part Four: 1939-1945

Aichi D3A1 'Val'   Japan

Photo: Aichi D3A1 serial 3179, alias CF-TZT, which was restored to fly by Bob Diemert.

Powerplant: One 1,075hp Mitsubishi Kinsei 44
Span: 47ft 1.25in
Length: 33ft 6.75in
Height: 10ft 11.25in
Wing area: 376sq ft

The original D3A1 entered production during 1937 and 478 were produced before production was switched to the more powerful D3A2 in 1942. The 'Val' was, more than any other type, the machine which predominated in the Japanese attack on Pearl Harbor. It was a navy dive-bomber and owed much to contemporary German designs, having been conceived after lengthy examination of the Heinkel He66, 70 and 74. It was extremely effective during the early part of the Pacific war but by the closing stages it had been outclassed and large numbers were lost in the Battle of Midway and the Solomons.

One D3A1, serial number 3179, was salvaged in the mid-1960s by Canadian Bob Diemert and restored to flying condition as CF-TZT. It has since been obtained by the Canadian National Aeronautical Collection and is exhibited at Rockcliffe, Ottawa.

Airspeed Oxford   UK

Photo: Oxford V3388/G-AHTW is maintained at Duxford with the Skyfame Collection.

Powerplants: Two 370hp Armstrong Siddeley Cheetah X
Span: 53ft 4in
Length: 34ft 6in
Height: 11ft 1in
Wing area: 348sq ft

Developed from the civilian Envoy airliner the Oxford entered service with the Central Flying School of the Royal Air Force in November 1937 to become the first monoplane, twin-engined, advanced trainer in RAF service. 400 were in service at the outbreak of war and by 1945 a total of 8,751 had been produced.

The 'Ox-box' was widely used within the UK and throughout the Commonwealth Air Training Plan in Canada, Southern Rhodesia, Australia, South Africa and New Zealand. With the cessation of hostilities the type was civilianised as the Airspeed Consul and others soldiered on with Advanced Flying Training Schools until 1954.

One Oxford is preserved with the Skyfame Collection at Duxford while the RAF Museum is rebuilding one from a collection of two Oxfords and a Consul at Cardington. A Consul is also displayed with the Canadian National Aeronautical Collection.

Arado Ar196A

Germany

Photo: One of two Arado Ar196As still surviving is this example which is stored at Silver Hill, Maryland, USA.

Powerplant: One 900hp BMW 132K
Span: 40ft 10.5in
Length: 36ft 1in
Height: 14ft 6in
Max speed: 193mph

Probably the most successful and certainly the most familiar seaplane to be used by the German naval air forces during World War 2 the Ar196 was the standard catapult seaplane of the German Navy for many years, 435 being manufactured. It was used for a wide range of duties which included submarine-hunting, light bombing and general reconnaissance. The prototype flew in 1936 and, during its service career, it was encountered all over the European theatre of operations, often being used on land-based coastal patrols as well as their sea-going missions. Two aircraft survive, both of which are in the United States; one is displayed at the Naval Air Station at Willow Grove, Pennsylvania and the other is stored at Silver Hill Maryland with the National Air & Space Museum.

Avro 652A Anson I

UK

Photo: Anson I N4877 is now preserved at the IWM collection at Duxford, Cambridgeshire.

Powerplants: Two 350hp Armstrong Siddeley Cheetah Mk IX

Span: 56ft 6in
Length: 42ft 3in
Height: 13ft 1in
Wing area: 410sq ft

The Anson prototype made its first flight on 24 March 1935 and was a military development of the six-passenger civil transport known as the 652. It was intended as a land-based coastal reconnaissance type and from 1936 until the outbreak of war the Ansons served with first-line squadrons of Coastal Command. The Anson was significant in that it was the first monoplane to enter the Royal Air Force under the expansion programme and it also featured the novelty of a retractable undercarriage. On 5 September 1939 an Anson of No 500 Sqn, Detling, carried out the first RAF action of World War 2 when it attacked a German U-boat. They were steadily replaced by Hudsons and Whitleys in the reconnaissance role from 1940 onwards, a few remaining in operational use as late as 1942, and relegated to training and communications duties, the later metal-winged versions being designed specifically for these roles and soldiering on with the RAF until the mid-1960s, a record for any type. One Anson I remains today, N4877/G-AMDA, which is preserved at Duxford Airfield, Cambridgeshire as part of the Skyfame Collection.

Avro Lancaster   UK

Photo: Lancaster BI PA474 seen landing at Duxford.

Powerplant: Four 1,460hp Rolls-Royce Merlin 20 or 22
Span: 102ft
Length: 69ft 6in
Height: 20ft
Wing area: 1,297sq ft

Without doubt the most famous British bomber of World War 2, the Lancaster prototype made its first flight in January 1941. It was a development of the twin engined Avro Manchester which was an abject failure because of the unreliability of its Rolls-Royce Vulture engines, the first aircraft (BT308) being a converted Manchester airframe modified to accept four Merlins. Initially expected to carry 4,000lb of bombs few could have foreseen the possibilities of carrying a 22,000lb Grand Slam bomb as was used in the final stages of the European war. Three main variants were built, the Mks I and III being externally identical — differing only in that the III had American-built Packard Merlin engines, while the Mk II had the 1,650hp Bristol Hercules VI radial engine, 300 of these were built by Armstrong-Whitworth.

After the war the Lanc soldiered on with Coastal Command on maritime reconnaissance duties, eventually being replaced by the Shackleton, and it also carried on with both the French and Canadian armed forces on similar duties until being finally retired in the early 1960s.

At least nine Lancs survive, in the UK, Canada, Australia and New Zealand, four aircraft being displayed in the UK. These are R5868, a Mk I at the Royal Air Force Museum, Hendon; KB976 (G-BCOH) a Canadian-built Mk 10 with the Strathallan Collection, Perthshire; NX611 (G-ASXX) an ex-French Aeronavàle Mk 7 which is displayed at the famous Scampton Dambuster base in Lincolnshire; and finally PA474, a Mk I which flies with the Battle of Britain Memorial Flight from RAF Coningsby, Lincolnshire.

Avro York

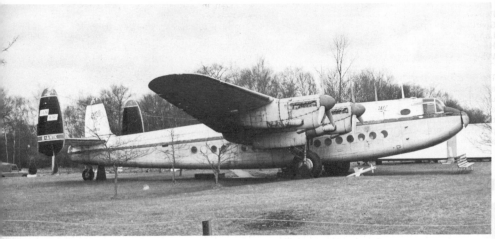

Photo: G-ANTK is preserved by Dan-Air at Lasham, Hampshire.

Powerplants: Four 1,280hp Rolls-Royce Merlin XX
Span: 102ft
Length: 78ft 6in
Height: 17ft 10in
Wing area: 1,297sq ft

The York was a transport derivative of the famous Lancaster bomber in which the Lancaster's wings, engines, undercarriage and tail unit were married to a new, box-like fuselage with twice the capacity of the Lancs. Because of a wartime agreement which gave priority to American transports the York did not start to appear in any numbers until after the war and it was to give sterling service during the Berlin Airlift, making 29,000 sorties and carrying 230,000 tons of supplies.

Yorks were also delivered to BOAC for airliner duties but were soon relegated to freighters with the development of specialised airliners such as the Handley Page Hermes. Many small charter companies started operations with the York and some were still in service carrying outsize loads into the early 1960s. Two have survived, G-AGNV restored as TS798 at the Aerospace Museum, RAF Cosford and G-ANTK is preserved by its last operators, Dan-Air, at their Lasham headquarters in Hampshire.

Bell P-39 Airacobra

Photo: P-39Q N969B is flying with the Harlingen-based Confederate Air Force.

Powerplant: One 1,150hp Allison V-1710-E-4
Span: 34ft 0in
Length: 34ft 2in
Height: 9ft 3.25in
Wing area: 213sq ft

The Airacobra was laid out to fulfil a specification for a fighter aircraft with maximum firepower and was unusual in that it sported a tricycle undercarriage and a mid-mounted Allison V-1710 engine which drove the propeller via a long extension shaft. The prototype flew in 1939 and the first production aircraft were destined for the French Air Force. With the fall of France in 1940 these machines were diverted to the Royal Air Force which received its first aircraft in the summer of 1941. The P-39D entered service with the USAAC in February 1941 but the type was not a success as a fighter, the RAF machines were withdrawn after two months and most of the American machines were diverted to the Middle East where its 20mm cannon, firing through the propeller hub, made it a useful tank-buster. The Airacobra also saw limited service with the Free French but over half the 9,558 produced were Lease-Lent to Russia. At least 19 Airacobras survive in the United States but of these only one, N696B/43-19597, is known to be active, a P-39Q with the Confederate Air Force, Harlingen, Texas.

Bell P-63 Kingcobra   USA

Photo: This Kingcobra has been specially prepared for air racing in the USA.

Powerplant: One 1,325hp Allison V-12
Span: 38ft 3in
Length: 32ft 7in
Wing area: 248sq ft
Max speed: 408mph

Although sharing the sleek lines, tricycle gear and mid-mounted engine of the Airacobra the P-63 was a new aeroplane which actually bore only superficial resemblence to the earlier type. Although 3,303 were built none of them saw combat with the USAAF and two-thirds of them were sent to Russia. The Kingcobra also saw service with the French Air Force.

Seven P-63s survive in the USA with the National Air & Space Museum, the US Air Force Museum, Yesterday's Air Force and the Confederate Air Force, of these only the CAF's N191H is currently airworthy having been restored in French markings.

Boeing B-17 Fortress

USA

Data: B-17G

Powerplants: Four 1,200hp Wright Cyclone GR-1820-97
Span: 103ft 9in
Length: 73ft 0in
Height: 15ft 6in
Wing area: 1,486sq ft

The Flying Fortress was designed to the requirements of the US Army Air Corps and the XB-17, tested in July 1935, was a blending of the Model 247 airliner and XB-15 prototype bomber. By 1941 over 100 had been delivered to the US forces but the first to go into combat were the Fortress Is (B-17C) of No 90 Sqn RAF. In British service the early C model was found to be inadequate for a number of reasons and European operations were abandoned.

With the introduction of the vastly improved B-17E in 1942 the US Army Eighth Air Force commenced its daylight raids on Europe, the first being held on 17 August, it was later joined by the B-17F, which had a modified bombardier's position, and the B-17G with chin-turret.

The Fortress is probably the most famous American bomber of World War 2 and 12,731 were eventually built, mainly by Lockheed and Douglas, many survive worldwide, especially in North America, and several exist in Europe. Two Fortresses, both B-17Gs, are kept at the Imperial War Museum's airfield at Duxford, Cambridgeshire, '44-72258'/G-BEDF is airworthy and owned by Euroworld Ltd, whilst 44-83735 is being rebuilt to static display standard for the IWM.

Boeing B-29 Superfortress

USA

Photo: Boeing B-29A Superfortress 44-61748 at the end of its last flight on arrival at Duxford, Cambridgeshire.

Powerplants: Four 2,200hp Wright Cyclone Eighteen R-3350
Span: 141ft 3in
Length: 99ft
Height: 27ft 9in
Wing area: 1,738sq ft

Designed as a very-long-range heavy bomber the B-29 prototype first flew on 21 September 1942 and a total of 4,221 was delivered to the USAAF before production ended in 1946. A modified version, the B-50, and a Russian copy, the Tupolev Tu4, were also manufactured.

The B-29 was used for the bombing of Japan from bases in the Pacific, its normal range of 2,850 miles with a 6,000lb bomb load making this a worthwhile exercise. The Japanese raids culminated with the Atomic attacks on Hiroshima and Nagasaki by *Enola Gay* and *Bockscar*, both these machines surviving in the United States, the former in store with the National Air & Space Museum whilst the latter is displayed at the US Air Force Museum.

Two B-29s are airworthy in the USA, the Confederate Air Force's *Fi-Fi*, N4249/44-62070, being one example and the American Air Museum Society's *Fertile Myrtle*, N91329/45-21787 being the other. In addition to these two the Imperial War Museum has acquired 44-61748 which was restored to fly and delivered by air from California to Duxford, Cambridgeshire, as G-BHDK in February-March 1980.

Boulton Paul Defiant

UK

Photo: The last Defiant is preserved in the Battle of Britain Museum, Hendon.

Powerplant: One Rolls-Royce Merlin III of 1,030hp
Span: 39ft 4in
Length: 35ft 4in
Height: 12ft 2in
Wing area: 250sq ft

The Defiant was unique in that it was a two-seat fighter in which the four 0.303in Browning machine guns were installed in a power-operated turret with no forward armament carried at all. The prototype flew in 1937 and the first production aircraft reached No 264 Sqn in December 1939. The Defiants went into action on 12 May 1940 and by the end of the month they had accounted for some 65 enemy aircraft, mainly bombers shot down over Dunkirk. Once the Defiants had lost their surprise advantage the German fighters swiftly realised that the heavy

Defiant was no real match for them, especially with its lack of forward armament, and against a background of ever-increasing losses the Defiants were withdrawn from daylight operations in August 1940.

Relegated to night operations the Defiant was fitted with AI radar and became the outstanding nightfighter of 1940-1941. Production ceased in early 1943 after 1,064 had been manufactured and in the later stages of the war the type was used for target-towing (TT III) and Air-Sea Rescue duties. Some were used at Air Gunnery Schools, Operational Training Units and a few were even tried in the Army Co-operation role for a short time.

The sole survivor, N1671, was delivered to No 307 (Polish) Sqn in September 1940, later serving with Nos 153 and 285 Sqns before being struck off charge at RAF St Athan in 1947. Somehow it survived and is today preserved in the Battle of Britain Museum, Hendon.

Brewster Buffalo   USA

Photo: The Valtion Humu was a Finnish copy of the Buffalo, one of which survives at Tampere Air Force Base, Finland.

Powerplant: One 1,200hp Wright Cyclone GR-1820-G 205A
Span: 35ft
Length: 26ft
Height: 12ft 1in
Wing area: 208.9sq ft

The Buffalo originated during 1938 and went into service with the US Navy the following year as the F2A-1. Following a visit by the British Purchasing Commission the type was selected for the RAF and a contract for 180 was placed, the British name Buffalo being applied. The RAF version was the Brewster Type 339, which corresponded to the US Navy's F2A-2, and the first aircraft arrived at Liverpool in July 1940 and were assembled at Burtonwood. 38 aircraft originally destined for Belgium were also delivered to the RAF, these being a later version, the Type 439, which corresponded to the US Navy's F2A-3.

Following service trials the Buffalo was rejected for European use and the type was instead delivered to the Far East where it equipped four squadrons, in the defence of Singapore, where it was hopelessly outclassed by the Japanese Zero.

One Buffalo is known to survive in semi-complete state with the Victory Air Museum of Mundelein, Illinois, USA, but a Finnish-built copy, the Valtion Humu, is preserved by the Finnish National Aeronautical Collection at Tampere Air Force Base.

Bristol Blenheim IV and Bolingbroke   UK & Canada

Photo: Although marked as L8756 this aircraft is a Canadian-built Fairchild Bolingbroke IVT and not a Blenheim IV.
Data: Blenheim IV

Powerplants: Two 920hp Bristol Mercury XV
Span: 56ft 4in
Length: 42ft 7in
Height: 9ft 10in
Wing area: 469sq ft

The original Blenheim I was a military development of the advanced Bristol Type 142 'Britain First' which had been built to the personal order of Lord Rothermere in 1935. The long-nosed Blenheim IV replaced the Mk I in production during 1939, it was a light bomber with a crew of three and was distinguished as the first British aircraft to cross the German frontier during World War 2 when N6215 of No 139 Sqn, Wyton, flew a recce mission on 3 September 1939.

Blenheim IVs served with the squadrons of No 2 Group on daylight raids over occupied Europe until superseded by Bostons and Mosquitos in 1942. Overseas they served in the Western Desert and in the Far East — including the defence of Singapore.

Today only one Blenheim IV remains, this being aircraft BL-200 of the Finnish Air Force which is preserved at Jyvaskyla, several Canadian-built versions, known as Bolingbrokes, survive and four are preserved in the UK. These are all ex-RCAF aircraft but most have been or are being restored as Royal Air Force Blenheim IVs including 'L8756' at the Battle of Britain Museum, Hendon; 9896 and 10038 at Duxford; and 9940 at Strathallan.

Bristol Beaufighter

UK

Photo: RD253 is a Beaufighter TFX which was brought back from Portugal and restored for display at the RAF Museum, Hendon.
Data: Mk X

Powerplants: Two, 1,770hp Bristol Hercules XVIII
Span: 57ft 10in
Length: 41ft 8in
Height: 15ft 10in
Wing area: 503sq ft

The Beaufighter had its origins in a private-venture by the Bristol Aeroplane Company which intended to use the wings, rear fuselage and empennage of the Beaufort torpedo-bomber together with a new nose

and cockpit to create a high-performance long-range fighter. The design proved attractive to the Air Ministry and Specification F17/39 was issued to cover the construction of four prototypes and an initial batch of 300 production aircraft. The Beaufighter had both the speed and fire-power that was necessary for it to take advantage of the new AI radars then coming into service and it thus became an extremely formidable night-fighter as well as distinguishing itself in the anti-shipping role armed with rockets and torpedoes as well as its 20mm cannon.

In the night-fighter role the type was eventually superseded by the Mosquito and the final production version, the Mk X, was delivered to Coastal Command for anti-shipping duties. This version was powered by two 1,770 Bristol Hercules XVIII radials, could carry a torpedo, rockets, bombs or a combination of all three and carried ASV radar in a thimble nose radome. 2,205 production Mk Xs were built, the last being converted to TT 10 target-tugs which continued in RAF service until May 1960 at Singapore.

At least five Beau's are known to survive, three Mk X and two Mk XIC: the Xs are RD253 exhibited at the RAF Museum, Hendon; RD867 with the Canadian National Aeronautical Collection at Rockcliffe; and BF-10 with the Museo do Ar, Alverca do Ribatejo, near Lisbon, Portugal. The two Mk XICs are A19-144 and A19-148, both ex-No 31 Sqdn RAAF, which were recovered from Kalumburu, N.T., Australia in 1981. One of these is to be restored to flying condition.

Cant Z506S Airone   Italy

Photo: MM45425 at Vigna di Valle.
Data: Cant Z506B

Powerplants: Three 750hp Alfa Romeo 126RC34 radials
Span: 86ft 11in
Length: 63ft 1.5in
Height: 22ft 2.5in
Wing area: 936sq ft

The original Cant Z506 was a large, 12-passenger floatplane which appeared in 1935 and was powered by three 610hp Piaggio Stella IX RC nine-cylinder radials. The Piaggio units were replaced with 750hp Alfa Romeo 126 RC 34 radials in the Z506A 18-seater and the Z506B and S military versions. The B model featured a ventral gondola containing a bomb-aimer, bomb load and a rear-mounted defensive machine gun and there was a semi-retractable dorsal turret over the trailing edge of the wing.

When Italy entered World War 2, two groups of the Regia Aeronautica were equipped with the Z506B and they served throughout on sea patrol, reconnaissance and anti-shipping operations; some were even used as troop and cargo transports. By the tail end of hostilities the type was becoming increasingly obsolescent and could only operate when escorted by large numbers of fighters. With Italy's capitulation several remained to serve with the Co-Belligerent Air Force and after 1945 several were converted into Z506S rescue aircraft which continued to serve with the 83°, 84° and 85° Gruppi di Soccorso Aereo until retired in 1959. One of these machines, MM45425, is preserved with the Museo Storico dell' Aeronautica Militare Italiana at Vigna di Valle on the southern shores of Lago di Bràcciano about 25km North West of Rome.

Cessna T-50 Bobcat   USA

Photo: A privately-owned Cessna Bobcat, N30L.

Powerplants: Two 225hp Jacobs L4MB radials
Span: 41ft 11in
Length: 32ft 9in
Height: 9ft 11in
Max speed: 195mph

Designed as a light-twin to sell at $30,000 the Cessna T-50 made its first flight in March 1939 with the company president, Dwane Wallace, at the controls. Only a small batch was constructed before production was switched to fulfil a large order from the Royal Canadian Air Force, in whose service the type was known as the Crane I, and following this came an American order for 33 AT-8 bomber-trainers. Other versions of the basic airframe were the AT-17 Bobcat series and the UC-78 transport variant. Total production came to 5,402 and about 50 are still airworthy in the US whilst one is reported to be still flying in Switzerland.

Chance-Vought Corsair   USA

Data: F4U-5

Powerplant: One 2,300hp Pratt & Whitney R-2800-32W Double Wasp
Span: 40ft 11.75in
Length: 34ft 6.5in
Height: 14ft 9.25in
Wing area: 314sq ft

Design work was started on the prototype XF4U-1 fighter in June 1938 and when it made its maiden flight, on 29 May 1940, the Corsair was the most powerful naval fighter yet built, with a Pratt & Whitney XR-2800-4 of 1,850hp. One of the most characteristic features of the type was the unusual 'gull-wing' which was necessitated by the need for a large-diameter propeller to absorb the power of the engine coupled with the need for a short undercarriage to allow wing-folding for stowage on the hangar decks of the carriers of the US Navy.

The Corsair introduced a considerable number of new features which were fairly radical at the time and by the time that the first production versions were reaching the squadrons, in 1942, fairly extensive changes had been incorporated; these included lengthening the fuselage, moving the cockpit back, installing six guns in the wings rather than two in the fuselage and the substitution of the more powerful R-2800-8 engine of 2,100hp.

The first Corsairs to see action were those of the US Marine Corps Squadron VMF124 at Guadalcanal on 15 February 1943. The type was then swiftly taken into service by other US units as well as being supplied under Lend-Lease to the Fleet Air Arm.

The Corsair was an outstanding aircraft and one which was subjected to a programme of continuous development in order to realise its full potential. When production finally ceased on 24 December 1952, 981 major engineering changes had been incorporated into the design. The type continued to give outstanding service after 1945, serving with distinction in Korea and in Indo-China as late as 1954. The French Navy received 94 F4U-7s and they served until replaced by the Etendard in 1964! Small air forces such as those of El Salvadore and the Argentinian Navy continued to operate the type well into the 1960s.

One Corsair, a Goodyear-built FG-1 Corsair IV KD431, is preserved at the Fleet Air Arm Museum, Yeovilton, Somerset and another has been acquired by Lindsay Walton of Sutton Bridge, Lincolnshire, it is in flying condition and will be an interesting sight at UK air shows. Many others are to be found world-wide. The photograph depicts one operated by the Confederate Air Force, Harlingen, Texas, USA.

Consolidated PBY Catalina

USA

Photo: An ex-Royal Danish Air Force PBY-6A which is now part of the Confederate Air Force collection at Harlingen, Texas.

Data: PBY-5A

Powerplants: Two 1,200hp Pratt & Whitney R-1930-92 Twin Wasps
Span: 104ft
Length: 63ft 10in
Height: 18ft 10in
Wing area: 1,400sq ft

The PBY-1 entered service with the US Navy in 1936 as a long-range patrol bomber. By 1940 the type had evolved into the PBY-5 and it was this model which was ordered for the RAF as the Catalina I. The 4,000-mile range and 17hr 30min endurance meant that the type was ideally suited for long-range maritime patrol duties and on 26 May 1941 a Catalina of No 209 Sqn RAF spotted the German battleship *Bismark* after she had been lost by surface forces, she was subsequently shadowed by an aircraft of No 240 Sqn.

An amphibious development, the PBY-5A, was manufactured both in the USA and in Canada — where it was called the Canso — and a later variant, the PBY-6A, was distinguished by its taller fin and rudder.

Catalinas served for many years after the war in both the military and civilian fields but most are now relegated to commercial operations in otherwise inaccessible areas. The Danish Air Force operated PBY-6As on Air-Sea Rescue duties in Greenland until fairly recently and one of these machines, L-866, is now exhibited at the Aerospace Museum, RAF Cosford, near Wolverhampton.

Consolidated B-24 Liberator

USA

Data: B-24H

Powerplants: Four 1,200hp Pratt & Whitney R-1830-43 Twin Wasp
Span: 110ft
Length: 67ft 1in
Height: 17ft 11in
Wing area: 1,048sq ft

Of the two classic American bombers of World War 2 the Liberator was a far more advanced aircraft than the earlier Fortress, the Liberator having been conceived some five years after its Boeing stablemate. It had a tricycle undercarriage and a special high aspect ratio, thin-section wing known as the 'Davis Wing' after its originator David R. Davis. It was the wing which gave the B-24 its extremely long range.

The first Liberators to see service were from a batch of 120 which had been ordered by the French Government, as France was overrun before the aircraft could be delivered they were diverted to the RAF and started to arrive during 1941. As a consequence of experience gained with the RAF the Liberator was modified to mount extra defensive guns, had additional armour plate fitted and the fuel tanks were changed to non-inflammable types, this version was the XB-24B — known in RAF service as the Liberator I.

The B-24C (Liberator II) mounted two power-operated gun turrets and became the first really effective bomber variant whilst the B-24D became the first variant to enter mass-production for the USAAF. This model had the dorsal turret moved forwards to a position just behind the cockpit and was the first to be fitted with exhaust-driven turbochargers to maintain power up to 36,000ft. The

B-24E was similar to the D but was built at the Willow Run factory whilst the B-24H and J models mounted power operated turrets in the nose and a Sperry ball turret ventrally.

The Liberator served with distinction with both the USAAF and RAF and the last survivors were still being used in the maritime reconnaissance role by the Indian Air Force well into the 1970s. Two of these ex-Indian machines are today preserved in the UK, KN751 is displayed at the Aerospace Museum, RAF Cosford, near Wolverhampton and a second, KH191, was flown in to Stansted Airport, Essex, *inside* a TAC Heavylift Shorts Belfast on 6 May 1982. This aircraft was subsequently moved by road to join Doug Arnold's Warbirds Museum at Blackbushe, Hants. Several other examples exist in the USA. The photograph depicts the Confederate Air Force's very early LB-30A transport variant.

Curtiss C-46 Commando   USA

Photo: C-46, N5370N, was in service with Rich International when photographed at Miami, Florida, in August 1974.

Powerplants: Two 2,000hp Pratt & Whitney R-2800-51 or -75
Span: 108ft 1in
Length: 76ft 4in
Height: 21ft 9in
Wing area: 1,360sq ft

Design of the CW-20 civil transport was commenced at St Louis in 1935 and the aeroplane that finally emerged was a very large 36-seat, all-metal, pressurised, twin-engined airliner which could carry an additional 8,200lb of cargo inside its capacious 'double-bubble' fuselage. The twin-finned prototype was eventually converted to standard configuration and sold to BOAC as G-AGDI *St Louis* and a further 3,182 were built between 1942-1945.

The Commando was not so well-known as the C-47 but nevertheless served with distinction, especially in the Far East on the 'Hump' run from India to China. Postwar the large (it has 4ft greater span than a B-17) transport found favour mainly with specialised freight airlines such as the Flying Tiger line and is still popular in this role today — especially in Latin America where its pair of 2,000hp Twin Cyclones give it that extra pull in the rarefied air of the Andes.

Curtiss P-40   USA

Photo: P-40N of the Confederate Air Force
Data: Curtiss P-40C

Powerplant: One 1,040hp Allison V-1710-33
Span: 37ft 4.5in
Length: 31ft 8.5in
Height: 10ft 7in
Wing area: 236sq ft

The prototype XP-40 was a modified Model 75 Hawk fitted with a 1,150hp Allison V-1710-19 liquid-cooled V-12. It made its maiden flight on 14 October 1938 and was the forerunner of 13,738 production variants which were variously known as Tomahawks, Kittyhawks and Warhawks. Available in larger numbers than any other US Army fighter from 1941-1943 the P-40 was obsolete by European standards, British P-40s gave a good account of themselves in the North African and Mediterranean theatres but the most famous operations were those of the American Volunteer Group 'Flying Tigers' in China.

A major modification designed to overcome the P-40's limitations was the installation of the Rolls-Royce Merlin engine in place of the Allison, Merlin-powered variants were the P-40F, L and N. Several examples of the P-40E, M and N exist in both museums and private hands in the USA, Canada and Australia.

Curtiss SB2C Helldiver   USA

Photo: Helldiver of the Confederate Air Force

Powerplant: One 1,900hp Wright Cyclone R-2600
Span: 49ft 7in
Length: 36ft 7in
Wing area: 422sq ft
Max speed: 295mph

The Helldiver originated in a 1938 US Navy specification which led to a Navy Dive-Bomber Competition. In its anxiety to get new aircraft into the air for its 1940 expansion programme the Navy took the then unprecedented step of ordering the type 'off the drawing board', an initial order for 370 SB2C-1s being placed on 29 November 1940,

several weeks before the maiden flight of the prototype.

Many problems were encountered with the type which combined to prevent its joining the Fleet until November 1943 but 'The Beast', as it was nicknamed by its crews, finally earned a good reputation for itself and over 6,130 were built — including 900 for the USAAF as A-25A Shrikes.

The Confederate Air Force of Harlingen, Texas maintains the sole airworthy survivor and several non-flying examples are preserved in other US museums.

De Havilland DH98 Mosquito UK

Photo: RR299/G-ASKH maintained in flying trim by British Aerospace.
Data: B35

Powerplants: Two 1,710hp Rolls-Royce Merlin 113 or 114
Span: 54ft 2in
Length: 40ft 9.5in
Height: 15ft 3in
Wing area: 435sq ft

Using experience gained in the construction of the Comet racer and Albatross airliner, the de Havilland company put forward its idea for a fast, unarmed bomber of wooden construction in 1938. These plans were dismissed by a sceptical Air Ministry but de Havilland pressed ahead with the idea and at the end of 1939 were rewarded with an order to go ahead with the design of a light unarmed bomber to have a range of 1,500 miles and a bomb load of 1,000lb. Design work was centred on Salisbury Hall in Hertfordshire and on 1 March 1940 a contract for 50 aircraft was finally placed.

The first prototype, W4050, was built in a small hangar at Salisbury Hall, it was then dismantled and taken by road to Hatfield where it made its maiden flight on 25 November 1940, less than 11 months after the start of design work. It had an astounding performance and after only two test flights the manufacturers were themselves amazed at its fighter-like performance. Following three months of official trials the Mosquito was confirmed as the world's fastest operational aircraft type — an honour which it held until the advent of the first jets $2\frac{1}{2}$ years later.

The Mossie was built in bomber, fighter and photo recce versions, the Mk IV bomber being the first bomber version to enter service following the production of 10 Mk I photo-reconnaissance machines. The Mk IV carried a bomb load of four 500lb bombs — double the design load! By February 1944 the Mosquito was carrying a single 4,000lb bomb in a bulged bomb bay — *four* times the original design load!

The fighter version of the Mosquito was initially produced as a radar-equipped night fighter but the Mk VI fighter-bomber became the most widely used fighter variant, the Srs 2 being capable of mounting four 20mm cannon and four 0.303in guns in the nose together with two 500lb bombs in the rear of the bomb bay and two 500lb bombs or eight rocket projectiles under the wings! The rockets when fired as a salvo were the equivalent in striking power to the broadside from a 10,000ton cruiser.

Minor modifications to the aircraft ran into hundreds and the Mosquito continued to serve operationally with the postwar RAF well into the 1950s, eventually being supplanted by Canberras and Meteors. In the target-towing role the Mosquito served at Exeter until retired in 1961.

Several Mosquitos survive, including the prototype W4050 which is preserved in the Mosquito Aircraft Museum at Salisbury Hall, Herts, and three remain in flying condition; RR299 with British Aerospace at Chester, RS712 with Kermit Weeks and RS709 at Blackbushe, Hants.

Dornier Do24T-3   Germany

Photo: HD.5-4 preserved in the Dornier museum, Neues Schloss.

Powerplants: Three 1,000hp BMW-Bramo 323R-2 Fafnir
Span: 88ft 7in
Length: 72ft 4in
Height: 18ft 10.5in
Wing area: 1,162.5sq ft

The Do24 was a large, sea-going flying boat built to the specifications of the Dutch Marine Luchtvaartdienst (MLD) for service in the Dutch East Indies. Twelve aircraft were ordered from Dornier and plans were put in hand for the licence-production of a further 60 by Aviolanda and De Schelde in Holland. The first Dutch Do24K-2s were accepted in the late spring of 1939 and were shipped from Rotterdam to Surabaya where they were re-erected.

In the meantime the first two Jumo-engined prototypes were in store at Dornier's factory at Friedrichschafen but with the outbreak of war and with the formulation of plans for the German invasion of Denmark and Norway the two boats were readied for operations and taken over by the Luftwaffe. With the occupation of Holland in May 1940 the Do24K manufacturing facilities were taken over intact with several aircraft still in the works and others in various states of production. The type was evaluated in the Air-Sea Rescue role and pronounced ideal for the task, being re-designated Do24N-1, the first two boats being delivered to the Luftwaffe in August 1941.

Stocks of the American Wright Cyclone engines were sufficient to allow the production of 11 aircraft before the BMW-Bramo 323R-2 Fafnir engine was substituted to create the Do24T-1. Production was increased in 1942 by the takeover of the CAMS factory at Sartrouville, France but relatively few machines were completed there before the Allied take over of the plant in 1944. Subsequent production was for France's Aeronavale.

In spring 1944 the German government offered to supply neutral Spain with a number of Do24T-3s for Air-Sea Rescue duties. The ulterior motive behind this generous gesture being that with the loss of German bases on Sicily the Luftwaffe was hard-pressed to maintain an effective rescue service in the Mediterranean. The 12 aircraft were based at Pollensa, Majorca and the survivors were not withdrawn until the 1970s. HD5-2 is today preserved at the Spanish Museo del Aire at Cuatro Vientos, Madrid and HD5-4 is with the Dornier Museum at Neues Schloss near Frederichschafen, whilst HD5-1 arrived at Hendon during July 1982 as an interesting addition to the RAF Museum.

Dornier Do335A Pfiel   Germany

Photo: The sole surviving Do335A after restoration in 1976.

Powerplants: Two 1,900hp Daimler-Benz DB 603E-1
Span: 45ft 3.3in
Length: 45ft 5.25in
Height: 16ft 5in
Wing area: 414.4sq ft

The Do335 Pfiel (Arrow) was unique amongst twin-engined fighters in that it utilised tandem 'Push and Pull' engines. The reason for the unusual engine arrangement was that it gave the power of a twin with the handling qualities of a single-engined fighter, asymmetrical thrust problems associated with engine failure in a conventional twin were also resolved and the wing was left free of the clutter from any engine nacelles.

A development contract was awarded in 1942 for a single-seat unarmed intruder capable of carryng a 1,100lb bomb load at speeds of up to 495mph but the specification was soon amended to become a multi-role fighter. The necessary redesign was swiftly accomplished and when the first Do335 V1 flew on 26 October 1943 contracts had been placed for 14 experimental aircraft, 10 pre-production Do 335A-O and 11 production Do335A-1 single-seat fighter-bombers, and three Do335A-10 and A-12 tandem two-seat dual control trainers.

The B-series aircraft was a more heavily armed version for ground attack and all-weather interception — the latter being a two-seater. In the event only small numbers were built of all types before the Oberpfaffenhofen factory was overrun.

Several examples were taken to both the UK and the USA for evaluation and the second of 10 Do335A-O pre-production fighter-bombers survived long-term storage at Silver Hill, Marlyand, USA to be restored by Dornier in 1976. It is currently loaned to the Deutsches Museum.

Douglas SDB Dauntless

USA

Photo: N54532 is an SBD-5 kept in flying trim by the Confederate Air Force.

Powerplant: One 1,200hp Wright Cyclone
Span: 41ft 5in
Length: 32ft 1in
Wing area: 325sq ft

A progressive development of the Northrop XBT-1 and Gamma, the Dauntless project was in the hands of Edward Heinemann and the first XBT-2s (SBDs) were delivered to the US Navy in August 1938. The Dauntless was to become the most widely-used dive-bomber in the fleet, sinking more enemy shipping than all other *weapons* combined and having the lowest loss ratio of any carrier aircraft in the Pacific Theatre.

5,936 were built as SBDs for the US Navy and a further 863 land-based A-24s were delivered to the USAAF. At least eight remain in existence today, A-24 42-60817 being on display at the US Naval Aviation Museum, Pensacola, Florida, SBD-5 N54532 being in flying condition with the Confederate Air Force at Harlingen, Texas and another SBD-5 being maintained in flying condition at the US Marine Corps Museum, Quantico, Virginia.

Douglas A-20 Havoc (Boston)   USA

Photo: 43-22200 is an A-20G displayed at the USAF Museum, Wright-Patterson AFB.
Data: Boston III

Powerplants: Two 1,600hp Wright Double-Row Cyclone GR-2600-A5B
Span: 61ft 4in
Length: 47ft 0in
Height: 15ft 10in
Wing area: 465sq ft

The Boston/Havoc first appeared as the private venture Douglas DB-7 and was initially ordered for the French Armee de l'Air. Only a few reached France before the capitulation in 1940 and the remainder of the French order was diverted to the RAF and a further order of 1,335 was placed by the British Government. The first Boston Is were used as trainers and the Boston IIs were all converted into Havocs for the night-intruder role, this left the Boston III as the first version to see service in its designed role as a light attack bomber. The Boston IV was delivered from August 1944 by which time the aircraft was also serving with the USAAF as the A-20G and A-20J Havoc. The Boston V was the final version to be delivered to the RAF. Four A-20s survive in the USA.

Douglas B-23 Dragon   USA

Photo: One of several executive conversions of the B-23. This one was seen at Harlingen, Texas.

Powerplants: Two 1,600hp Wright R-2600-3 Cyclone
Span: 92ft
Length: 58ft 4in
Height: 18ft 6in
Wing area: 993sq ft

A development of the B-18A Bolo, the Dragon first flew in July 1939, 38 having been ordered for the USAAC. It was a great improvement aerodynamically over the Bolo and incorporated the latest American ideas on defensive armament — including a tail gun position.

After serving only briefly on coastal patrol work the Dragons were relegated to the transport and training role, 12 being converted into UC-67 transports in 1942. Most survived the war and a civil conversion was approved in 1945 which enabled a fair proportion of them to be converted into corporate transports with accommodation for two crew and up to 14 passengers. Several of these conversions are still in existence and at least one, owned by World Airways, has been superficially restored to its original USAAC condition.

Douglas B-26 Invader   USA

Photo: Douglas A-26C Invader N3710G was owned by Euroworld Ltd and often seen at Duxford, Cambridgeshire.

Powerplants: Two 2,000hp Pratt & Whitney R-2800-79
Span: 70ft
Length: 50ft
Height: 18ft 6in
Wing area: 540sq ft

The Invader first flew in prototype form (XA-26) on 10 July 1942. It was a development of the A-20 Havoc and it became operational with the US 9th Air Force in Europe during November 1944. 2,451 were eventually built in a number of different versions, the B variant carrying eight 0.5in guns in a solid nose whilst the C variant has a transparent nose section. All versions carried six 0.5in guns in the wings and the internal weapons bay could accommodate

4,000lb of bombs whilst rocket projectiles could be carried on racks under the wings.

The designation A-26 was changed to B-26 in 1948 and the type was active with the USAF in both Korea and Vietnam in the counter-insurgency role. The B-26K Counter-Invader is an improved version produced by the On Mark Engineering Company which was built to a specification issued by the USAF Special Air Warfare Center, it differed from the conventional aircraft in that it comprised a re-manufactured airframe with water-injected engines, dual controls, a 6,000lb st JATO pack, heavy duty brakes, 14 0.5in guns and eight external pylons on a stengthened wing. Forty of these conversions were ordered, the first flying in May 1964.

One A-26C, 43-22612/N3710G, was maintained in flying condition within the UK by Euroworld Ltd, and based at Duxford aerodrome, Cambridgeshire, until destroyed in a fatal accident.

Douglas C-54 Skymaster

USA

Photo: This Douglas C-54 Skymaster is one of a handful preserved in American museums.

Powerplants: Four 1,450hp Pratt & Whitney R-2000-2SD-13G
Span: 117ft 6in
Length: 93ft 11in
Height: 27ft 6.25in
Wing area: 1,463sq ft

The C-54 is a military equivalent of the DC-4A airliner, 60 of which had been ordered by US airlines when America entered World War 2 in 1941. The DC-4A was a 42-seat airliner which had been developed as a scaled-down version of the original DC-4, the sole example of which was eventually sold to Japan.

The first C-54 flew in April 1942 and entered service with the USAAF the following year. Production continued after the war and a further 79 had been built by the time that it eventually ceased in favour of the DC-6 in 1947. A handful of DC-4s, most of which are actually ex-military C-54s, are still operated, mainly in Latin and North America on freight duties. Few survive in Europe although they are occasionally seen and several have been converted into bars and nightclubs. The last British examples were G-BANO and G-BANP which were used as examples at the CAA Fire Training School at Stansted Airport, Essex.

EKW (Swiss Federal Aircraft Factory) C-3503 Switzerland

Photo: This EKW C-3603 is exhibited in the Swiss Transport Museum at Lucerne.
Data: C-3603-1

Powerplant: One 1,000hp Hispano-Suiza HS-51 12Y
Span: 45ft 1.5in
Length: 36ft 9.5in
Height: 13ft 1in
Wing area: 307.8sq ft

The prototype C-3601 was built during 1938-39 as a two-seat, long-range reconnaissance and ground support aircraft, powered by a single Hispano Suiza HS-77 12 Ycrs engine of 860hp. Initial tests indicated that more power was needed but the prototype was destroyed before this could be rectified. The second prototype, the C-3602, incorporated several modifications and was fitted with the more powerful HS-51 12Y engine which gave 1,000hp. Trials with the C-3602 led to an order for 10 C-3603-0 pre-production machines and 142 C-3603-1 combat aircraft, these entered service with the Swiss Air Force in 1942 and served operationally for 10 years.

On their withdrawal from front-line duties many aircraft were converted to the target towing role but by the mid-1960s the aircraft were experiencing difficulties with their antique Hispano Suiza engines. Several alternative types were considered as replacements but the solution was found in 1968 when aircraft C-502 was converted to take the Lycoming T-53-L7A gas turbine of 1,115hp. This conversion proved entirely successful and a further 23 aircraft were converted under the designation C-3605 'Schlepp'. Aircraft C-534 is preserved at the Swiss Air Force Museum, Dubendorf, and C-537 is exhibited at the Verkehrshaus (Transport Museum) at Lucern.

Fairchild Cornell   USA

Photo: The enclosed cabin model was designated PT-26, this example was photographed in the USA.
Data: PT-19 & PT-26

Powerplant: One 200hp Ranger 6-440C-5
Span: 35ft 11.75in
Length: 27ft 8in
Height: 7ft 6in
Wing area: 200sq ft

The Cornell was the production version of the M-62 tandem, two-seat, primary trainer which was first flown in March 1939. The name 'Cornell' was applied to Canadian versions of the design but is now widely used in association with all surviving aircraft. More than 8,000 were built in the USA, Canada and Brazil in three basic versions; the PT-19 and PT-26 (M-62A), both powered by the 200hp Ranger L-440 in-line; and the PT-23 which was powered by the 220hp Continental R-670-4 radial.

Considerable numbers of Cornells remain active in North America and there are one or two in Europe, non-airworthy examples being stored at the Historic Aircraft Museum, Southend and for the Royal Air Force Museum.

Fairey Battle   UK

Photo: R7384 is the only complete Fairey Battle in the World and is part of the Canadian National Aeronautical Collection.

Powerplant: One 1,030hp Rolls-Royce Merlin I, II, III or V
Span: 54ft
Length: 52ft 1.75in
Height: 15ft 6in
Wing area: 422sq ft

The Battle was ordered against Spec P27/32, issued in April 1933, as a replacement for the biplane Hart and Hind light bombers. As a monoplane with twice the bomb load of its predecessors the type was expected to be outstanding and was one of the designs chosen for the expansion of the RAF in the late 1930s. In the event the Battle proved to be underpowered and poorly defended and was obsolescent by the outbreak of war in 1939.

The Battle entered squadron service in May 1937

when the first examples joined No 63 Sqn at Upwood, by the following year they equipped 15 squadrons of Bomber Command and there were over 1,000 in service at the outbreak of war. Battles of the Advanced Air Striking Force made some of the earliest operational sorties of the war and a Battle of No 88 Sqn claimed the first German aircraft shot down on 20 September 1939. The type was, however, totally unsuitable for daylight operations without an escort, a type of operation which was abandoned after 30 September when four out of five Battles of No 150 Sqn were downed by German fighters.

Probably the most famous battle 'op' was the attack of the Maastricht Bridges which was made on 10 May 1940 by aircraft from No 12 Sqn. Two posthumous VCs were awarded to the crew of one Battle, P2204, the first awarded to members of the RAF in World War 2.

Soon withdrawn from front-line duties the Battle soldiered on in the training and target-towing roles. Large numbers were shipped to Canada where they were used at Air Gunnery Schools under the Commonwealth Air Training Plan and it is one of these machines, R7384, which is currently the only Battle on public display anywhere in the World, being preserved by the Canadian National Aeronautical Collection at Rockliffe. Three incomplete Battles are preserved in the UK L5343, P2183 and R3950, but none are currently viewable.

Fairey Fulmar

UK

Photo: Fulmar prototype N1854 at Yeovilton.
Data: Mk I

Powerplant: One 1,080hp Rolls-Royce Merlin VIII
Span: 46ft 4.5in
Length: 40ft 3in
Height: 14ft
Wing area: 342sq ft

The eight-gun, two-seat Fulmar entered service with the Fleet Air Arm in the summer of 1940 and was the first aircraft to join the Fleet which had the fire power of the land-based Spitfires and Hurricanes.

The prototype, N1854, made its maiden flight at Ringway on 4 January 1940, being a development of the P4/34 light bomber prototype from which it differed mainly in carrying the Merlin VIII engine, arrester gear, eight guns, catapult points, folding wings and having a non-continuous canopy for the pilot and navigator.

The first Fulmars joined No 808 Sqn at Worthy Down in June 1940 and the type had reached its operational peak by 1942, from 1943 onwards it was steadily replaced by the far superior Seafire. The type saw service in almost all the theatres of war, being used against the Italian fleet in the Med, on

Malta convoy defence duties and in the Middle and Far East. Fulmars of No 800Z Sqn embarked on board HMS *Victorious* were instrumental in shadowing the German pocket battleship *Bismark* in May 1941.

The Fulmar was a useful type which lacked the speed of a single-seat fighter on account of the navigator, who was considered essential in the early war years when the chances of returning successfully to a carrier at sea were thought to be marginal without specialised navigational help. Its top speed of 280mph meant that the Fulmar pilot had to be on target the first time, he rarely had the speed to try another pass, especially against fast German opposition.

The prototype Fulmar, converted to Mk II standard, was used for many years as a manufacturer's communications aircraft with the civil registration G-AIBE. It is today preserved at the Fleet Air Arm Museum, Yeovilton.

Fairey Firefly I   UK

Photo: Firefly I Z2033/G-ASTL is preserved at Duxford Cambridgeshire.
Data: F1

Powerplant: One 1,730hp Rolls-Royce Griffon IIB or 1,990hp Griffon XII
Span: 44ft 6in
Length: 37ft 7.25in
Wing area: 328sq ft

Designed to Naval Spec N5/40 the Firefly was a fast, well-armed, two-seater combining the roles of both fighter and reconnaissance aircraft, in this respect it was a descendant of the Fulmar, its immediate predecessor from the Fairey stable. First flown on 22 December 1941 the Firefly bore a superficial resemblance to the Fulmar but its Griffon engine gave it a top speed some 40mph faster and its four 20mm cannon had far greater punch than the eight 0.303in machine guns.

The basic Mk I Firefly was built in a number of versions; the FI was followed by the FRI which mounted ASH ship and submarine-detection radar, the NF2 night-fighter and the NFI night-fighter. The NF2 was the earlier of the two night-fighter versions but it was abandoned after only 37 had been built as it had been discovered that more compact radar could be installed in the FRI airframe to produce the NFI without the need for the considerable structural

mods which had been needed to produce the original NF2.

The final operational variant was the FIA, an FI converted to FRI standards.

Fireflies embarked on board a carrier for the first time in 1943, No 1770 Sqn forming at Yeovilton in October of that year. The aircraft of that unit were embarked on HMS *Indefatigable* the following year and were operational during attacks on the *Tirpitz* in July 1944. The first major actions in which Fireflies played a part were with carriers attached to the Ceylon-based East Indies Fleet, Fireflies of No 1770 Sqn carrying out rocket attacks on the Japanese oil refineries in Sumatra in early January 1945 prior to the main fleet attack later in the month.

With the arrival of VJ-day 658 Fireflies had been built and the type equipped eight squadrons, four of which were with the British Pacific Fleet. All these units were disbanded by June 1946 and by this time the Mk I had been superseded by the Mk 4 on the production lines.

Four Mk I Fireflies are known to exist today: Z2033/G-ASTL, an FRI with the Skyfame Collection, Duxford; DT989/SE-BRG, a TT1 at Arlanda, Sweden; MB410, an FI with the Royal Thai Air Force Museum, Bangkok; and PP392/SE-CAW, a TT1 at the Tekniska Museet, Malmo, Sweden. The latter aircraft is said to be for disposal.

FIAT CR42 Falco
Italy

Photo: FIAT CR42 Falco MM 5701 is on show in the Battle of Britain Museum, Hendon.

Powerplant: One 840hp FIAT A741C-38
Span: 31ft 9.75in
Length: 27ft 2.75in
Height: 10ft 10in
Wing area: 241sq ft

Although comparable in several ways with the Gloster Gladiator, the CR42 was a later design. The CR32, first flown in 1933, had proved to be highly manoeuvrable and had been used with some success during the Spanish Civil War. When the Italian Air Ministry issued new specifications for new fighters in July 1935 Celestine Rosatelli designed a new biplane which incorporated several features of its predecessor. The prototype was completed in 1938 and an initial batch of 200 ordered with first deliveries being made in 1939 — after the entry into service of the FIAT G50 monoplane fighter! A top speed of 267mph and excellent manoeuvrability won the type a number of export orders: Hungary received

an unknown number in late 1939, Belgium received 25 out of an order for 34 by May 1940 and Sweden took delivery of 72 aircraft which received the local designation J11 and which flew alongside Sweden's Gloster Gladiators (J8s).

When Italy entered World War 2 on 10 June 1940 some 290 CR42s were in operational service. Several Stormi participated in the brief Italian campaign against France and in September 1940 the Corpo Aero Italiano was sent to Belgium to assist Luftwaffe attacks on the UK. Three bomber units were accompanied by 50 CR42s and 48 G50s as escort fighters. The poor weather and the slower speeds of the Italian fighters contrived to make operations difficult for the Italians and it was not until 11 November that their only major attack was mounted. One of the CR42s shot down that day was MM5701 which was repaired and flown for evaluation as BT474, it is today exhibited at the Battle of Britain Museum, Hendon. One of the Swedish machines, 2543, is preserved at the Swedish Air Force Museum, Linkoping.

Fieseler Fi156 Storch
Germany

Photo: Storch D-EKMU is exhibited at the Historic Aircraft Museum, Southend, in North African desert camouflage as 'CB+VD'.

Powerplant: One 240hp Argus As 10C-3
Span: 46ft 9in
Length: 32ft 5.75in
Height: 9ft 10in
Wing area: 279.862sq ft

The Storch was designed with Army Co-operation duties very much in mind, the prototype flying in 1936, and was thus broadly comparable with the British Westland Lysander with which it shared extensive high-lift devices on the wing and associated slow flying qualities. Whereas the

Lysander was not outstanding in its designed role the Storch most certainly was and was to be found on every front throughout World War 2.

It entered production as the Fi156A-1 in 1936, a proposed civilian version designated Fi156B was abandoned, and the C series appeared in 1939. The C-1 was intended for short-range reconnaissance, the C-2 as an air ambulance and the D series were for various army co-op duties. The experimental Fi156E was fitted with a caterpillar type tracked undercarriage for operation off rough terrain.

With the low priority afforded to non-combat types the production of the Storch was eventually transferred to German controlled factories in France and Czechoslovakia, the French-built examples continuing in production for the Armee de l'Air as the

Morane Saulnier MS500 Criquet. Probably the best known Storch operation was the rescue of Benito Mussolini from his mountain-top prison in 1943.

Several Storchs survive of German, French and Czech origin, world-wide; in the UK the Royal Air Force Museum maintains a genuine wartime example, Wk Nr 475081, at St Athan; another is exhibited at the Historic Aircraft Museum, Southend; and a French-built Criquet, G-AZMH, is maintained in flying condition by the Hon Patrick Lindsay at Booker.

Focke Wulf Fw190 Germany

Photo: Fw190D-9, Wk Nr 601088, in the markings of JG3 'Udet' Geschwader, is owned by the Smithsonian Institution but exhibited at the USAF Museum, Dayton, Ohio.
Data: Fw 190A8

Powerplant: One BMW 801D-2 Rated at 1,700hp for take-off and 1,440hp at 18,700ft
Span: 34ft 5.5in
Length: 29ft 4.5in
Height: 13ft
Wing area: 196.98sq ft

Although the Messerschmitt Bf109 is probably the most well-known German fighter of World War 2 the Focke Wulf Fw190 was a far superior machine and is widely regarded as the best German fighter of the period. The type was unusual in that it was Germany's first radial-engined monoplane fighter, Kurt Tank having persuaded the German Air Ministry that the radial had three points in its favour when compared with the liquid-cooled Daimler-Benz: it was less likely to suffer battle damage as it had no cooling system, was in less demand that the

Daimler-Benz and it was producing more power in prototype form than the developed Daimler-Benz.

The prototype flew in June 1939 and after initial problems with the engine over-heating the type proved to be markedly superior to anything else flying at the time. The type entered Luftwaffe service in the summer of 1941 and was first seen over the UK in August of that year. It could outfly the Spitfire V and was the main cause of the development of the 'stop-gap' Spitfire IX with the Merlin 61 engine.

The initial production variant was the Fw190A, fitted with the BMW 801 engine of 1,440hp at 18,700ft. The sub-types in this series differed mainly in their armament whilst the 190F was a ground-attack development and the 190G was a fighter-bomber. The first major change in the airframe came with the 190D which was powered by the liquid-cooled Jumo 213 engine. The longer nose neccesitated a rear fuselage stretch to compensate for the increased moment arm but the 'A' wing was retained. This model was introduced in 1943 and led to the development of the ultimate Fw190 variant, the Ta152, powered by the Daimler-Benz DB603LA of 1,820hp and with a speed of over 460mph at

35,000ft the heavily-armed Ta152H appeared too late to have any real effect on the outcome of the war.

Two Fw190s are preserved in the UK Wk Nr 733682 is an A8 sub-type on show at the Imperial War Museum while Wk Nr 584219 is a rare two-seat trainer version of the F8 which is displayed with the RAF Museum Regional Collection at RAF St Athan. Further examples are preserved in France, Jugoslavia, South Africa and the USA.

Gloster E28/39   UK

Photo: The sole E28/39, W4041/G, preserved at the Science Museum, South Kensington.

Powerplants: Various but currently fitted with a 1,700lb st Whittle W2/500
Span: 29ft
Length: 25ft 2in
All up weight: 3,700lb
Max speed: 340mph

Designed around the experimental Whittle W1 gas turbine engine, which had been bench-run during 1937, the E28/39 was constructed in considerable secrecy at Hucclecote and Cheltenham and made its maiden flight on 15 May 1941 at Cranwell. It was thus the first Allied type to fly on the power of a jet engine. W4041/G was the first prototype, a second was flown on 1 March 1943 but was lost in an accident only four months later, the original aircraft being fitted with engines of increasing power until the 1,700lb thrust W2/500 was finally installed. It was transferred to the Royal Aircraft Establishment at Farnborough in April 1944 and remained there for almost two years before being retired in January 1946 and was presented to the Science Museum, London, on 28 April 1946 where it remains on exhibition today.

Gloster Meteor (F9/40)   UK

Photo: F9/40 prototype, DG202/G, which is preserved at the Aerospace Museum, RAF Cosford.
Data: Fl

Powerplants: Two 1,700lb thrust Rolls-Royce Welland I
Span: 43ft
Length: 41ft 4in
Height: 13ft
Wing area: 350sq ft

The Meteor was the first British jet aircraft to enter service and also the only jet to fight on the Allied side during World War 2. Designed to meet Air Ministry Spec F9/40 the Gloster team produced their twin-jet Thunderbolt — the name was changed in 1942 after objections from the USA that the name was already being used for the P-47.

The first Meteor was DG202/G which was fitted with Rover-built W2B turbojets which failed to deliver the required thrust for flight and so the honour of being the first to fly fell to the fifth prototype, DG206, which was fitted with early versions of the de Havilland Goblin turbojet. All the prototypes were fitted with different engines in order to assess their relative merits.

The first production Meteor Is were delivered to No 616 Sqn on 12 July 1944 and the first sortie was against V-1 flying bombs on 27 July. The first 'op' was a failure as the guns failed to fire correctly but on 4 August Fl Off Dean managed to destroy a V-1 by tipping it up with his wingtip and thus toppling its gyros.

In October 1944 Meteors were used in simulated attacks against American bombers in order that the Mustang and Thunderbolt pilots could assess the

best way of dealing with the Messerschmitt Me262s then beginning to appear and in January 1945 a flight of No 616 Sqn moved to Belgium, later to be joined by No 504 Sqn. These aircraft were attached to the 2nd Tactical Air Force and were of the improved Mk III variety which had flown in September 1944.

The Meteor was later to become one of the mainstays of the postwar RAF and a small number are still flying with the Royal Aircraft Establishment at Llanbedr. The prototype, DG202/G, somehow survived and is today preserved with the Aerospace Museum, RAF Cosford.

Grumman F4F Wildcat (Martlet) USA

Photo: FM-2 Wildcat, N681S, operated by the Confederate Air Force in the markings of US Navy Sqdn VF-41, USS *Ranger*.
Data: Martlet I

Powerplant: One 1,200hp Wright Cyclone G-205A
Span: 38ft
Length: 28ft 10in
Height: 9ft 2.5in
Wing area: 260sq ft

The XF4F-2 prototype made its maiden flight on September 2, 1937 and the first production aircraft, known as F4F-3s, were received by the US Navy and US Marine Corps in August 1940. These early aircraft were characterised by the lack of any wing-folding mechanism, a development which did not appear until the advent of the F4F-4.

The first F4F aircraft to see combat were those of the Fleet Air Arm, in whose service they adopted the name Martlet I. These machines were Grumman G-36A models originally ordered by France, with the fall of France in 1940 the contract was taken over by the British Purchasing Commission and 81 Martlets were delivered in 1940. A further 10 were shipped in 1941 to replace 10 lost at sea during delivery.

In American service the name Wildcat was officially adopted on 1 October 1941, the British name Martlet surviving in use until 1944 when it was changed to coincide with American nomenclature.

Wildcat variants went up to the -8 but the most widely produced version was the FM-2, this being the production version of the F4F-8 built by the Eastern Aircraft Division of General Motors. Martlets were generally straightforward equivalents of the American types with the exceptions of the Mks I-III, the Mk I being the French model, the Mk II being a compromise with folding wings and the single-stage two-speed R-1830-S3C-4G engine, and the Mk III being a batch of 30 F4F-3A originally destined for Greece. The Martlet IV was the equivalent of the F4F-4 but with the engine of the F4F-5, the Martlet V was an FM-1 and the Martlet VI was an FM-2.

At least 15 Wildcats survive worldwide, two of which are in Europe; Martlet I AL246 is a static exhibit in the Fleet Air Arm Museum at Yeovilton, Somerset, and F4F Wildcat N47201 was delivered by air to its new owner, Stephen Gray, in June 1982, it will be based in Switzerland alongside his Bearcat and Mustang.

Grumman F6F Hellcat   USA

Photo: Hellcat N1078Z, owned by Cols Ed Messick and Ken Wynn of the Confederate Air Force, Harlingen, Texas.
Data: F6F-5

Powerplant: One 2,000hp Pratt & Whitney R-2800-10W Double Wasp
Span: 42ft 10in
Length: 33ft 7in
Height: 14ft 5in
Wing area: 334sq ft

Although bearing a superficial resemblance to the Wildcat, the Hellcat was a totally different aeroplane which originated as a collaborative project between Grumman's engineering staff and US Navy fighter pilots who had experience with the Wildcat in operations against the Japanese.

The Hellcat appeared on the production lines during 1942, it was 50mph faster than the earlier machine, climbed faster, carried more ammunition, possessed a greater range and ceiling and carried more armour plate for the pilot's protection. Perhaps the most notable structural change was the alteration of the undercarriage so that it now retracted into the centre-section rather than into the belly in time-honoured Grumman tradition.

The first production Hellcats reached the squadrons in November 1942 and early the following year the type became available to the Fleet Air Arm under Lend-Lease agreements. 1,182 of the 10,000 built were delivered to the FAA over the three years that the type was in production, the first 252 Hellcat Is being known as Gannets until the names were standardised. The Hellcat I was the equivalent of the F6F-3 with the R-2800-10 Double Wasp and the Hellcat II was the equivalent of the F6F-5 which was fitted with the -10W engine. 74 Hellcat IIs were fitted with a wing-mounted radome and finished in midnight blue for night-fighter operations, these were F6F-5Ns in US nomenclature.

At least 14 Hellcats survive in museums and private hands, mainly in the USA, but Hellcat II, KE209, which was still flying in the mid-1950s at Lossiemouth, is preserved at the Fleet Air Arm Museum, Yeovilton.

Grumman F8F Bearcat   USA

Photo: F8F-2P, N7825C/BuAer 122674, is maintained in flying condition by the Confederate Air Force, Harlingen, Texas.
Data: F8F-1

Powerplant: One 2,100hp Pratt & Whitney R-2800-34W Double Wasp
Span: 35ft 10in
Length: 28ft 3in
Height: 13ft 10in
Wing area: 244sq ft

The Bearcat was the last of the classic piston-engined Grumman navy fighters to come from the offices of Ralston Stalb, previously responsible for the Wildcat and Hellcat. Flight-testing of the XF8F-1 prototype began in August 1944 and initial deliveries

to the US Navy were being made a mere five months later but the type did not actually see operational service in World War 2. Production ran to 1,265, including two civil aircraft, and the type saw service with the US Navy and with the armed forces of France, Thailand and Vietnam.

Several examples were civilianised and came on to the American civil register, the most famous of which is Darryl Greenamayer's highly-modified *Conquest One* in which he took the World Speed Record for piston-engined aircraft. This famous aircraft is now preserved by the Smithsonian Institution, Washington, DC and several others are preserved in the USA plus one in Thailand, whilst Steven Gray has recently acquired N700H which he bases in Switzerland.

Grumman TBM Avenger USA

Photo: TBM-3E Avenger N6583D/BuAer 53503 is maintained by the Confederate Air Force, Harlingen, Texas.
Data: Avenger AS4

Powerplant: One 1,750hp Wright R-2600-20 Cyclone
Span: 54ft 2in
Length: 40ft
Height: 15ft 8in
Wing area: 490sq ft

The Avenger design appeared during 1940 and the prototype XTBF-1 was being tested at the time of the Japanese attack on Pearl Harbor. Conceived as a replacement for the Douglas Devastator the Avenger was armed with a 22in torpedo and was the first single-engined American type to boast a power-operated gun turret. The first production aircraft, the TBF-1, was delivered in early 1942 and in June of that year six participated in the Battle of Midway — it was a disastrous start to an auspicious career in that none of them sank any shipping and five were

shot down.

The parent company built over 2,000 aircraft but the vast majority were built by the Eastern Aircraft Division of General Motors at Trenton, New Jersey, these Trenton-built machines were distinguished by the TBM designation.

Avengers were delivered to the Fleet Air Arm under Lend-Lease and were operational both in home waters and in the Far East, the last aircraft being withdrawn with the disbandment of No 828 Sqn on 3 June 1946. This was not the end of the Avenger in British service however as a number of Avenger AS4s were delivered under the MDAP scheme to supplement the Royal Navy's anti-submarine forces in 1953. These aircraft were the equivalent of the US Navy's TBM-3E and they remained in service until supplanted by Gannets in 1955. One aircraft, XB446, was still flying in the early 1960s and is today preserved by the Fleet Air Arm Museum, Yeovilton. Two further Avengers are preserved in the UK, at Duxford and Blackbushe and many are still flying in the USA and Canada as fire-fighting borate bombers.

Grumman J2F Duck

USA

Photo: One of several Ducks still flying in the USA is seen here in R. W. Harrison's photo.
Data: J2F-6

Powerplant: One 1,050hp Wright R-1820-54 Cyclone
Span: 39ft
Length: 34ft
Height: 12ft 4in
Wing area: 409sq ft

The first Duck was the XJF-1 prototype of 1933 which was a direct descendent of the Leoning XO2L-2. The aircraft was basically a combination of Grumman's Model B amphibious float married to a stretched FF-1 airframe to create an amphibious utility floatplane. Nine versions were produced for the US Navy, the US Coast Guard, the US Marine Corps and for export to Argentina before production ceased in 1945. Pressure of work with the Hellcat and other front-line designs caused the parent company to transfer production to Columbia Aircraft Corporation and this concern built more J2F-6s between 1942 and 1945 (330 aircraft) than the parent company had built of all versions (315) previously.

Several Ducks remain in flying condition in the USA, probably the best-known of which is the example owned by Tallmantz Aviation which starred in the film *Murphy's War*.

Handley Page Halifax BII

UK

Powerplants: Four 1,390hp Rolls-Royce Merlin XX
Span: 98ft 10in
Length: 70ft 1in
Height: 20ft 9in
Wing area: 1,250sq ft

Tracing its ancestry back to an Air Staff requirement of September 1936 the Halifax prototype made its maiden flight on 25 October 1939 and deliveries commenced in late 1940 to No 35 Sqn at Leeming. The first operational sortie by the squadron was on the night of 11/12 March 1941 when six Halifaxes bombed Le Havre, the first daylight attack was made on Kiel on 30 June 1941 but the type was withdrawn from daylight operations after an attack on the German battle-cruisers *Scharnhorst* and *Gneisenau* at the end of that year.

The Halifax was the second four-engined heavy bomber to enter RAF service, being preceded into squadron service by the Short Stirling, and it was soon overtaken by the more illustrious Lancaster. With the Lancaster the Halifax shared the Bomber Command night offensive against Germany between 1941 and 1945 but made only about half the sorties (75,532 as against 156,000). Despite the apparent secondary role in Bomber Command the Halifax was an outstanding bomber which was put to numerous other duties not shared by the Lancaster, these included that of a glider-tug associated with airborne invasions and as a general reconnaissance aircraft with Coastal Command. Specialised transport versions were also built.

Despite the fact that 6,176 Halifaxes were built for the RAF no whole aircraft were thought to exist until the spectacular recovery of BII Srs 2, W1048, in June 1973. This aircraft was shot down on 28 April 1942 after No 35 Sqn had attacked the German battleship *Tirpitz* in Trondheim Fjord, crash-landing on the frozen surface of Lake Hoklingen the blazing starboard outer engine melted the ice and the Halifax sank shortly after the crew scrambled to safety. It lay at the bottom of the lake until a team of divers raised it on 30 June 1973 and beached it successfully. It was then transported to the RAF Museum store at Henlow and restored for display in the new Bomber Command Museum at Hendon.

Hawker Hurricane

UK

Photo: Hurricane IIC PZ865 was the last of the type to be built, in September 1944, and was operated by the Hawker Aircraft Co Ltd for many years as G-AMAU *The Last Of The Many* it is now maintained with the Battle of Britain Memorial Flight.

Data: Mk IIC

Powerplant: One 1,280hp Rolls-Royce Merlin XX
Span: 40ft
Length: 32ft
Height: 13ft 1.5in
Wing area: 257.5sq ft

The Hurricane, first of the RAF's eight-gun fighters, first flew on 6 November 1935 and the following June a contract was placed for the production of 600 aircraft, this was increased to 1,000 in November 1938 and by 7 August 1940 — the height of the Battle of Britain — 2,309 had been delivered to form the equipment of 32 squadrons. The Battle of Britain was probably the Hurricane's 'Finest Hour' as the type was responsible for bringing down more enemy aircraft than all other defences combined. It later won fame in the defence of Malta, in the Western Desert and in the Burma Campaign. In all these operations the Hurricane bore the brunt of the fighting yet the type has always seemed to be somewhat overshadowed by its more magical partner the Spitfire.

Construction of the Hurricane followed traditional Hawker lines with a welded steel tube fuselage to which wooden formers and stringers were added to carry the fabric covering. The wings of the early aircraft were also fabric-covered but metal skinning was introduced with effect from Hurricane Mk I N2423, three-bladed variable speed airscrews replacing the fixed-pitch, two-bladed wooden varieties to absorb more power from the increasingly powerful Marks of Merlin engine fitted over the years.

Although the method of construction made the Hurricane a remarkably tough aeroplane capable of

absorbing considerable damage it also led to its eventual demise as it left no room for improvement. The all-metal monocoque fuselage, typified by the Spitfire, had far more development potential and Hawkers adopted this method of construction for the Hurricane's successors, the Typhoon and Tempest.

By 1942 the Hurricane was outclassed on normal fighter operations but the adoption of rocket-projectiles and 40mm guns turned it into a formidable ground-attack aircraft which had considerable success in the European Theatre until supplanted by the even more potent Typhoon. In the Western Desert the Hurricane became a 'Tank-Buster' armed with two 40mm Vickers 'S' guns and a similar role was assumed in Burma against Japanese armour.

The final production variant was the Mk IV which appeared in 1943 and which featured a so-called 'universal' wing capable of mounting various combinations of offensive armament, it also carried extensive armour plating and was much used on low-level ground attack. The RAF's last Hurricane squadron, No 6, took its Mk IVs from Italy to Palestine after the war and remained there until October 1946.

The Hurricane rapidly disappeared from the postwar RAF and is today poorly represented when compared with the Spitfire, the Battle of Britain Memorial Flight maintain two Mk IIs in flying condition, PZ865 and LF363 — the former being the 12,780th and final aircraft to be built; the Strathallan Aircraft Collection has a flyable Canadian-built Mk X, G-AWLW/'P3308'; and several static examples remain. Two further examples are being rebuilt to fly in the USA and the Shuttleworth Collection's Sea Hurricane, Z7015, is undergoing a similar restoration to flying condition at Duxford, Cambs.

Hawker Typhoon Ib   UK

Photo: The sole surviving Typhoon, MN235 at the RAF Museum, Hendon

Powerplant: One 2,260hp Napier Sabre IIC
Span: 41ft 7in
Length: 31ft 11in
Height: 15ft 3.5in
Wing area: 279sq ft

The Typhoon was designed as an interceptor to take advantage of the more powerful 24-cylinder Napier Sabre engine. As such it was the first fighter to enter service with the RAF to boast a top speed of more than 400mph but repeated engine failures and a structural weakness in the tail assembly plagued the type with accidents after its entry into service in September 1941. The problems were so bad that there was talk of its being withdrawn from use altogether but common sense prevailed, the teething troubles were sorted out and the Typhoon became a devastatingly effective ground-attack aircraft.

The high-altitude performance of the Typhoon was also below the expected standard so the first real operations were by No 609 Sqn from Manston in November 1942. The area had been plagued by Focke Wulf Fw190 'Tip and Run' raiders which were too fast for the Spitfires then in service, within a week No 609 had downed four Fw190s. The low-level potential of the type was quickly realised and one of the Typhoon's specialities was that of 'train-busting', by the middle of 1943 some 150 locos being destroyed per month!

It was the build up of the 2nd Tactical Air Force which led to the Typhoon's greatest achievements, by D-Day 26 squadrons were equipped with the type which now carried a massive 2,000lb bomb load or eight rocket projectiles. With the advance across France and the Low Countries in the autumn and winter of 1944 the Typhoon really came into its own, reaching its zenith during the ground battles of Caen and Falaise where they annihilated the German Panzer divisions and cleared the ground for the Allied advance.

With the end of the war in Europe the Typhoon's role vanished and by the end of 1945 there were none left in front-line units. The type became extinct, except for a cockpit section in the Imperial War Museum, until a solitary survivor was discovered in a crate at the Smithsonian Institution's Silver Hill storage facility just outside Washington DC. This aircraft had been sent to the USA for evaluation in March 1944. It was exchanged for a Hurricane and returned to the UK for preservation with the Royal Air Force Museum in 1968.

Hawker Tempest   UK

Photo: Tempest V NV778 seen at RAF Gaydon in September 1969
Data: Mk V

Powerplant: One 2,180hp Napier Sabre II
Span: 41ft
Length: 33ft 8in
Height: 16ft 1in
Wing area: 302sq ft

Conceived as an enlarged Typhoon the Tempest first flew in prototype form on 2 September 1942. The main production variants were the Mks II and V, the former powered by the radial Bristol Centaurus engine while the latter was fitted with the same 24-cylinder Napier Sabre as was used in the Typhoon. The Mk V bore a marked resemblance to the earlier type but differed mainly in the use of a new thin section eliptical wing which necessitated a longer fuselage to house the fuel tanks banished from the wings.

The first Tempest Wing was commanded by Wg Cdr Roland Beamont, who had led No 609 Sqn's Typhoons from Manston, and was formed at Newchurch, Kent, in April 1944. Following initial successes on ground-attack and train-busting operations the fast (427mph) fighters came into their own when used against V-1 flying bombs, destroying 638 out of the RAF total of 1,771 between June and September 1944. With the formation of the 2nd TAF the Tempests fought their way across Europe, where they were credited with 20 Me262 jet fighters, and postwar served for many years in the high-speed target towing role, some remaining in use at Sylt, Northern Germany, until 1953.

Two Tempests survive: Mk V NV778 is displayed in the Royal Air Force Museum, Hendon, and is a composite made up from a number of components which were retrieved from the Proof & Experimental Establishment, Shoeburyness, in 1958. No 33 Sqn used these to construct a whole aircraft, serialled SN219, for its Standard Presentation ceremony at Middleton St George in April that year, it was then used as a gate guardian at Middleton and Leeming until rebuilt for the RAF Museum by No 27 MU at Shawbury in 1968.

Mk II, LA607, was the second prototype Tempest and spent most of its life on development work before being allocated to the College of Aeronautics, Cranfield, in the late 1940s. It was acquired by the Skyfame Museum in July 1966 and moved to Staverton from where it moved to Duxford in 1978. In addition to these two the fuselage of Mk V, EJ693, is held in store by the RAF Museum.

Heinkel He111H   Germany

Photo: Spanish-built CASA 2111D, G-BDYA, was one of 15 command-transport versions built for the Spanish Air Force, imported into the UK in 1976 it was later sold in the USA.
Data: He111 H-23

Powerplants: Two Junkers Jumo 213A-1 rated at 1,776hp at take-off
Span: 74ft 1.75in
Length: 53ft 9.5in
Height: 13ft 1in
Wing area: 931.07sq ft

First appearing in 1935 the He111 was said to be a civil transport and mailplane but in 1936 the He111B was being delivered to the Luftwaffe and by the following year the type was involved in bombing missions in the Spanish Civil War. The early versions featured a conventional stepped windscreen and nose but the HE111P, which was powered by Daimler-Benz DB601 engines, introduced the characteristic 'glasshouse' nose that was to become the hallmark of the type.

Despite a promising start in the Spanish Civil War the lightly-armed bombers fared badly sent over on lightly-escorted daylight raids during the Battle of Britain. Rushed installations of additional armour and defensive guns did little to help the situation and the Heinkels were soon switched to the less hazardous duties of night bombing, mine laying and torpedo carrying and by 1943 it was out of date and withdrawn from offensive roles.

Lack of any suitable replacement kept the type in production as late as 1944 but the final versions, such as the H23, were used as combined transports and paratroop carriers instead of bombers. An interesting variant was the He111Z, 12 of which were built, and which consisted of two He111H-6 machines joined together by a new wing section which carried a fifth Jumo 211 engine. This unusual edifice was used as a tug aircraft for the Messerschmitt Me321 Gigant glider.

Two genuine Heinkel He111s are known to exist, an He-111E, B2-82, is preserved at the Spanish Air Force Museum, Quatro Vientos, Madrid, and, an H-23 transport version, survives and is displayed at the Battle of Britain Museum, Hendon. Several Spanish-built CASA 2111 derivatives powered by Rolls-Royce Merlin engines are displayed in Europe and America, one of which is at the Historic Aircraft Museum, Southend Airport, Essex.

Heinkel He162   Germany

Photo: Wk Nr 120227 is preserved at RAF St Athan, South Wales.

Powerplant: One BMW 003E-1 or -2 turbojet rated at 1,764lb st for take-off
Span: 23ft 7.5in
Length: 29ft 8.3in
Height: 8ft 6.3in
Wing area: 120.5sq ft

The He162 'Volksjager' or People's Fighter was one of the most remarkable aircraft of the last war. Conceived as a last-ditch weapon in the closing stages of the war the He162 was flown within 90 days of work starting on Heinkel's Projekt 1073. The aircraft was lightly built from non-strategic materials and designed for construction in large numbers by unskilled labour; the fuselage was a light metal monocoque with a plywood nose cap and the one-piece wing was mainly of wood with detachable

downturned tips. The BMW 003 turbojet was mounted on top of the fuselage and attached by just three bolts, the exhaust gases ejecting between the twin fins and rudders of the tail assembly.

The He162 V1 prototype first flew on 6 December 1944 and attained a speed of 522mph at almost 20,000ft, the flight was brought to an abrupt end when an undercarriage door tore away due to faulty construction but on the whole the flight proved satisfactory. Four days later it was destroyed when the leading edge of the starboard wing failed in flight. The story was to repeat itself during the type's short career and in the event very few were encountered on operations. Several He162s were brought over to the UK and USA for evaluation after the war and two survive in this country, 120235 is preserved with the Imperial War Museum and 120227 with the RAF Museum Regional Collection at St Athan, South Wales.

Ilyushin Il-2 Shturmovik   USSR

Photo: Ilyushin Il-2M3 in the Polish Army Museum, Warsaw.
Data: Il-2M3

Powerplant: One 1,6Q0hp Mikulin AM-38F
Span: 47ft 10in
Length: 38ft
Max speed: 257mph at 6,560ft

The Il-2 was designed with ground attack and anti-tank operations in mind in the aftermath of the 1938 Munich Crisis and Soviet Intelligence reports of mass production of tanks and armoured vehicles in Germany. The first two prototypes were two-seaters and both were beset with problems but the third prototype, the TsKB-57, was a single-seater. This version was fitted with the 1,600hp AM-38 engine, the space for a second crew member was replaced with an additional fuel tank, it carried greater armour

protection for the pilot and had a much greater weapons-carrying capacity. Following State Acceptance Trials the type was ordered into production in March 1941 and the first batch of pre-production aircraft was rushed into service to combat the German invasion which began the following June. The type proved so successful that Stalin sent a telegram to the Ilyushin plant which read, 'The Red Army needs the Il-2 as much as it needs bread!'

Service use showed that the type was vulnerable to attack from the rear and as a result a two-seater appeared in 1942 in which the second crew member was armed with a 12.7mm gun for rearward defence. This model was extremely successful and led to a much improved derivative known as the Il-10 which continued in service with the Air Forces of the Eastern Bloc well into the 1950s.

Junkers Ju86K-4

Germany

Powerplants: Two 820hp Nohab-built Bristol Pegasus III radials
Span: 73ft 9.75in
Length: 58ft 7.5in
Height: 16ft 7.25in
Wing area: 882.64sq ft

The Ju86 was designed to the same specification as the Heinkel He111 in that it was intended as a fast, twin-engined all metal transport aircraft with the capability of being rapidly converted into a bomber should the need arise. The prototype flew at Dessau on 4 November 1934, four months ahead of its rival, and was seen to be a departure from the traditional Junkers corrugated, multi-spar construction technique in that it boasted smooth skinning and a two spar wing. The A series was the bomber variant and the B series the transport variant.

In the event the type was found to suffer from considerable handling problems and the Heinkel product was adopted for mass production for the Luftwaffe, the Ju86 being assigned to the transport role and later for use as a trainer and (Ju86P) high-altitude reconnaissance aircraft.

Overseas interest in the type was high at first and the K and Z suffixes were assigned to export bomber and transport variants respectively. The Swedish Air Force took delivery of a number of variously-powered K models, some of which were assembled in Sweden under German supervision, and a small number were wholly-built in Sweden by the SAAB concern under the designation Ju86K-13 (locally known as B3Cs or B3Ds.).

After the war the Swedish aircraft soldiered on as 12-seat transports until the mid-1950s and one aircraft, serial Fv155, is preserved with the Flygvapnets Flygmuseum at Malmslätt, west of Linköping, which is open on Sundays during the months of August and September.

Junkers Ju87 Stuka

Germany

Powerplant: One 1,400hp Junkers Jumo 211-1
Span: 49ft 2.5in
Length: 37ft 8.75in
Height: 12ft 9.25in
Wing area: 362.6sq ft

The infamous Stuka — an abbreviation for Sturzkampfflugzeug, a term meaning dive bomber — probably shares the honours with the Bf109 as being the most widely remembered German aircraft of World War 2. Its reputation was already made when it was unleashed upon the south coast of Britain

during the Battle of Britain but it was a myth which was soon exploded. It had swept across the relatively undefended skies of Poland, France and the Low Countries with comparative ease but it was more than vanquished by the Hurricanes and Spitfires of Fighter Command which found its ugly, cumbersome bulk easy prey.

Once its vulnerability in its designed role as a dive bomber was uncovered the Junkers designers came up with specialised versions such as the D-3 and D-4 for ground attack duties, the G was an anti-tank conversion of the long-span D-5, fitted with two 37mm cannon and the Ju87H was a two-seat trainer.

As with very many other Luftwaffe aircraft the Stuka was kept in operational service well past its time and was really obsolescent by the middle of the

war, there was however no suitable alternative owing to poor forward planning on the part of the German Air Ministry, by the time production ceased in 1944 some 5,000 had been built in various sub-types, two of which survive today.

A Ju87B is displayed in the Experimental Aircraft Association's Museum at Hales Corner, Wisconsin, USA and a Ju87G-2 converted from a D-5 is displayed at the Battle of Britain Museum, Hendon.

Junkers Ju88   Germany

Photo: Wk Nr 360043 a radar-equipped Ju88R-1 is preserved at Hendon.
Data: Ju88R-1

Powerplants: Two 1,700hp BMW 801MA radials
Span: 65ft 7.5in
Length: 47ft 1.3in
Height: 16ft 7.5in
Wing area: 586.63sq ft

The Ju88 was one of the most outstanding medium twins on either side during World War 2 and was a design which lent itself to considerable numbers of modifications and conversions, in this respect it was comparable to the de Havilland Mosquito.

The prototype flew in December 1936, only 11 months after design work had commenced, and was powered by a pair of 900hp DB600 in-line engines within annular cowlings. Production of the bomber series, the A series, began in 1938 and the Ju88A-1 was in service at the outbreak of war in 1939. Further development continued throughout the conflict in order to keep the aircraft competitive and both wingspan and engine power were increased in order to increase both the bomb load and the

number of guns carried. Parallel with the A series was the B series which never achieved full production status, although the streamlined nose of the B-1 appeared on the developed Ju188 which entered production as the E-1 during 1941. The final bomber versions were the S series which featured a smooth nose, no ventral gondola and reduced bomb load and defensive armament, they were powered by the BMW 801G radial of 1,700hp.

The fighter versions were the C series which were distinguished from the bombers by virtue of their solid noses which carried three 7.9mm guns plus a 20mm cannon with two more 20mms in a detachable mounting beneath the nose. The D series was comparable to the A-4 bomber and was intended as a long-range reconnaissance version while the G was a specialist night-fighter which entered service in 1944 and which carried an extra crew member to operate its radar equipment. The H series was characterised by a stretched fuselage of 58ft, the H-1 being a recce version and the H-2 a fighter, several of these aircraft were used as the lower half of the Mistel composite, a 'piggyback' Focke Wulf Fw190 guiding the explosive-packed 88s on their final missions.

A total of over 15,000 Ju88s was built of which two survive, together with a single Ju 388: Ju88D-1, Wk Nr 880430650 is preserved at the US Air Force Museum, Wright-Patterson AFB, Ohio; and Ju88R-1 360043, a radar-equipped night-fighter, is exhibited at the Battle of Britain Museum, Hendon. The 388 is exhibited at the Smithsonian Institution's storage and restoration centre at Silver Hill, Maryland, USA.

Kawasaki N1K2-J Shiden — Japan

Photo: Shiden 62387 is displayed by the US Air Force Museum at Wright-Patterson AFB, Ohio, it was donated by the City of San Diego in 1959.

Powerplant: One 1,990hp Nakajima Homare 21
Span: 39ft 4in
Length: 30ft 8in
Height: 13ft
Max speed: 369mph at 18,370ft

The Shiden (Violet Lightning), known to the Allies as 'George 21' was a formidable land-based naval fighter which appeared in the later stages of the war and of which only 428 were completed. Its history was complex as it was conceived as a simplified version of the N1K1-J ('George 11') which itself was a land-based derivative of the N1K1 ('Rex') floatplane fighter of 1942.

As with many Japanese fighters the Shiden possessed an excellent rate of climb and was supremely manoeuvrable, it incorporated only two-thirds the structural components of its predecessor, from which it varied chiefly in its low-set rather than mid-set mainplane. The fuselage was also streamlined and lengthened whilst the fin and rudder were both reshaped. The first prototype flew on 31 December 1943 but production was severely hampered by the escalating level of B-29 bombing raids on the eight factories assigned to its production.

Three N1K2-Js have survived together with three N1K1 Kyofus. The Shidens are preserved at the Tucson Air Museum, the US Air Force Museum and at NAS Willow Grove, all in the USA while one Kyofu is also displayed at Willow Grove, another at Frederiksburg, Texas, and the third in store at Silver Hill.

Kawasaki Ki61-11 Hien — Japan

Photo: K161-II preserved at the Kotsu Transportation Museum.
Data: Ki61-IC

Powerplant: One 1,175hp Kawasaki Ha40
Span: 39ft 4in
Length: 29ft 4in
Height: 12ft 1.75in
Max speed: 348mph at 16,400ft

Known to the Allies as 'Tony' the Hien (Flying Swallow) was unusual as it was the first fighter to serve with the Japanese Army Air Force to have an in-line, liquid cooled engine. The total absence of such types prior to the appearance of the Hien in operational squadrons, in the late summer of 1942, led to the initial belief that it was a licence-built derivate of the Messerschmitt Bf109. This theory was soon disproved although it was discovered that

the Kawasaki Ha40 engine was a light-weight adaptation of the DB601 and that early armament comprised German manufactured Mauser MG151 cannon.

The -I version remained in production from 1942 until early 1945 whilst the -II made its appearance in the late autumn of 1942, powered by the 1,500hp Ha140 this version also featured a larger wing and a changed cockpit canopy. Problems with the engine limited production of the -II to only eight and a total re-design was needed before the Ki61-IIa and -IIb entered production. The final derivative eventually appeared as the Ki100 which is described separately.

One Ki61 is known to be exhibited at the Kotsu Transportation Museum in Tokyo and it is believed to be a -II derivative, the exact model is unknown.

Kawasaki Ki100-1b Japan

Photo: The sole surviving Ki100-1b seen undergoing restoration in the colours of the 5th Fighter Squadron at the Aerospace Museum, RAF Cosford.

Powerplant: One 1,500hp Mitsubishi Ha112-II Type 4
Span: 39ft 4.25in
Length: 27ft 9in
Max speed: 367mph at 32,800ft

With increasing American attacks on the Japanese islands the manufacturing industry was being hit harder and one factory to fall to the B-29 was the engine plant which produced the Ha140 for the Kawasaki Ki61-II. With some 270 airframes waiting for their engines it was decided to fit the readily-available Ha112-II radial instead and the first conversion was flown on 1 February 1945. The revised aircraft was designated Ki100-Ia and 256 had been assembled by the end of May 1945. The type was such a success that a refinement with a cut-down rear fuselage was introduced as the Ki100-Ib and 99 were built before the factory was destroyed in an American bombing raid. Employed mainly as a home-defence fighter the type had provision for the carriage of two 550lb bombs but with the lack of a supercharger it was found lacking in performance at high altitude. To counteract this problem several prototypes of the Ki100-II are known to have been built with a supercharged engine but this version never entered production.

The type was in service with the 5th, 17th, 59th, 111th and 244th Sentais and the sole survivor is preserved in the markings of the 5th Sentai (Fighter Squadron) which was based at Chefu and Yakkaichi although its actual history and serial are both unknown.

Lavochkin La-7   USSR

Photo: La-7 '77' on show at Prague-Kbely, Czechoslovakia.

Powerplant: One 1,775hp ASh-82FN
Span: 32ft 1.25in
Length: 27ft 10.75in
Height: 9ft 3in
Max speed: 413mph

The La-7 appeared in 1943 as a development of the earlier La-5AV, it was powered by the 1,775hp ASh-83FN radial and armed with three 20mm cannon — one firing through the propeller boss and the other two mounted within the top cowlings. The basic design could be traced back to the I-22 of 1939 which in modified form had entered production as the LaGG-1 in 1940, this aircraft had a comparatively short life and was replaced by the LaGG-3 the following year. This fighter was of all-wooden construction, was very rugged but was considered to be lacking in manoeuvrability. The La-5 appeared early in 1942 as the result of the decision to boost the performance of the LaGG-3 by the installation of the 1,600hp ASh-82A radial engine in place of the 1,100hp Klimov M-105

in-line. The earliest versions retained the built-up rear fuselage of the -3 but the La-5FN of 1943 introduced the cut-down fuselage and other refinements, the La-7 being a generally 'cleaned-up' derivative with a top speed of 413mph.

One La-7 is known to survive and this is displayed at the Letecka Expozice Vojenskeho Muzea at Prague-Kbely, Czechoslovakia.

Lockheed 414 Hudson   USA

Photo: The RAF Museum's Hudson IV, A16-199/G-BEOX.
Data: Hudson IV

Powerplants: Two 1,200hp Pratt & Whitney Twin Wasp S3C4-G two row radials
Span: 65ft 6in
Length: 44ft 4in
Height: 11ft 10.5in
Wing area: 551sq ft

The Hudson was a military adaptation of the Model 14 Super Electra airliner which was produced in response to an enquiry from the British Purchasing Commission in June 1938. Lockheed produced the layouts in such a quick time that they won a contract for 200 Hudsons to replace the Anson I in Coastal Command service. At the time the order was considered controversial as it was thought to be a slap in the face for the British aircraft industry.

The first Hudsons were delivered by sea to

Liverpool in February 1939 and the Mk I entered service with No 224 Sqn at Gosport that summer. The Model 14 was already familiar as it was in service with British Airways Ltd and the Hudson differed only in the provision of nose glazing, twin machine guns in the nose, a ventral bomb bay and accommodation for a Boulton Paul turret in the rear fuselage. By November 1940 deliveries were reaching a peak and the first trans-Atlantic ferry flight was successfully accomplished by seven Hudson IIIs which arrived at Aldergrove on 11 November after a 10½hr delivery flight from Gander.

As the war progressed the Hudson was replaced in Coastal Command and relegated to air-sea rescue and transport duties, being the first aircraft to carry an airborne lifeboat although from 1942 onwards the type was assigned to No 161 Sqn, Tempsford, for its clandestine operations with the SOE and was frequently used for night-landings in occupied France.

Over 800 Hudsons of various Marks were delivered against British contracts before it became available on Lend-Lease, it was also used by the USAAF, under the designations A-28, A-29 and AT-18, whilst the US Navy used an anti-submarine version in the Caribbean known as the PBO-1. The Royal Australian Air Force used large numbers of Hudsons and one of these, Hudson IV serial A16-199, was flown to the UK in 1973 to join the Strathallan Aircraft Collection, but despite its being registered G-BEOX it never flew again and in July 1981 it was sold to the RAF Museum and has since been moved by road to Hendon.

Lockheed Model 18 Lodestar, Ventura and Harpoon USA

Data: Ventura II

Powerplants: Two 2,000hp Pratt & Whitney Double Wasp GR2800 S1A4-G
Span: 65ft 6in
Length: 51ft 2.5in
Height: 11ft 10.5in
Wing area: 551sq ft

The Loadstar transport was introduced in September 1939 as a stretched version of the Super Electra with more power and a bigger payload. With the prospect of war on the horizon the Army Air Corps took delivery of over half the 625 aircraft produced as C-60 military transports and in the summer of 1940 a contract was received for a bomber derivative for the Royal Air Force which was designated Ventura.

Compared with the earlier Hudson the Ventura had the dorsal turret moved forward to give a better field of fire, the underside was re-profiled to incorporate a ventral gun position behind the bomb bay and more powerful Double Wasp engines replaced the Wright Cyclones of the Hudson I. Although 675 were ordered for the RAF deliveries were late, commencing in mid-1942, and ceased after the 394th aircraft as experience on daylight operations with Bomber Command had shown that the type was not particularly suited to its designed role. The Ventura was withdrawn from Bomber Command in 1943 and diverted to Coastal Command where the GRI and GR5 were used on general reconnaissance and meteorological flights.

Large numbers were used by Commonwealth air forces and the basic type was also delivered to the USAAF as the B-34 Lexington and the US Navy as the PV-1 and PV-2 Harpoon.

Lockheed P-38 Lightning

USA

Span: 52ft
Length: 37ft 10in
Max speed: 414mph

One of the most distinctive aircraft to see combat during World War 2, the P-38 was eventually built in a total of 18 different versions and production ended after 9,924 had been constructed.

Initial layouts were prepared in 1935 but the design did not commence in earnest until the Army Air Corps held a fighter competition in 1937. Lockheed's unorthodox entry was the winner and the prototype flew in January 1939 and entered service in mid-1941. 143 were ordered for the Royal Air Force in March 1940 and the first was delivered in December 1941, however an embargo on the supply of superchargers for the Allison engines meant that the performance of the British machines was inferior and the type was rejected for RAF service and handed back to the USAAF as the P-322.

The Lightning won fame as a long range escort fighter accompanying the daylight bombers of the 8th Air Force over occupied Europe although it met with considerable success in the Pacific Theatre and was also used in the light bomber and photo-reconnaissance role. In the latter role the nose was greatly enlarged to carry camera gear and the designation was changed to F-5.

Several Lightnings remain in flying condition in the USA together with a number displayed statically in museums.

Photo: This P-38, named *Scatterbrain Kid*, was flown by the Confederate Air Force but has since been destroyed in a fatal accident.
Data: P-38L

Powerplants: Two 1,475hp Allison V-12 supercharged

Macchi MC202 Folgore

Italy

Photo: The MC202 Folgore exhibited in realistic pose in the National Air & Space Museum, Washington, DC, USA.

Powerplant: One 1,200hp licence-built Daimler-Benz DB601N
Span: 34ft 9in
Length: 29ft 0.3in
Height: 9ft 10in
Max speed: 369mph at 17,056ft

The Folgore (Thunderbolt) was a straightforward conversion of the existing MC200 Saetta (Lightning) airframe to accept the more powerful, low-drag, liquid cooled Daimler-Benz DB601 engine in place of the bulky and low powered Fiat A74RC38 radial which had handicapped this otherwise excellent fighter. The first Folgore was a converted Saetta and flew in August 1940, flight testing was very encouraging and the decision was taken to put the DB601 into licence production and adapt the Saetta

to take it, the first aircraft entering squadron service with the Regia Aeronautica during 1942.

The performance and armament of the Folgore was far superior to its predecessor and was, in fact, not far short of the best Allied fighters of the time and it was in an effort to boost performance that the Macchi company produced the DB605A-powered MC205V Veltro (Greyhound) in 1943. Structurally identical to the Folgore this aircraft benefited from the extra horsepower available but appeared too late to have any real effect against the Allied forces.

Armed with two 20mm wing cannon and two 12.7mm nose machine guns the Veltro could also carry two 330lb bombs in the fighter-bomber role.

Examples of all three types survive in the Italian Air Force Museum at Vigna di Valle, near Rome, and one MC202 is exhibited in the National Air & Space Museum, Washington, DC, USA. One Veltro, MM92214, has been restored to flying condition by a team of engineers from Aermacchi and made its maiden flight on 24 April 1981, it is believed to be the only flyable World War 2 Italian aircraft.

Martin B-26 Marauder   USA

Photo: The US Air Force Museum displays B-26G, 43-34581, which was obtained from the Air France training school near Paris in June 1965.
Data: B-26G

Powerplants: Two 2,000hp Pratt & Whitney Double Wasp R-2800-43
Span: 71ft
Length: 57ft 6in
Height: 20ft
Wing area: 664sq ft

The B-26 medium bomber was designed for the USAAF and made its first flight on 25 November 1940, its design showing such promise that 1,131 had already been ordered the previous September. Combat missions were started in the South-West Pacific in the spring of 1942 but most Marauders were subsequently assigned to the European and Middle Eastern areas.

Operating with the US Ninth Air Force from bases in south-east England and East Anglia the Marauder was used from medium altitudes of 10,000-15,000ft and enjoyed the lowest attrition rate of any Allied bomber — less than 0.5%. By the end of the war the type had flown more than 110,000 sorties and had dropped 150,000 tons of bombs.

The Marauder was also delivered to both the Royal Air Force and the South African Air Force which used them exclusively in the Mediterranean area, aircraft of the Desert Air Force being used in direct support of the Allied forces invading Sicily, Sardinia and Italy. Although originally dubbed something of a 'hot ship' the Marauder was honed into a fine fighting aircraft which was capable of withstanding considerable amounts of punishment.

Six Marauders are known to exist today, all but one of them in the USA. The National Air & Space Museum has a B-26B, 41-31773 *Flak Bait*; the Confederate Air Force has a B-26C, N5546N, which was in flying condition until recently; the USAF Museum has a B-26G, 43-34581; and Yesterday's Air Force is restoring two crashed aircraft at Chino, California. One ex-French Air Force B-26 is stored at Villacoublay for the Musee de l'Air.

Messerschmitt Bf109

Germany

Photo: This Bf109E-4 Wk Nr 4101 made a wheels-up landing at Manston on 27 November 1940. It is now preserved at the Battle of Britain Museum, Hendon.
Data: Bf109E-4

Powerplant: One Daimler-Benz DB601A rated at 1,175hp for take-off.
Span: 32ft 4.5in
Length: 28ft 4.5in
Height: 8ft 2.3in
Wing area: 176.53sq ft

Undoubtedly the most famous German aircraft of World War 2, the Messerschmitt Bf109 flew in prototype form in September 1935 and remained in continuous production until the German surrender in 1945. The prototype was powered by an imported Rolls-Royce Kestrel of 695hp but subsequent machines were powered by the 610hp Jumo 210A, 635hp Jumo 210D (Bf109B-1) and eventually the 1,100hp Daimler-Benz DB601A (Bf109E).

As with most German military types of the period the early 109s were used by the Condor Legion in the Spanish Civil War and it was experience in this campaign which led to the development of the Bf109E which replaced all previous versions and became the standard German fighter for the first three years of the war. Despite its Spanish trials the E was outclassed by the Spitfire — although fairly evenly matched with the Hurricane — and was switched to defensive rather than offensive missions in the form of the Bf109F (1,200hp DB601N) which was recognised by its more streamlined fuselage and

reduced armament. With the development of the later G model the Fs were modified to mount underwing rocket projectiles and returned to the fray as ground attack aircraft.

The Bf109G Gustav appeared in the summer of 1942, was powered by the DB605 engine, and can be considered as the definitive version as it was eventually built in greater numbers than all the other models combined. Sub-types went as far as the G-12 and varied greatly in armament, engine, photographic equipment and other details such as pressurised cockpits.

The H was an abandoned high-altitude version, the K was similar to the G but for minor structural changes, the L was a long-span version fitted with a Jumo 213 engine which only reached the project stage and the T was a navalised version fitted with increased wing area and other modifications.

Spanish-built versions of the 109 continued to be built into the 1950s by Hispano Aviacion SA and the last of these Merlin-engined fighters were not withdrawn until the early 1960s, many being used in the fim *The Battle of Britain* alongside Spanish-built Heinkel He111 bombers. At least 12 genuine Bf109s are known to exist worldwide with no less than four in the UK. E-3 1190 is under restoration at Hurn airport, E-4 4101 is exhibited in the Battle of Britain Museum, Hendon, G-2 10639 is under restoration at Northolt — possibly to flying condition, and 'FE-124', believed to be a 109K, is being restored at Blackbushe. In Germany, MBB have restored an HA 1112M1L to near-109G standard as D-FMBB and this flew on 23 April 1982.

Messerschmitt Bf110G-4   Germany

Photo: The sole surviving Bf110 is exhibited in the Battle of Britain Museum, Hendon.
Data: Bf110G-4d/R-3

Powerplants: Two Daimler-Benz DB605B-1 rated at 1,475hp for take-off
Span: 53ft 3.75in
Length: 42ft 9.75in
Height: 13ft 8.5in
Wing area: 413.334sq ft

Conceived as a strategic fighter, the Bf110 was intended to have a high performance, mount heavy armament and be able to act as a long range bomber escort as well as maintain standing patrols far from base and carry out deep-penetration offensive raids into enemy territory. Unfortunately the 110 fell foul of the far more nimble Hurricanes and Spitfires during the Battle of Britain and ended up being itself escorted by Bf109Es! This rather abysmal start tended to give the 110 a 'failed' label in Allied eyes

but in fact it was in continuous service throughout the war and went through six major production variants from B to G. In its numerous roles the 110 was a competent aircraft and deserves far more credit than it generally afforded.

As a result of the delay experienced in obtaining suitable powerplants the 110 did not partake in the Spanish Civil War and was therefore at a disadvantage when compared with some of its German contemporaries. The Bf110C first saw active service in the Polish campaign where it was used in the ground attack role in support of the advancing troops but with its failure against the British fighters in 1940 it was adapted to other roles including bomber interception and as a long-range fighter. It was really to find its forté as a night-fighter and with the F-4 and later models such as the G-4 it was extensively used in this role. The surviving aircraft is an example of a radar-equipped night-fighter, the Bf110G-4d/R-3, this particular type being the last G series night-fighter to be produced.

Messerschmitt Me163B Komet   Germany

Photo: Wk Nr 191904 is part of the RAF Museum Collection and is displayed at St Athan.
Data: Me163B-1a

Powerplant: One 3,750lb thrust Walter HWK 509A-2 bi-fuel rocket motor
Span: 30ft 7.3in
Length: 19ft 2.3in
Height: 9ft 0.6in
Wing area: 199.132sq ft

The Me163 was one of the most unorthodox aircraft to see service on either side during World War 2. A rocket-powered interceptor, its origins lay in a prewar experimental project and the first prototype flew as early as August 1941 but extensive delays with the development programme meant that the first operational Me163Bs were not encountered until 28 July 1944 when five aircraft of 1/JG 400 attacked a formation of B-17s in the vicinity of Merseburg.

The high speed of the Me163B and poor armament meant that the pilots had less than three seconds to operate their cannon before they had to break away from their targets, this meant that new tactics had to be devised if they were to have any hope of pressing home an attack. The Komet also had an unendearing habit of bursting into flames on touch-down and more were lost in this way than in combat.

With further development the Komet could have had a devastating effect upon Allied daylight raids, but with the turning tide of the European war, time was not on Germany's side and the aircraft was of little consequence.

Ten Komets exist in museums in the UK, USA, and Germany, the British examples numbering five which are exhibited at Duxford, Cosford, St Athan, the Science Museum and the Royal Scottish Museum of Flight, East Fortune.

Messerschmitt Me262 Germany

Photo: Me262A-1a Wk Nr 112372 preserved at RAF Cosford, Staffordshire.
Data: Me262A-1a

Powerplants: Two 1,980lb thrust Junkers Jumo 004B-1-2 or 3 turbojets
Span: 40ft 11.5in
Length: 34ft 9.5in
Height: 12ft 7in
Wing area: 234sq ft

The Me262 will for ever be remembered as the first jet aircraft to gain operational status, this distinction being awarded to the Test Detachment which was formed at Lechfeld in April 1944 under the command of Hauptmann Thierfelder. Known as EKdo262, it had claimed two P-38s and a Mosquito before final confirmation of its operational status was obtained on 25 July 1944, two days before

No 616 Sqn, RAF, received clearance for its Diver patrols against V-1 flying bombs.

Conceived in 1938 as a test vehicle with operational potential, the Me262 was designed around the new BMW P3302 axial-flow turbojet then under development. The first engines should have been available by December 1939 but as the 003, as it was designated, had run into serious difficulties the Junkers Jumo 004 was selected as an alternative powerplant. This too encountered problems and the decision was taken to complete the first Me262 prototype with two Walter rocket motors; in the event this idea was abandoned and the Me262 V1 made its maiden flight on the power of a Junkers Jumo 210G 12-cylinder liquid-cooled engine which was mounted in the nose.

There has been much said about the revolutionary Me262 which would suggest that with more official backing and with less meddling from the Führer it

could have turned the tide of aerial superiority in favour of the Luftwaffe once more. With the benefit of hindsight it now seems clear that the type could not have entered service any sooner than it did, owing to insuperable delays in the powerplant development programme, and that it finally fell victim to the decay which was well set into the Third Reich by the summer of 1944.

Conceived as an interceptor the Me262A-1 series began to leave the production lines in May 1944 but Hitler demanded that the type be produced as a bomber and as a result it suffered considerable delays before entry into service in a role to which it was totally unsuited. The fighter-bomber was known as the Me262A-2, the first examples leaving the lines in July 1944 and carrying two 551lb or one 1,102lb bomb. Of over 1,400 built probably only 100 actually saw service, other variants included the Me262B-1 dual-control trainer, the B-2 two-seat night-fighter, the Me262C with rocket booster and the 262D and E rocket-armed bomber interceptors.

Eight Me262s survive plus one Czechoslovakian-built Avia S92, six are single-seaters and two are two-seaters, the S92 being equivalent to an Me262A-1. One Me262A-1, Wk Nr 112372, is preserved in the Aerospace Museum, RAF Cosford.

Messerschmitt Me410   Germany

Photo: Wk Nr 420430 is part of the RAF Museum Collection and is displayed at the Aerospace Museum, RAF Cosford.
Data: Me410A-1/U2

Powerplants: Two Daimler-Benz DB603A rated at 1,750hp at take-off
Span: 53ft 7.5in
Length: 40ft 11.5in
Height: 14ft 0.5in
Wing area: 389.687sq ft

The 410 was the final development of the earlier 210 which had displayed such poor flying qualities that Messerschmitt's Chief Test Pilot, Fritz Wendel, had said that it had all the least desirable attributes an aeroplane could possess. The 210 was unstable both longitudinally and directionally, it had a very violent stall and at low airspeeds was liable to flick into a spin without the least warning.

Following extensive redesigning the type re-emerged as the 410 Hornisse in the latter part of 1943, the revised type possessed none of the vices of its predecessor and was spinproof. It also showed a considerable advance over the elderly Bf110 which it was intended to replace.

The Me410 was quite widely used, although total production — including Me210 conversions — only amounted to some 1,900 aircraft; it was used in a number of roles including fighter, fighter-bomber, photo-reconnaissance and torpedo-bomber. The principal sub-types were the A-1 fighter-bomber, the A1/U2 and A-2 'heavy' fighters and the A-3 photo-recce aircraft. Two A-1 fighter-bombers survive, Wk Nr 420430 is preserved at the Aerospace Museum, RAF Cosford, and another example 'FE-499' is stored by the National Air & Space Museum at Silver Hill, Maryland, USA.

Miles M38 Messenger UK

Photo: Messenger 2A G-AIEK was converted to look like a Messenger I in 1973 and flown as 'RG333' in the markings of an aircraft used by Field Marshal Lord Montgomery. It is now being rebuilt at Bristol.
Data: Messenger I

Powerplant: One 145hp DH Gipsy Major 1D
Span: 36ft 2in
Length: 24ft
Height: 7ft 6in
Wing area: 191sq ft

The Messenger was a development of George Miles' M28 Mercury which was intended for Air Observation Post duties in the light of discussion with several army officers who were not satisfied with the Taylorcraft Austers then in use. The Messenger prototype was built in some secrecy as a private venture and made its first flight from Woodley on 12 September 1942. Characteristically the authorities were not pleased with the Miles brothers unconventional approach and despite the type's excellent short-field performance it was not adopted for its intended AOP role. Instead some 21 were built to Spec 17/43 for light liaison and communication duties as the Gipsy Major-powered Messenger I.

Following the end of hostilities the Messenger was produced as a civil aircraft, powered by the Blackburn Cirrus Major 3 and designated Messenger 2A. Production continued at Woodley and Newtownards until the company's demise in the winter of 1947-48 and ex-RAF Messenger Is were declared redundant in 1948 to become Messenger 4As after civilianisation.

Eighteen Messengers are known to survive in the UK in varying states of preservation, three of which are ex-RAF Mk 4As; these are G-AKVZ (ex-RH427) under reconstruction at Biggin Hill, G-ALAH (ex-RH377) stored with the RAF Museum at Henlow, and VP-KJL (ex-RH371 and G-ALAR) the fuselage of which is stored by the Midland Air Museum at Baginton.

Mitsubishi A6M Zero-Sen Japan

Photo: The only truly authentic flyable Zero is this aircraft which is part of Ed Maloney's Planes of Fame museum at Chino Airport, California.
Data: A6M5b

Powerplant: One 1,130hp Nakajima Sakae 21
Span: 36ft 1in
Length: 29ft 9in
Height: 9ft 2in
Max speed: 351mph at 19,685ft

The Zero fighter stands out in the Pacific Theatre as did the Messerschmitt Bf109 or Focke-Wulf Fw190 in the European. It was a formidable opponent and one which outstripped all other Japanese types at the time of its introduction in 1939. Built in a variety of sub-types in order to keep it abreast of development, the Zero's production run ended after 10,611 had been built, of which Mitsubishi built 3,879 and Nakajima 6,215.

Two A6M1 prototypes, powered by the lightweight 780hp Mitsubishi Zuisei 13, were built and the type's maiden flight was on 1 April 1939, both had been accepted by the Japanese Navy by the end of the year. The third prototype was powered by the 925hp Nakajima Sakae 12 and was designated A6M2. 64 were built as Model 11s, some seeing service in China, before production was switched to the Model 21 which featured folding wingtips and of which 740 were eventually manufactured. A two-seat trainer, designated A6M2-K, was built by the Hitachi and Sasebo factories but the next major production variant was the A6M3 powered by the 1,130hp Sakae 21. This eventually entered production as the Model 32 with the folding wingtips removed to give clipped wings, it become operational in 1942 and 343 were built by Mitsubishi plus a further 560 full-span Model 22s.

The major production variant was the A6M5 which appeared during 1943 as the Model 52. This

type featured the clipped-wing of the Model 32 but with the tips rounded off, and the Sakae 21 engine was boosted to push the top speed up to 358mph, sub-types included the 5a, 5b and 5c, which varied in the firepower and armour protection fitted, whilst the A6M5-K trainer only reached the testing stage. The A6M6, powered by the Sakae 32, was rejected as sub-standard but a further adaptation of the basic type produced the A6M7 which was entering production in the spring of 1945. The final variant, only two prototypes of which were flown, was the A6M8 which was powered by Mitsubishi's own 1,560hp Kinsei 62 radial.

At least 11 Zeros survive together with parts of others and several examples have been or are in the process of being recovered from abandoned Pacific airfields and other sites. Amongst the museums which display complete aircraft are the Planes of Fame Museum, California; Auckland Institute & Museum, New Zealand; the Marine Corps Museum, Quantico, Virginia; the National Air & Space Museum, Washington, DC; and the San Diego Aerospace Museum. The cockpit and centre-section of an A6M5 is displayed at the Imperial War Museum, London.

Mitsubishi J2M3 Raiden   Japan

Photo: The only Raiden known to exist is on show in the Planes of Fame museum at Chino Airport, California.

Powerplant: One 1,820hp Mitsubishi Kasei 23a
Span: 35ft 5in
Length: 31ft 10in
Max speed: 371mph at 19,360ft

First flown as a prototype on 20 March 1942 the Raiden was basically a good design but it was plagued with production, structural and powerplant difficulties which combined to prevent the manufacture of more than about 500. The three J2M1 prototypes were powered by the 1,460hp Kasei 13 and were followed by 155 Kasei 23-powered J2M2s armed with two 20mm cannon and

two 7.7mm machine guns. The J2M3 featured four 20mm cannon and no machine guns whilst only two J2M4 high-altitude versions were built, these featuring a turbo-charged engine and six-cannon armament.

The J2M5 was flown in May 1944, it was powered by the 1,820hp Kasei 26 and armed with two 20mm cannon, its top speed was in the region of 380mph but only 30-40 were built. The J2M6 and M7 were modifications of earlier models, the M6 being an M3 with a revised canopy and the M7 being an M2 powered by the Kasei 26.

One Raiden is known to survive, this being a J2M3, serial 3014, which is maintained by Ed Maloney's Planes of Fame museum at Chino, California, USA.

Mitsubishi Ki46-III   Japan

Photo: Believed to be serial No 5439 the St Athan 'Dinah' is officially known as 8484M and BAPC-84.

Powerplants: Two 1,500hp Mitsubishi Ha112-II
Span: 48ft 2in
Length: 37ft 8.25in
Height: 10ft 10in
Max speed: 395mph

Known to the Allies as 'Dinah' the Ki46 was produced as a fast reconnaissance type to a Japanese Army specification, in whose service it was known as the Type 100. Technically and aerodynamically it was a superb aeroplane and was so far in advance of Allied fighters that the single defensive machine gun was soon dispensed with. The prototype flew in November 1939 and was powered by the 850hp Mitsubishi Ha26-I radial, this engine was also used in the first production aircraft which had a top speed of 312mph at 26,250ft. The Ha102 was introduced with the Ki46-II which became the principal operational version and which had a top speed of 375mph at 19,000ft, the performance of this version was so good that a German technical mission assessed it with a view to licence production of the type!

The final major version was the Ki46-III, one of which survives, this was distinguished from the earlier models by its smooth glazed nose and cockpit which gave an unbroken line to the fuselage; the IIIA was the basic reconnaissance model whilst the IIIKAI was a solid-nosed interceptor and the IIIB a ground-attack version. Production of all types reached a total of 1,738 which included three Ki46-IVAs which featured exhaust-driven superchargers, the ground-attack IVB was not produced.

The surviving aircraft is thought to have been in service with the Japanese 81st Reconnaissance Group in Burma where it was probably captured and later test-flown. It is known that it was flown at Farnborough and by the Empire Test Pilot's School and then put into storage at Fulbeck, Biggin Hill and Henlow before moving to St Athan where it was refurbished for static display with the RAF Museum Regional Collection

Noorduyn Norseman   Canada

Photo: Norseman IV, QT-787, preserved by the Canadian National Aeronautical Collection at Rockliffe.

Powerplant: One 600hp Pratt & Whitney R-1340-AN-1 or -S3H1 Wasp
Span: 51ft 8in
Length: 32ft 4in
Height: 10ft 1in
Wing area: 325sq ft

The Norseman was designed specifically for the exceptionally hard life of a 'bush-flyer' in Northern Canada where the aeroplane was the only convenient method of communication between scattered settlements. Fitted out either as a light freighter or 8-10 seat light transport the prototype flew in 1935 on the power of a Canadian Wright R-975-E3 and entered production in this form as the Norseman II. The Norseman IV appeared during 1937 and featured the more powerful 600hp Pratt & Whitney R-1340-S3H1 Wasp. This version entered service with the RCAF for radio and navigational training duties and was also adopted for the USAAF as the C-64A, 746 being delivered from 1942.

Noorduyn was taken over by Canadian Car & Foundry (CCF) in 1946 and the final production version, the Norseman V, remained in production until 1950.

North American AT-6 USA

Photo: 'FX301' is an AT-6 Harvard III, ex-EX915, SAAF7439 and FAP1502. It is civil-registered as G-JUDI and owned by Tony Haig-Thomas.
Data: T-6G

Powerplant: One 550hp Pratt & Whitney R-1340-AN-1
Span: 42ft 0.25in
Length: 29ft 6in
Height: 11ft 8.5in
Wing area: 253.7sq ft

Known to the American forces as the Texan and to the British as the Harvard, the AT-6 was a development of the NA-16 trainer prototype of 1937. Originally designated BC-1 in the Basic Combat classification the AT-6 Advanced Trainer designation was applied in 1940 when the earlier classification was discontinued and over 10,000 were eventually built both in the US and in Canada where the designation AT-16 was applied to distinguish locally-manufactured aircraft. The type was the standard allied advanced trainer and more allied airmen received their advanced training on it than on any other type.

It was one of the first American aircraft to be ordered for the RAF, the first examples entering service in December 1938, remaining standard equipment at Flying Training Schools for over 16 years, even after their withdrawal in 1955 the Harvard remained in service with University Air Squadrons and in an operational role against Mau Mau terrorists in Kenya. Two still serve with the Aircraft & Armaments Experimental Establishment at Boscombe Down.

After the war 2,068 were re-manufactured as T-6Gs and went into service with over 40 air forces, considerable numbers are still flying throughout the world and a considerable number of ex-Portuguese Air Force machines have recently appeared in private hands in the UK.

North American P-51 Mustang   USA

Photo: Two P-51Ds of the Confederate Air Force, Harlingen, Texas.
Data: P-51D

Powerplant: One 1,695hp Packard Merlin V-1650-7
Span: 37ft 0.25in
Length: 32ft 3in
Height: 8ft 8in
Wing area: 235sq ft

Probably the most widely-known American fighter of World War 2 the Mustang was unusual in that it was designed to a British specification. North American Aviation commenced design work in April 1940 following a visit from the British Purchasing Mission and the first prototype was built in just over 100 days, flying in September 1940. Powered by the 1,150 Allison V-1710-39 the Mustang's performance was far better than its American contemporaries, mainly due to the advanced aerodynamics which had been put into the design

such as the laminar-flow wing and aft-mounted radiator intake to ensure a smooth nose entry.

The first Mustangs were delivered to the RAF in November 1941 but despite an excellent performance at low and medium altitudes the type was handicapped by the lack of power from the Allison engine at higher altitudes and was intially used for ground attack duties, supplanting Tomahawks of Army Co-operation Command and entering service with No 2 Sqn in April 1942. The Allison-powered version was also used by the USAAF, initially in the ground-attack role where it was known as the A-36A Invader, but it was the installation of the Packard-built Rolls-Royce Merlin which realised the full potential of the type's advanced aerodynamics and produced the P-51C and P-51D which with their ultra-long range were to become the most versatile fighters in the USAAF inventory.

Although the Merlin-powered models were used by the RAF, as the Mustang Mks III and IV, the type was mainly operated by the USAAF as a long-range escort fighter for the B-17 and B-24 daylight formations and as a formidable strike fighter in its own right. The type remained in production after the end of the war and the final production versions were the P-51H and K which had redesigned fuselages and taller fins and rudders. Some of the more bizarre Mustang developments include the P-82 Twin Mustang in which a pair of standard aircraft, complete with pilots, was joined by a common centre-section for ultra-long range missions in the Pacific Theatre, and the Cavalier Mustang III which was powered by a Rolls-Royce Dart turboprop and intended as a low-budget strike aircraft for emerging nations of the Third World.

Many Mustangs survive world-wide including the XP-51 prototype, serial 41-038, which was restored to fly as N51NA by the Experimental Aircraft Association of the USA. In the UK several Mustangs are maintained at the Imperial War Museum's Duxford Airfield in Cambridgeshire, some of which are under restoration to flying condition, while Doug Arnold has P-51D G-PSID restored as a camouflaged RAF Mk IV at Blackbushe, Hants, and Steven Gray has N6340T based in Switzerland but frequently seen at UK air displays.

North American B-25 Mitchell   USA

Photo: TB-25J N94947 seen at Duxford after the filming of *Hanover Street* in 1978.
Data: B-25J

Powerplants: Two 1,700 Wright Cyclone R-2600-29
Span: 67ft 6.75in
Length: 52ft 11in
Height: 15ft 9.75in
Wing area: 610sq ft

Developed from the experimental NA-40 attack bomber of 1938 the first B-25 for the USAAC made its maiden flight on 19 August 1940. Sixty four B-25 and B-25As were delivered before the introduction of the B-25B in August 1941, this being the model which was to enter service with the Royal Air Force as the Mitchell Mk I. The B-25C or D was known in RAF service as the Mitchell Mk II while the Mitchell Mk III was the equivalent of the B-25J, this version being identified by the dorsal turret which was

moved forward to a position just behind the cockpit.

Probably the most famous Mitchell operation was that by General Doolittle's 16 'Tokyo Raiders' which were flown off the deck of the carrier USS *Hornet* to attack targets in Tokyo and elsewhere mainly as a morale-boosting exercise when the US was smarting after the attacks on Pearl Harbor and the Philippines.

The Mitchell had a long postwar career with many air forces, the Canadian Armed Forces operating one or two survivors into the 1960s but most of those flying today are either borate bombers or museum aircraft, one or two corporate executive conversions having been restored to semi-original condition. The Mitchell has also figured as a camera-ship for many aviation films and in 1978 several were to be seen in the UK for the filming of the movie *Hanover Street* one of which is still to be seen at Blackbushe, Hants, and which makes occasional air display appearances.

Two Mitchells are preserved in the UK; N7614C is a B-25J with the Imperial War Museum at Duxford and 'HD368'/N9089Z is a TB-25J with the Historic Aircraft Museum, Southend.

Northrop P-61 Black Widow

USA

Photo: P-61C, 43-8353, at the US Air Force Museum, Dayton, Ohio.

Powerplants: Two 2,100hp Pratt & Whitney R-2800
Span: 66ft
Length: 49ft 7in
Height: 14ft 7in
Max speed: 350mph

The Black Widow was the first American aircraft to be designed specifically as a night-fighter, making its maiden flight in 1942. Production examples appeared in 1943 and the type became operational with the US 9th Air Force from bases in the UK prior to the invasion of occupied Europe in June 1944. In the Pacific Theatre the Black Widow had the remarkable reputation that not one was lost to enemy action in over a year of combat.

The P-61 was notable in that it was the first night-fighter to carry a radar computer which automatically aimed, corrected and fired the four .50in calibre machine guns in its dorsal turret. A reconnaissance version known as the Reporter was also built but the last survivor crashed in the early 1970s.

Two Black Widows are known to survive, both P-61Cs, 43-8330 is in store with the National Air & Space Museum at Silver Hill, Maryland, USA while 43-8353 is on display at the US Air Force Museum, Wright-Patterson AFB, Dayton, Ohio.

Republic P-47 Thunderbolt

USA

Photo: P-47D, N47DA, after restoration by the Confederate Air Force.
Data: P-47D

Powerplant: One 2,300hp Pratt & Whitney Double Wasp R-2800-59
Span: 40ft 9.25in
Length: 36ft 1.75in
Height: 12ft 7.75in
Wing area: 308sq ft

A development of the Seversky P-35 and P-43 fighters the P-47 first flew on 6 May 1941 and became the first fighter of 2,000hp to enter US service. It was a massive aeroplane — known to its crews as 'The Jug' — and it entered service with US forces in Europe in May 1943 escorting B-17 and B-24 attacks in daylight. From March 1944 the Thunderbolts were equipped with drop tanks which allowed them to escort the bombers as far as Berlin and back and with the build up to D-Day the P-47 was increasingly used by the US 9th Air Force

escorting its Havocs and Marauders as well as operating on ground-attack and train-busting missions deep into occupied territory.

The original Thunderbolts had the built-up rear fuselage characteristic of the Seversky P-35 but with the introduction of the P-47D the Razorback was forsaken in favour of a bubble canopy and cut-down rear fuselage for improved vision. Thunderbolts were used by the Royal Air Force after September 1944 but they were exclusively operated by South East Asia Command against the Japanese, soon after VJ-Day the type was withdrawn from RAF service and it was also withdrawn from the USAAF although several Latin American Air Forces operated the type until the mid-1960s, notably the Peruvian Air Force. Six Peruvian P-47Ds were obtained by Ed Jurist in 1969 and restored over the following five years by the Confederate Air Force at Harlingen, Texas. The six were later sold to David Tallichet of California and one of them, N47DE/45-49205, has recently been flown to the UK for the Slymar Leasing Company based at Blackbushe, Hants.

Savoia-Marchetti SM79 Sparviero

Italy

Photo: MM45508 is exhibited at Vigna di Valle, it was previously LR-AMB and L-112 of the Lebanese Air Force.
Data: SM79-II

Powerplants: Three 1,000hp Piaggio PXIRC40 radials
Span: 69ft 6.75in
Length: 53ft 1.75in
Height: 13ft 5.5in
Wing area: 656.6sq ft

The SM79 originated in 1934 as an eight-passenger transport which was intended to compete in the 'MacRobertson' race from Mildenhall to Melbourne. The civil prototype was completed too late to participate but it was later used to establish several

closed circuit and load records and was eventually developed into the SM83 airliner.

Meanwhile development of the military version of the SM79 had proceeded apace and the initial model supplied to the Regia Aeronautica was the SM79-I which was powered by three Alfa Romeo 126 RC34 radials of 780hp each. The maximum internal bomb load was 2,750lb and the armament consisted of a variety of 12.7mm and 7.7mm machine guns; structurally it differed from the civil transport in the addition of a dorsal fairing behind the cockpit, a ventral bombardment gondolier and the deletion of the cabin windows along the fuselage sides.

The SM79-I saw service during the Spanish Civil War and by 1937 a torpedo-carrying variant was being proposed, this entered service in 1939 as the SM79-II and was widely regarded as the best land-

based torpedo bomber in its class. By mid-1940 the type formed the backbone of the bomber force of the Regia Aeronautica and it was widely used in the Mediterranean for anti-shipping, reconnaissance and bombing duties but by September 1943 only 61 remained in service, all as torpedo bombers, 34 of which joined the Allied Co-Belligerent Air Force following the Italian surrender.

A number of SM79s served with the postwar Italian Air Force as transports and three were sold to Lebanon in 1950 and one of these was obtained for permanent exhibition by the Italian Air Force Museum. It has now been completely refurbished in its original Italian markings and is displayed at Vigna di Valle near Rome.

Savoia-Marchetti SM82 Canguro Italy

Data: SM82PW

Powerplants: Three 1,217hp Pratt & Whitney Twin Wasp R-1830 radials
Span: 97ft 5in
Length: 74ft 4.25in
Height: 18ft 2.5in
Wing area: 1,276.1sq ft

First flown in 1938 the SM82 was a tri-motor bomber/transport and was reputed to be one of the best aircraft that Italy had at her disposal at the time of her entry into the war in June 1940. Originally powered by the 950hp Alfa Romeo 128RC21 radial it could accommodate up to 8,800lb in the transport role, typical loads being six aero engines, 40 fully-equipped troops or 600gal of fuel. The dimensions of

the hold were such that a dismantled FIAT CR42 could be carried and at least 50 are known to have been transported to North Africa in this way.

As a heavy bomber the type featured a semi-retractable bomb-aimer's position, a dorsal turret armed with one 12.7mm machine gun and three 7.7mm guns in nose and side positions, the bomb load was 8,800lb.

Following the Italian surrender 30 SM82s joined the Allied Co-Belligerent Air Force and further examples fought on under German control. After the war many were re-engined with 1,217hp Pratt & Whitney Twin Wasps and they continued to serve in the transport role as SM82PWs until supplanted by the C-119 Packet in 1960.

One SM82PW, MM61187, originally built in 1943 is under restoration at the Italian Air Force Museum at Vigna di Valle.

Short Sunderland

UK

Photo: Sunderland MR5, ML796 prior to being dismantled for shipping to Duxford.
Data: Sunderland MR5

Powerplants: Four 1,200hp Pratt & Whitney Twin Wasp R-1830.
Span: 112ft 9.5in
Length: 85ft 4in
Height: 32ft 10.5in
Wing area: 1,487sq ft

First flown as a prototype in October 1937 the Sunderland was a straightforward military adaptation of the Empire flying boats in service with Imperial Airways. The type entered service with Nos 230 and 210 Sqns during the summer of 1938 and was finally withdrawn 21 years later when the last two aircraft of No 205 Sqn, based at Seletar, Singapore, made their last sorties on 15 May 1959.

One of the features of the Sunderland was its strong defensive armament, it being the first British flying boat to mount power-operated turrets, it was on 3 April 1940 that a Sunderland first showed its remarkable teeth when one shot down one Ju88 in flames and forced another down in Norway after being attacked by six whilst on a North Sea patrol. Later in the war another Sunderland shot down three out of eight attacking Ju88s!

The Sunderland was built in four basic marks, the Mk I was the initial model which featured manually-operated defensive beam guns, the Mk II dispensed with the manual guns in favour of a dorsal, power-operated turret and this feature was continued in the Mk III which introduced a new planing bottom with a shallower forward step. All of these versions were powered by the 1,065hp Bristol Pegasus XVIII but the final mark, the Mk V, was fitted with Pratt & Whitney Twin Wasps. Only eight Mk IVs were constructed before the type was re-designated Seaford, most of those being assembled in civil form as Solents.

With the withdrawal of the Sunderland from RAF service the type became extinct in the UK although it continued to serve with the French Navy and the Royal New Zealand Air Force. It was left to private enterprise, in the shape of Peter Thomas, to establish the Short Sunderland Trust which arranged for an ex-French machine, ML824, to be flown back to Pembroke Dock in March 1961 where it was put on public display until 1971. It was then donated to the Royal Air Force Museum and is now exhibited in the Battle of Britain Museum, Hendon.

Another ex-French Sunderland, ML796, is being restored at Duxford for the Imperial War Museum and several examples survive in New Zealand.

Siebel Si204D

Germany

Photo: SE-KAL is a French-built NC701, c/n 159, exhibited at Arlanda Airport, Sweden.

Powerplants: Two 575hp Argus As411A-1 (Renault 12S00)
Span: 69ft 9in
Length: 39ft 4.75in
Height: 13ft 9.5in
Wing area: 495.14sq ft

The Si204 was a development of the prewar Fh104 Hallore medium-range transport which flew in prototype form for the first time during 1941.

Intended as a light communications aircraft the main production effort was centred on the Si204D which was produced as a crew trainer to supersede the Focke Wulf Fw58 Wheihe. As with other non-combat types the production of the type was assigned to factories in occupied France and Czechoslovakia, production continuing postwar at both centres, the French examples appearing as the NC701 and 702 Martinet, the latter being a civil transport derivative. In Czechoslovakia the postwar examples were the C3 and C3B for military use and the C103 commercial transport.

SAI KZIII

Denmark

Photo: KZIII, OY-DMO, seen at Sywell for a PFA rally in 1976.

Powerplant: One 100hp Blackburn Cirrus Minor 2
Span: 31ft 6in
Length: 21ft 6in
Height: 6ft 9in
Wing area: 140sq ft

The design of the KZIII two-seater was started in 1943 during the German occupation of Denmark. The first prototype was flown in 1944, the type being intended as an Air Ambulance for the Danish Air Ambulance Service, but the second was smuggled out to Sweden where it was test-flown.

Production commenced in 1945 and 64 were built during the next two years, only three of which were actually completed as ambulances, being equipped to carry a single stretcher which was loaded via a hinged panel in the port fuselage side.

A four-seat development, the KZVII Laerke, was flown on 11 November 1946 and this supplanted the earlier type on the production line the following year. 55 were subsequently built, components for a further 22 being destroyed in a factory fire, and the last was built in 1954.

Numerous examples of both the KZIII and KZVII exist in Scandinavia.

Sikorsky Hoverfly I

USA

Photo: The RAF Museum's Hoverfly I, KK995, seen at Henlow in 1970.

Powerplant: One 180hp Warner R-550-1
Rotor diameter: 38ft
Length: 35ft 5in
All up weight: 2,535lb
Max speed: 82mph

The Hoverfly first appeared in 1941 as the Sikorsky VS-316 and the initial deliveries were to the USAAF in whose service it was designated R-4. One of the first experimental XR-4 machines, 41-18874, is preserved by the Smithsonian Institution's National Air & Space Museum at Washington, DC. Delivered to the Royal Air Force and Fleet Air Arm from 1944-1945 a total of 52 was supplied under Lease-Lend

and the Hoverfly I entered service with the Helicopter Training School at Andover in early 1945. The Fleet Air Arm machines first appeared with No 771 Fleet Requirements Unit at Portland in September the same year.

The service use of the Hoverfly was not extensive but it is significant as the first Allied helicopter to attain production status and to enter military service on any form of scale. At least nine R-4 Hoverflies of various models are known to survive, all but one in the USA, and at least four R-6 Hoverfly IIs are preserved.

The aircraft on show at the Royal Air Force Museum, Hendon, is a composite made up from parts of both KL110 and KK995, it is shown in the markings of No 43 OTU, Andover, c1945.

Stinson L-5 Sentinel

USA

Photo: Model 105 Voyager, G-BCUM, seen at Biggin Hill.

Powerplant: One 185hp Lycoming 0-435-1
Span: 34ft
Length: 24ft 1in
Height: 7ft 11in
Wing area: 155sq ft

The L-5 Sentinel was an Air Observation Post which was developed from the civilian Model 105 Voyager in 1941. Initial deliveries were made to the US Army from 1942 under the designation 0-62 but this was changed to L-5 after the delivery of the 275th machine. Production of the L-5 totalled 1,731 but orders for later variants brought this up to a final figure of 3,283.

The L-5A differed in its electrical system from the standard aircraft, the L-5B was an air ambulance, the L-5C had a K-20 reconnaissance camera, the L-5E introduced drooping ailerons and the L-5G featured the 190hp Lycoming 0-435-11. Considerable numbers of L-5s were delivered to the RAF and they were extensively used in Burma. Large numbers are still flying in the USA and several are active in Europe. None are presently based in the UK but two civilian Model 105s are undergoing restoration to flying condition.

Supermarine Spitfire (Merlin-powered variants)   UK

Photo: Spitfire VC, AR501/G-AWII operated by the Shuttleworth Trust.
Data: Mk VC

Powerplant: One 1,440hp Rolls-Royce Merlin 45/46/50A/55/56
Span: 32ft 2in
Length: 29ft 11in
Max speed: 374mph

Probably the most famous fighter aircraft ever produced the Spitfire, as is well-known, owed its outstanding performance and potential for development to its racing ancestors — the S4, S5 and S6 seaplanes. The prototype, K5054, was built as a private venture as a result of designer R. J. Mitchell's dissatisfaction with the Supermarine F7/30, K2890, which had been built to an official specification.

The official Spec F37/34 was written around the prototype Spitfire which made its maiden flight on 5 March 1936 in the hands of 'Mutt' Summers, after that first flight the development was in the hands of Jeffrey Quill. Following initial flights which proved its outstanding flying qualities an official order was placed for 310 and production of the Mk I commenced in 1937. First deliveries were made to No 19 Sqn at Duxford in August 1938, where the type replaced the ancient Gloster Gauntlet biplane fighters, and by the outbreak of war Spitfires equipped nine full squadrons of Fighter Command with a further two squadrons partly-equipped with the type.

The initial Spitfires had four .303 machine guns and were known as the Mk I, the Mk IA featured eight guns and the Mk IB had four .303s and two 20mm cannon. 1,566 Mk Is of all types were built and they equipped 19 squadrons by July 1940, the average on strength during the Battle of Britain being 957 aircraft.

The Mk I was followed into service by the more powerful Mk II, 920 of which were built, and which mounted the 1,175hp Merlin XII in place of the Merlin II or III, the IIA and IIB had armament which corresponded to the appropriate Mk I sub-types while the IIC was a version used by Air-Sea Rescue squadrons.

It would be impossible to chart the progress of the innumerable Spitfire variants in a book such as this but it is worth mentioning that the main Merlin-powered variants were the Mks V, IX and XVI. The Mk V appeared on squadrons from March 1941, it was powered by the 1,440hp Merlin 45 series engine and was produced in A, B and C sub-types depending upon the armament installed. The Mk IX was a 'Stop-gap' version consisting of a Mk V airframe to which was fitted the 1,660hp Merlin 61 series powerplant intended for the all-new Mk VIII. In the event the Mk IX became the most widely-used Spitfire variant with 5,665 being built; the Mk XVI was identical but had the American Packard Merlin 266 engine installed, many of the later aircraft featuring a cut-down rear fuselage, bubble canopy and extended rudder. The Mk XVI served with the postwar Royal Auxiliary Air Force until 1950 and is today the most numerous example surviving.

Supermarine Spitfire (Griffon-powered)   UK

Photo: Spitfire PR19 PM631 preserved in flying condition by the Battle of Britain Memorial Flight at RAF Coningsby.
Data: PR19

Powerplant: One 2,050hp Griffon 65 or 66
Span: 36ft 10in
Length: 32ft 8in
Max speed: 460mph

In order to keep the Spitfire competitive the more powerful Rolls-Royce Griffon engine was eventually substituted for the Merlin, the first Griffon-powered Spitfire being an experimental Mk III, DP485. The first operational version of the Griffon-powered aircraft was the Mk XII which entered service with Nos 41 and 91 Sqns at Hawkinge in the spring of 1943. Its Griffon III or IV was optimised to give its full output at 1,000ft so that the type could effectively counter the Fw190 sneak raiders then plaguing the south coast and this it did with considerable success until the end of 1944.

Whereas the Mk XII had been based on the Mk V airframe the next major version, the Mk XIV, was based on the Mk VIII airframe and was intended as an interim before the introduction of the fully-revised Mk XVIII. the Mk XIV was powered by the 2,050hp Griffon 65 and its longer nose required a corresponding increase in fin area, the opportunity was also taken to move the ailerons inboard to improve lateral control and later aircraft had the

bubble hood and cut-down rear fuselage of the Mk XVI. A total of 957 were built in various sub-types, including the FR XIVE which was a clipped-wing, fighter-reconnaissance version, it was a very effective fighter and one of No 401 Sqn's machines became the first aircraft to down an Me262 jet fighter on 5 October 1944.

The Mk XVIII was just coming into service at the end of the war, it was fully revised and featured the bubble hood and a strengthened undercarriage to cope with its increased internal fuel tankage. 300 were built and they served postwar in the Middle and Far East, some being transferred to the Indian Air Force.

The PR XIX was the last unarmed photo-recce version built and was something of a hybrid being based on a Mk XIV fuselage and modified Mk VC wings. 225 were built and they served for many years after the war, two surviving in flying condition with the Battle of Britain Memorial Flight.

During 1944 the Spitfire was totally re-designed and emerged as the F21 which did not see war service. This was a completely new aircraft with a new wing planform and many other internal changes, it was followed by the F22 with cut-down rear fuselage and finally the F24 which featured zero-length rocket projectile launchers and four short-barrel 20mm Hispano cannon. Production of Griffon-powered Spitfires totalled 2,053 and the grand total of all Spitfires (excluding Seafires) was 20,351.

Taylorcraft Auster I   UK

Photo: Taylorcraft Plus D G-AHXE has been restored in its original colours as an Auster I, LB312, by John Pothecary. It is based at Shoreham.

Powerplant: One 90hp Blackburn Cirrus Minor 1

Span: 36ft
Length: 22ft 10in
Height: 8ft
Wing area: 167sq ft

The Auster I was a two-seat Air Observation Post, powered by the 90hp Blackburn Cirrus Minor 1, which was a straightforward adaptation of the civilian Taylorcraft Plus C. The design originated in America as the Models A and B, powered by the Continental A-40 and A-50 respectively, and licence production of the Anglicised Plus C began at Leicester in 1939. The 11th British machine was completed with a Cirrus Minor in place of the standard Lycoming 0-145-A2 and as such became the prototype Auster I, the 25th machine was finished to a similar standard as the civilian Plus D but with the outbreak of war the eight Plus Ds built were rapidly impressed for communications and AOP use.

An Air Ministry contract for 100 Auster Is was placed in 1941 following trials with the impressed Plus Cs and Ds but they had a very short service life and most were stored to be sold by public tender after the war and to reappear as Plus Ds.

Developments of the basic airframe were the Auster II (130hp Lycoming), Auster III (130hp Gipsy Major I), Auster IV (130hp Lycoming) and the Auster V which was a refined Auster IV with blind-flying panel and revised trim tabs.

Considerable numbers of wartime Austers of all models except the II are still flying and a prewar Plus C is under restoration for the Leicestershire Museum of Technology.

Tupolev Tu-2 USSR

Photo: This ex-Polish Air Force Tu-2 is preserved in the grounds of the Polish Army Museum in Warsaw.
Data: Tu-2S

Powerplants: Two 1,850hp Shvetsov ASh-82FNV radials
Span: 61ft 10.5in
Length: 45ft 3.5in
Max speed: 357mph at 12,000ft

The Tu-2 had its origins in a specification for a twin-engined, three-seat bomber to be capable of delivering its 4,400lb bomb load in both conventional and dive-bombing modes of operation. The two prototypes were known as the ANT-58 and ANT-59 respectively, differing from one another in minor detail, and both flew during the first half of 1941. Development flying revealed that more power was required and an extensive re-design produced the M-82 powered ANT-60 which flew in December 1941.

Development of the type was hindered by the German advance and such was the Russian situation that three pre-production aircraft were in service by September 1942, six months before the final acceptance trials! In service the Tu-2 was well-liked but it was found that the airframe was too complicated for mass production and accordingly a simplified version, known as the Tu-2S or ANT-61, was put into production in the winter of 1943-44.

The final versions of the type accommodated a crew of four, up to 5,000lb of bombs and was armed with two 23mm cannon and five Beresin 12.7mm machine guns. It was one of the best Russian designs to emerge from the period and was roughly comparable to the Junkers Ju88. Several Tu-2s survive throughout the countries of the Communist bloc.

Vickers Wellington   UK

Photo: MF628 is the sole survivor of 11,461
Wellingtons built, it is preserved at the RAF Museum,
Hendon.
Data: T10

Powerplants: Two 1,670hp Bristol Hercules XVIII
radials
Span: 86ft 2in
Length: 60ft 10in
Height: 17ft 5in
Wing area: 840sq ft

More than any other type, the Wellington formed the
backbone of Bomber Command during the first
critical years of World War 2, there being no less
than 21 squadrons equipped with the type during the
winter of 1941-42. The prototype was designed to
Air Ministry Spec B9/32 which was issued in
September 1932 and made its maiden flight some
four years later on 15 June 1936. Designed by
Barnes Wallis, the new bomber was famous for its
geodetic method of construction which was to give
its immense strength and the ability to absorb
tremendous amounts of punishment in later years.

By the autumn of 1943 the Wellington had
been replaced as a Front Line bomber by the Halifax
and Lancaster, its last operational sortie with
Bomber Command being made on the night of 8-9
October 1943 but 18 months earlier, in the spring of
1942, the Wellington Mk VIII had become the first of
a long line of general reconnaissance variants which
was to serve with Coastal Command. The Mk VIII
was powered by the Bristol Pegasus XVIII engine and
was fitted with ASV Mk II radar, some of them also
carrying Leigh lights for U-boat attacks at night.

The Wellington Mk X was the final bomber
variant, 3,804 being delivered, and it saw extensive
service with Bomber Command and in the Middle
East. It was an improved Mk III powered by Bristol
Hercules XVIII engines and after the war many were
reconditioned as crew-trainers by Boulton Paul
Aircraft Ltd. Known as the T10 in postwar service
these 'flying classrooms' soldiered on until 1953
when they were replaced by Valetta T3s. One of
them contrived to survive and was exhibited at
Biggin Hill for many years before being refurbished
for the RAF Museum, Hendon.

Vultee BT-13 Valiant   USA

Photo: BT-13 Valiant, N75004, ex-42-1779, is
preserved in USAAC blue and yellow colours by the
Confederate Air Force, Harlingen, Texas.

Powerplant: One 450hp Pratt & Whitney Wasp
Junior
Span: 42ft
Length: 28ft 8in
Wing area: 239sq ft

The Valiant was designed by Richard W. Palmer,
who had previously created the record-breaking
Hughes H-1 for Howard Hughes, and in 1939 was

selected as the US Army's new Basic Trainer under
the designation BT-13. Production commenced in
1940 and continued for four years, during which
time a total of 6,407 was constructed. During 1941-
1942 a shortage of 450hp Pratt & Whitney's
resulted in the BT-15 which was powered by the
450hp Wright, production of this version amounting
to 1,693. The Valiant was also built for the US Navy,
in whose service it was known as the SNV.

Several examples remain in the USA, both
airworthy and as museum exhibits, a number having
been reconstructed to resemble Japanese 'Kates' for
the filming of *Tora! Tora! Tora!*

Westland Lysander   UK

Photo: Lysander III, R9125, is exhibited in the Battle of Britain Museum, Hendon.
Data: Lysander III

Powerplant: One 870hp Bristol Mercury
Span: 50ft
Length: 30ft 6in
Height: 11ft 6in
Wing area: 260sq ft

Although designed for Army Co-operation and Artillery spotting the Lizzie will always be associated with the clandestine work of the SOE in dropping and picking up agents in occupied territory. The first Lysanders entered service with No 16 Sqn at Old Sarum in June 1938 and with the outbreak of war they were dispatched to France in their assigned role of artillery spotting and reconnaissance, however, in November 1939 it was a Lysander which brought down the first Heinkel over BEF territory! The Lysanders remained in action throughout the Dunkirk evacuation and were the last aircraft to leave for England after the withdrawal.

With the entry of Italy into the conflict Lysanders saw action in the Western Desert with No 208 Sqn and also saw service in the Greek campaign, in Palestine and in India.

Following their withdrawal in favour of P-40s from 1941 the Lysander was switched to Air-Sea Rescue and Target Towing duties as well as the agent-dropping activities which were centred on Nos 138 and 161 Sqns at RAF Tempsford.

One ex-161 Sqn aircraft is preserved at the Battle of Britain Museum, Hendon, in the markings of its first unit, No 225 Sqn and two ex-Royal Canadian Air Force machines have recently been restored to fly at Booker and Strathallan. Several other Lysanders exist in North America and an ex-Canadian machine is exhibited at the Indian Air Force Museum, New Delhi.

Yakovlev Yak-3 and Yak-9   USSR

Photo: This Yak-3 is exhibited at Le Bourget by the Musee de l'Air.
Data: Yak-9T

Powerplant: One 1,260hp Kilimov M-105 PF
Span: 32ft 9.75in
Length: 28ft 0.5in
Height: 8ft
Max speed: 363mph at 16,400ft

The Yak-1 prototype flew in mid-1940, entered production in 1941 and was in service by 1942. It was an outstanding fighter and led to a number of developments, two of which were the Yak-3 and Yak-9.

The Yak-9 was the first to appear, being a development of the Yak-7, and it became one of the most widely-used aircraft in the Communist bloc, equipping the Soviet Air Force and the air forces of Russia's satellites for many years after World War 2. Whereas the Yak-9 was developed from the Yak-7 the Yak-3 was a development of the Yak-1M, series production started in 1943 and they showed their superiority over the Bf109G during the Battle of Kursk.

Both the Yak-3 and Yak-9 were operated by the

French and Polish units serving within the Soviet Air Force and at the end of hostilities the surviving aircraft were presented to the appropriate countries. As a result of this gesture one Yak-3 survives with the Musee de l'Air and is currently exhibited at Le Bourget whilst several others survive throughout the museums of the Communist bloc.

Yokosuka MXY-8 Ohka   Japan

Photo: Ohka 11, 1-13, is exhibited at the US Marine Corps Museum at Quantico, Virginia, USA.
Data: MXY-8 Ohka 11

Powerplants: Three 588lb thrust type 4 Mk I Model 20 solid fuel rocket motors
Span: 16ft 5in
Length: 19ft 8.5in
Max speed: 570mph in final dive

With the increase in frequency of American attacks on the Japanese islands an elite suicide corps was formed, the Kamikaze (Divine Wind). Initially using conventional aircraft for their attacks on US Navy ships their success warranted the development of a specialised suicide aircraft, this was the MXY-8 Ohka ('Cherry Blossom') which was flown in the autumn of 1944. Production of the Ohka 11 started in September 1944 and 755 were completed by March 1945 before they were superseded by the revised Models 22, 33 and 43.

Only the Ohka 11 became operational, being carried on its mission beneath the belly of a G4M2e 'Betty' bomber and released at a height of some 27,000ft to commence its 230mph 50-mile glide towards the target before cutting in the rockets for its final dive. The Ohka 22 was a slightly smaller version powered by a 110hp piston engine which drove a compressor to give some 441lb thrust à la Campini; the Ohka 33 was powered by a 1,047lb thrust gas turbine and was intended for air launches from the G8N1 Renzan bomber but it was dropped in favour of the similar Ohka 43 which was intended for catapult launching. The MXY-7 was a non-powered pure glider version for training purposes.

Examples of the Ohka 11 are preserved at the Science Museum, London; the Aerospace Museum, RAF Cosford; and in store with the RAF Museum at Henlow. Others are exhibited world-wide.

Index